Spanish
Vocabulary

HANDBOOK

Mike Zollo

Spanish Vocabulary Handbook

The Author:
Mike Zollo is an experienced teacher, author and chief examiner. He is the chairman of the Association for Language Learning Spanish and Portuguese Committee.

The Series Editor:
Christopher Wightwick is a former UK representative on the Council of Europe Modern Languages Project and principal Inspector of Modern Languages for England.

Other titles in the Berlitz Language Handbook Series:

French Grammar Handbook
German Grammar Handbook
Spanish Grammar Handbook
Italian Grammar Handbook
French Verb Handbook
German Verb Handbook
Spanish Verb Handbook
Italian Verb Handbook

French Vocabulary Handbook
German Vocabulary Handbook
Italian Vocabulary Handbook

1st printing 1994

Printed in England by Clays Ltd, St Ives plc

CONTENTS

C   Appendices

D   Subject index

How to use this Handbook

This Handbook is a carefully ordered work of reference covering all areas of Spanish vocabulary and phrasing. It is based on the thesaurus structure of the Council of Europe's Threshold Level, expanded to include other major topics, especially in the fields of business, information technology and education. Unlike a dictionary, it brings together words and phrases in related groups. It also illustrates their usage with contextualized example sentences, often in dialogue form. This enables learners and users of the language to:

- refresh and expand their general knowledge of vocabulary;
- revise systematically for public examinations, using the word-groups to test their knowledge from Spanish to English and *vice versa*;
- extend their knowledge of authentically Spanish ways of saying things by studying the example sentences;
- support their speaking and writing on a given topic, when the logical arrangement of the sections will often prompt new ideas as well as supplying the means of expressing them.

THE STRUCTURE OF THE HANDBOOK

After the List of Contents, the Handbook is divided into four parts:

A   Introduction: Word building in Spanish

A concise account of the ways in which Spanish creates compound words and phrases in order to express more complex ideas. (For a more extensive treatment of this topic, see the Berlitz *Spanish Grammar Handbook*.)

B   The Topic Vocabularies

96 Vocabularies, grouped under 27 major areas of experience. Most Vocabularies are divided into a number of sections, so that words and phrases are gathered together into closely related groups. Almost all sections contain example sentences showing the vocabulary in use. Wherever it makes sense to do so, these sentences are linked together to form short narratives or dialogues which help to fix them in the memory. In some Vocabularies the lists of words and phrases are both extensive and more independent of context, so that the role of the example sentences is reduced.

C The Appendices

Lists of specific terms such as the names of countries or musical instruments. These would simply clutter up the main Vocabularies, but they are linked to them by clear cross-references.

D The Subject Index

An alphabetical index of topics and themes, enabling you to locate quickly the area you are interested in.

LOCATING THE RIGHT SECTION

The Handbook can be approached in two main ways.
• If you are not sure which topic will be best suited to your needs, start with the *List of Contents* on page iii. This will give you a general picture of the areas covered. You can then browse through the sections until you find the one you want.

• Alternatively, if you have a specific topic in mind, look it up in the *Subject Index* at the end of the book. This will take you directly to the relevant Vocabulary or Appendix. To help you find what you are looking for, topics are often listed more than once, under different headings. Within most sections there are cross-references to other, related areas.

A
INTRODUCTION

The vocabulary of the Spanish language

Conventions used in this Handbook

The vocabulary of the Spanish language

1   *The origins of Spanish*

Modern Castilian Spanish (**Castellano**) is derived from Vulgar Latin, the Latin spoken by ordinary Romans which also gave rise to other Romance languages, including other languages and dialects of the Iberian Peninsula. The Castilians won political and military dominance over much of Spain, so it was their dialect which eventually became the national language of Spain. Thus, Spanish comes from the same source as, for example, Italian, French and Portuguese, and almost all other Iberian Peninsular languages, such as Catalán, Valenciano and Gallego.

Much vocabulary in English also comes from Latin, either via Norman French, from other Romance languages, or direct from Latin in more recent times (largely in the fields of science or culture). Hence, Spanish and English have a lot of vocabulary in common, and many words new to you in Spanish will be recognizable from English or any other Romance language you may know.

Spanish has also imported words from many other languages over the centuries, among them Arabic (e.g. **algodón** 'cotton'), French (e.g. **boutique**), English (e.g. **márketing**) and Latin American Indian languages (e.g. **tomate** 'tomato'). Many of the more recent importations are from English, mostly in the fields of sport, pop-music, business, science and computing. It is worth noting that verbs based on imported words are almost always in the **-ar** verb family, e.g. **dopar, esnifar, xerocopiar.**

Some imported words keep more or less their original spelling, but with pronunciation adapted to Spanish: this is usually the case with words adopted in written form e.g. 'iceberg'. Words imported through spoken language on the other hand tend to do the opposite, and have spelling adapted to keep the pronunciation similar, such as is the case with **fútbol**. It is interesting to compare two words with similar meanings – **jersey** and **suéter**: the former was probably adopted from written English and is now usually pronounced in Spanish as something like 'hersei'; the latter was obviously adopted in spoken form, and a form of spelling was evolved which produces the right sound when said aloud.

2 *Important grammatical features*

Awareness of these will help you to categorize words and get to their base form. (For full treatment of Spanish structures, consult the Berlitz *Spanish Grammar Handbook*.)

2a *The noun phrase*

(i) *Gender*

All Spanish nouns are either **masculine** or **feminine** in gender. As a general rule:

• most words for actual female people or animals are in the **feminine** group, and most male people and animals are in the **masculine** group.

• most masculine words end in **-o**, and most words ending in **-o** are masculine

• most feminine words end in **-a**, and most words ending in **-a** are feminine

BUT there are exceptions:

el taxista, *el* mapa, *la* radio, *la* foto

(ii) *Plurals*

All nouns and adjectives add **s** to form their plural, unless they end in a consonant, in which case they add **-es.**

el niño – los niños	**la carta – las cartas**
el papel – los papeles	**la mujer – las mujeres**

There are a few exceptions. For these, consult the Berlitz *Spanish Grammar Handbook*.

(iii) *Articles*

There are four words for 'the' in Spanish:

el = masculine singular	**el chico, el perro, el papel**
la = feminine singular	**la chica, la vaca, la verdad**
los = masculine plural	**los chicos, los gatos, los taxis**
las = feminine plural	**las chicas, las ratas, las fotos**

Nouns listed in this Handbook are accompanied by **el/la**, **los/las** to show you which gender they belong to.

There are four words for 'a/some' in Spanish:

un = masculine singular	**un chico, un perro, un papel**
una = feminine singular	**una chica, una vaca, una verdad**
unos = masculine plural	**unos chicos, unos gatos, unos taxis**
unas = feminine plural	**unas chicas, unas ratas, unas fotos**

(iv) Agreement of Adjectives

Adjectives have to match the noun they describe in **gender** and **number**. Therefore they can have four forms: masculine singular and plural, feminine singular and plural, except those ending in **-e** which have the same form for masculine and feminine. This often gives rise to apparent rhyming phrases - learn the following as useful examples to remind you:

el niño malo	**unos toros bravos**
una paloma blanca	**las islas bonitas**

BUT

un hombre inteligente	**unas casas grandes**

Note that the masculine singular form is usually listed in this Handbook.

2b Verb forms

Different verb forms exist for each person referred to and for each tense, and the verb ending is crucially important. On the whole, Spanish does not use subject pronouns – words such as **yo** 'I', **él** 'he', **nosotros** 'we' and so on – because the actual verb form reveals who is doing the action as well as what is being done and when. Since Spanish pronunciation is very faithful to its spelling and vice-versa, Spanish has never really developed the need to use subject pronouns all the time, and reserves them for emphasis or to avoid ambiguity.

• Here are the six forms of a typical regular verb of the **-ar** verb family in the Present Tense, with the subject pronouns given in brackets. You will see that the verb forms are all clearly different and that most end in a vowel, an **n** or an **s**.

hablar	to speak
(yo) hablo	I speak
(tú) hablas	you speak (familiar singular)
(él/ella/usted) habla	he/she/ speaks, you speak (formal singular)

(nosotros/as) habl*amos*	we speak
(vosotros/as) habl*áis*	you speak (familar plural)
(ellos/ellas/ustedes) habl*an*	they speak, you speak (formal plural)

• Some verbs are affected by the spelling change described as vowel stretching (see Section 4). Here is an example – note that not all forms are affected.

pensar	to think
(yo) p*ie***nso**	I think
(tú) p*ie***nsas**	you think (familiar singular)
(él/ella/usted) p*ie***nsa**	he/she/ thinks, you think (formal singular)
(nosotros/as) pensamos	we think
(vosotros/as) pensáis	you think (familar plural)
(ellos/ellas/ustedes) p*ie***nsan**	they think, you think (formal plural)

Apart from the **-ar** verb family, other regular verbs belong to the **-er** and **-ir** verb groups. For other forms and for more information, consult the Berlitz *Spanish Verb Handbook*.

• In this Handbook, verbs are usually given in the 'I' form of the Present Tense (e.g. '*I* speak' **hablo**). If you come across a particular verb form, you need to work back to this form to find it in this Handbook, or to the general name part of the verb – the infinitive – to find out its meaning in a dictionary.

3   Guessing unknown words

For various reasons, several letters or combinations of letters changed in written form in the transition from Latin to modern Castilian Spanish. If you are aware of these, you can quite easily work out the meanings of many words which are similar in English but not otherwise easily recognizable. Often the changed Castilian form and a form closer to Latin exist side by side, though sometimes with slightly different meanings.

(i)   'vowel stretching' of **e**, **o** and **u**.

e → ie, and o → ue; and in addition, sometimes e → i, o → u and u → ue.

e → ie: b***ie***n	= well; c.f. Latin/Italian 'b*e*ne', English 'b*e*neficial'
o → ue: b***ue***no	= good; c.f. French 'b*o*n', English 'b*o*unty'
e → i: p***i***do	= I ask for, from **pedir**; c.f. 'p*e*tition'

o → u: d**u**rmió = he slept, from **dormir**; c.f. 'd**o**rmitory'
u → ue: ag**üe**ro = aug**u**r

(ii) *sc, sp, st*

You may notice that some native speakers of Spanish speaking English tend to put an 'e-' on the front of words beginning 'sc-', 'sp-', 'st-'. This is because many such words in English, French, and so on tend to begin in Spanish with **esc-, esp-, est-**;

e + sc: **e***sc***uela** = *sc*hool
e + sp: **e***sp***añol** = *Sp*anish
e + st: **e***st***udiante** = *st*udent

(iii) *ll*

Castilian Spanish often uses **ll** instead of 'cl', 'fl', and 'pl' at the beginning of words.

cl → ll: *ll***amar** = to call; c.f. *cl*aim (call)
fl → ll: *ll***ama** = *fl*ame (also the South American animal)
pl → ll: *ll***ano** = flat, *pl*ain

(iv) *f/h*

Castilian Spanish often uses **h** instead of 'f', and two words with similar meanings but different spellings often coexist.

h ↔ f: *h***ogar** = hearth +
 ·   *f***uego** = fire; c.f. '*f*ocus'
 ·   *h***ijo** = son; c.f. '*f*ilial' and French '*f*ils'

(v) *w/g*

Especially at the beginning of words, Spanish tends to use **gu** instead of 'w'.

w → g: (el País de) *G***ales** = *W*ales; c.f. **Galicia**
 ·   *gu***erra** = *w*ar; c.f. **guerrilla/guerrillero**
Note also: *w*hisky is often pronounced or written *gu***isky**.

(vi) *x/j*

Spanish usually uses **j** where English uses 'x'.

x → j: **Mé***j***ico** = Mexico   **fi***j***o** = fixed

(vii) g/h

Spanish sometimes begins words with **h** instead of 'g'

g → h: hermano   = brother; c.f. 'germane'

Note: In Latin American pronunciation, **g** with **e** and **i** sounds like **h**.

(viii) ph/f

Spanish does not allow 'ph' spellings, and uses **f** instead.

profeta	= prophet
geografía	= geography
farmacia	= pharmacy

(ix) *Double consonants*

Spanish has far fewer double consonants than English. However, **cc, ll, rr** are all very common, and **ll** even has its own section in the dictionary. **nn** occurs in a few words, usually ones beginning with the prefix **in-**.

innecesario   unnecessary (**in-** negating/opposite)

innovar   to innovate (**in-** meaning into)

4 Cognates and derivatives

Many Spanish words can be identified in a straightforward way, either because of their similarity to known words in Spanish or other languages (*cognates*), or through being derived from known words, with bits added at the beginning or end of the word (*derivatives*). In the case of the latter, you can often predict the existence of a word by knowing how similar words are built up from a base word, and you can work out the meaning of a word by 'undressing' it to get back to the base word at its core. Beware though of **falsos amigos** - words which look the same but have different meanings.

4a Cognates

(i)   English words absorbed into Spanish without change of meaning.

álbum, record, líder, fútbol, mánager

Note: many have spellings adapted into Spanish as we have seen before.

(ii)   Spanish words with common equivalent in English or ones which English has borrowed from Spanish.

paella, matador, fiesta, aficionado

(iii)   Words identical in form to their English equivalent and with comparable pronunciation.

casual, panorama

(iv)   Words similar in form to their English equivalent and with comparable pronunciation.

documento, militar, sistema, clima, movimiento, millón

(v)   Verbs whose stem is identical or similar in form to the English equivalent.

admirar, contener, consistir, aplaudir

(vi)   Words with frequently occurring suffixes with English equivalents.

libertad, posibilidad, indicación, potencia

Note the equivalent English – Spanish suffixes:

-dad	=' -ty' e.g. **ciudad** 'city'; **capacidad** 'capacity'
-ción	= '-tion' e.g. **acción** 'action'; **elección** 'election'
-ía, ia	= '-y' e.g. **energía** 'energy'; **farmacia** 'pharmacy'

4b   *Derivatives: word-building and undressing*

(i)   Words whose meaning is determined by common prefixes or suffixes, but whose base element is already known or easily identifiable.

con-: contener	**des-: deshacer, desnudo**
dis-: disuadir	**in-/im-: incorrecto, imposible**
re-: revolver	**sub-: submarino, subcontinente**
-able: salud > saludable	**-ería: zapatero > zapatería**
-miento: pensar > pensamiento	**-oso: arena > arenoso**

(ii)   Nouns denoting people and other concepts, with endings such as -ero/a, -or/a, -ista.

-ero/-era: zapatero, niñera
-ista: pianista, taxista
-or/-ora: pintor, pescador

These are mostly based on another noun or a verb.

(iii)   Adverbs formed by adding the ending **-mente** to adjectives.

totalmente, activamente

> **Note:** in Spanish most adverbs end in **-mente**, just as in English most end in '-ly'. This ending is usually added to the feminine form of the adjective.

(iv)   Adjectives with ending **-able**, equivalent to English '-able' or '-ible'.

imaginable, admirable

(v)   Adjectives with ending **-oso/-osa**, equivalent to English '-ous'.

religioso, furioso, vigoroso, vicioso

(vi)   Adjectives with ending **-és/esa, -(i)ense, -eno/a, -eño/a,** equivalent to English '-ese' or '-(i)an', usually indicating place of origin.

inglés, japonesa, canadiense, chileno, brasileña

(vii)   Diminutives ending in **-ito, -illo, -ico**

señorito, panecillo, casita, perico

(viii)   Augmentative and pejorative suffixes such as **-ón/ona, -azo, -ucho.**

hombrón, mujerona, manotazo, casucha

(ix)   Compound nouns, consisting of combinations of known words.

abrelatas, sacacorchos, cortacésped

(x)   Words derived from adjectives.

tranquilizar, ensuciar, limpieza

(xi)   Words mainly derived from verbs, with endings **-ante** or **-ente, -iente.**

cantante, oyente, comiente

(xii)   Common acronyms and initials, often in a different order.

UNO	**ONU** - Organización de las Naciones Unidas
NATO	**OTAN** - Organización del Tratado del Atlántico del Norte
Note:	
USA	**EEUU** - **los Estados Unidos** (plural words have doubled-up letters when given as acronyms)

Conventions used in this Handbook

a) Nouns
Nouns are given in the singular form preceded by the definite article.

el (pl. **los**) indicates masculine gender
la (pl. **las**) indicates feminine gender
Feminine words beginning with stressed **a-** or **ha-** are usually used with **el**.

Nouns referring to professions are generally given in only the masculine form, except for the list of professions App.14b, where the feminine is included.

b) Verbs
Verbs are in the first person, except when inappropriate. In the example sentences both familiar and polite forms of 'you' are used as appropriate in that particular context. Sometimes both are given.

c) Adjectives
Adjectives are in the masculine singular form.

Abbreviations

adj	adjective	m	masculine
adv	adverb	pl	plural
f	feminine		

Symbols

( )	a part of a translation which is optional: **el juzgado (de lo) penal**
/	alternative word(s): **el historia/el cuento de terror** = **el historia de terror** or **el cuento de terror**
,	an alternative translation: 'I resign' **dimito, renuncio**
[ ]	an alternative used in Latin American Spanish: 'computer' **el ordenador, [el computador]**
➤	a cross-reference to a Vocabulary or chapter

B
VOCABULARY TOPICS

Functional words

Articles

a   **un, una**
the   **el, la, los, las**
some   **unos, unas**
    algunos, algunas

Demonstrative adjectives/pronouns*

this   **este, esta**
that   **ese, esa, aquel, aquella**
these   **estos, estas**
those   **esos, esas, aquellos,**
    aquellas
this one   **éste, ésta**
that one   **ése, ésa**
those ones   **ésos, ésas, aquéllos,**
    aquéllas
the red one   **el rojo, la roja**

Emphatic subject pronouns*

I   **yo**
you *(fam sing)*   **tú**
    (fam pl)   **vosotros/as [ustedes]**
    (formal sing)   **usted**
    (formal pl)   **ustedes**
he   **él**
she   **ella**
it   **ello**
we   **nosotros/as**
they   **ellos/as**

Personal object pronouns (accusative & dative)

me   **me**
you *(fam sing)*   **te**
    (fam pl)   **os, [les]**
    (formal sing)   **lo, la, le**
    (form pl)   **los, las, les**
him   **lo, le**
her   **la, le**
it   **lo, la, le**

us   **nos**
them   **los, las, les**
one   **lo, la, le**

Reflexive pronouns

myself   **me**
yourself *(fam sing)*   **te**
    (fam pl)   **os, [les]**
    (formal sing/pl)   **se**
him/herself   **se**
itself   **se**
ourselves   **nos**
themselves   **se**
oneself   **se**
each other   **se**

Prepositional pronouns*

me   **mí**
you *(fam sing)*   **ti**
    (fam pl)   **vosotros/as [ustedes]**
    (formal sing)   **usted**
    (form pl)   **ustedes**
him   **él**
her   **ella**
it   **ello**
...self, ...selves   **sí** *(reflexive)*
us   **nosotros/as**
them   **ellos/as**
one   **uno**

Possessive adjectives*

my   **mi, mis**
your *(fam sing)*   **tu, tus**
    (fam pl)   **vuestro/a/os/as, [su,**
    sus]**
    (formal sing/pl)   **su, sus**
his   **su, sus**
her   **su, sus**
its   **su, sus**
our   **nuestro/a/os/as**
their   **su, sus**

For further guidance on the use of words in sections marked with an *,
►Berlitz *Spanish Grammar Handbook*.

one's   **su, sus**

Possessive pronouns*

mine   **el mío, la mía, los míos, las mías**
yours *(fam sing)*   **el tuyo,** etc.
   (fam pl)   **el vuestro,** etc., **[el suyo,** etc.]
   (formal sing/pl)   **el suyo,** etc.
his/hers   **el suyo** etc.
ours   **el nuestro** etc.
theirs   **el suyo** etc.
this is mine   **este/a es mío/a**
mine is better   **el mío/la mía es mejor**

Relative pronouns*

who   **que**
      quien, quienes
      el/la que, los/las que
      el/la cual, los/las cuales
which   **que**
      el/la que, los/las que
      el/la cual, los/las cuales
that   **que**
      quien, quienes
      el/la que, los/las que
      el/la cual, los/las cuales
what   **lo que, lo cual**
what you say is true   **lo que dices es verdad**

Indefinite pronouns

somebody/one   **alguien**
no one   **nadie**
anybody/one   **cual(es)quiera**
nobody   **nadie**
each   **cada (uno/a)**
everybody/one   **todos/as**
something   **algo**
anything   **algo, alguna cosa, cualquier cosa**
   (after negative)   **nada**
nothing   **nada**
everything   **todo**
all (of them)   **todos/as**

both (of them)   **los/las dos, ambos/as**
some (of them)   **algunos/as**

Questions

when?   **¿cuándo?**
where?   **¿dónde?**
how?   **¿cómo?**
how much?   **¿cuánto/a?**
how many?   **¿cuántos/as?**
how far?   **¿a qué distancia?,
   [¿qué tan lejos?]**
how long?   **¿durante cuánto tiempo?**
how hot?   **¿qué temperatura?**
why?   **¿por qué?**
who?   **¿quién(es)?**
whom?   **¿a quién(es)?**
to whom?   **¿a quién(es)?**
whose?   **¿de quién(es)?**
what?   **¿qué?**
what ...?   **¿qué ...?, ¿cuál(es) ...?**
which (one)?   **¿cuál?**

Common prepositions and conjunctions

about   **a eso de, acerca de**
also   **también**
although   **aunque**
and   **y**
as *(since)*   **puesto que**
because   **porque**
but   **pero**
if   **si**
in   **en**
in order that/so that   **para que**
on   **en, sobre**
only   **sólo, solamente**
or   **o**
since   **puesto que**
so   **pues**
too   **también**
until   **hasta (que)**
with   **con**
without   **sin**

2 Where? – position & movement

2a Position

about **alrededor**
about *(adv)* **por todas partes**
above **encima de**
across **a través (de)**
after **después (de)**
against **contra**
ahead **delante, [adelante]**
ahead of **delante de**
along **a lo largo de**
among **entre**
anywhere **en cualquier sitio**
around *(adv)* **alrededor de, por**
  around the garden **por el**
  jardín
as far as **hasta**
at **en**
  at home **en casa**
  at school **en el colegio**
  at work **en el trabajo**
back **detrás, atrás**
  at the back (of) **detrás (de), a**
  la espalda (de), [atrás, en la
  parte trasera]
  to the back **hacia atrás**
backwards **hacia atrás**
behind **detrás (de)**
below **debajo (de)**
  below **debajo, [abajo]**
beside **al lado de, [junto a]**
between **entre**
beyond **más allá (de)**
bottom **el fondo**
  at the bottom (of) **al fondo (de)**
centre/center **el centro**
  in the centre/center **en el**
  centro (de)
direction **la dirección**
  in the direction of Murcia **en la**
  dirección de Murcia
distance **la distancia**

in the distance **en la distancia**
distant **distante, distanciado,**
  lejano
down there **allí abajo**
downstairs **abajo**
edge **el borde**
  at the edge **al borde (de)**
end **el final**
  at the end **al final (de)**
everywhere **en todas partes, por**
  todas partes, en todos los
  sitios
far **lejos**
  far away (from) **lejos (de)**
first **primero**
  first (of all) **primero (de todo)**
  I am first **estoy primero**
forward(s) **hacia**
from **de, desde**
front **el frente**
  at the front **al frente**
  I am in front **estoy al frente**
  in front of **delante de, al frente**
  de
  to the front **hacia delante, al**
  frente
here **aquí**
  here and there **aquí y allí**
in **en**
  in there **allí dentro**
inside **dentro**
  inside **adentro**
into **dentro**
last **último**
  last of all **por último**
  last of all *(adv)* **últimamente**
  I am last **soy/estoy el último**
left **izquierda**
  on the left **a la izquierda**
  to the left **hacia la izquierda**

middle **medio**
in the middle (of) **en (el) medio (de)**
I move **me muevo**
movement **el movimiento**
near **cerca**
near(by) **cercano**
neighbourhood/neigborhood **el vecindario, las cercanías**
in the neighbourhood/neigborhood of **en las cercanías**
next **próximo, al lado**
next (adv) **próximamente**
next to **al lado de**
nowhere **en ningún sitio**
on **en, sobre**
onto **en**
opposite **opuesto, en frente (de)**
out of **fuera de**
out there **allí fuera, [allá afuera]**
outside **fuera**
outside **afuera**
over **encima**
over there **allí, [allá]**
past **pasado**
right **derecho**

the right **la derecha**
on the right **en la derecha**
to the right **a la derecha**
round/around **alrededor (de)**
round/around the tree **alrededor del árbol**
side **lado**
at the side **al lado**
at both sides of **a ambos lados de**
somewhere **en alguna parte, en algún sitio**
there **allí**
to **a, hacia**
top **arriba, encima**
top (of mountain) **la cima**
at the top **encima**
on top **encima**
towards **hacia**
under **debajo (de), bajo**
up here/there **allí arriba**
upstairs **arriba**
where? **¿dónde?**
where from? **¿de dónde?**
where to? **¿hacia dónde?, ¿adónde?**
with **con**

Over there in the distance is the river. It's not far away – about 1 km from our house.
Opposite the houses is the church and nearby are the shops/stores.

At the top of the hill is a farm and in the middle of the village is the bank.
The first house in the high/main street is near the river. Our house is the last. The next village is about five kilometres/kilometers away.

Allá a lo lejos está el río. No es lejos – a un kilómetro más o menos de nuestra casa.
Enfrente de la casa está la iglesia, y las tiendas están cerca.

En lo alto de la colina hay una granja, y en el centro del pueblo está el banco.
La primera casa de la calle principal está cerca del río. Nuestra casa es la última. El pueblo más cercano está a unos cinco kilómetros.

2b Directions & location

Points of the compass

atlas **el atlas**
east **el este, [el oriente]**
   east *(adj)* **del este, oriental**
   in the east **en el este**
   to the east **al este**
compass **la brújula**
latitude **la latitud**
location **la situación, la posición**
longitude **la longitud**
map **el mapa**
north **el norte**
   north *(adj)* **del norte, nórdico**
   in the north **en el norte**
   to the north (of) **al norte (de)**

northeast **el noreste, [el nororiente]**
northnortheast **el nornoreste, [el nor-nororiente]**
northwest **el noroeste, [el noroccidente]**
northnorthwest **el nornoroeste, [el nor-noroccidente]**
point of the compass **la cuarta**
south **el sur**
   south *(adj)* **del sur, sureño**
   in the south **en el sur**
   to the south **al sur**
southeast **el sureste, [el suroriente]**

Santiago is south of Coruña. Right in the south is Pontevedra. I prefer the south of Galicia to the north.

Santiago está al sur de Coruña. Precisamente en el sur está Pontevedra. Prefiero el sur de Galicia al norte.

Look on the map. You go north(wards).

Mire el mapa. Usted sigue hacia el norte.

To the south of the wood you can see the church spire.

Hacia el sur del bosque se ve la aguja de la iglesia.

– How do I get to Pamplona?
– Go straight on to the second crossroads/intersection.
Turn right at the lights and take the road to Vitoria. It's 25 kilometres/kilometers from here.

– ¿Cómo se va a Pamplona?
– Siga todo derecho hasta el segundo cruce.
Doble a la derecha en el semáforo y tome la carretera para Vitoria. Está a 25 kilómetros de aquí.

– Is there a bank nearby?
– It's behind the supermarket.
– Where is the tourist office?

– ¿Hay un banco cerca de aquí?
– Está detrás del supermercado.
– ¿Dónde está la oficina de turismo?

– Opposite the town hall.

– En frente del ayuntamiento.

southsoutheast   **el sursureste, [el sur-suroriente]**
southwest   **el suroeste, [el suroccidente]**
southsouthwest   **el sursuroeste, [el sur-suroccidente]**
west   **el oeste, [el occidente]**
west *(adj)*   **del oeste, occidental**
in the west   **en el oeste, [al occidente]**
to the west (of)   **al oeste (de), [al occidente de]**

Location & existence

I am   **soy, estoy**
there is   **hay**
there isn't (any)   **no hay**

ninguno
it is ready   **está listo, está preparado**
it amounts to   **hace, [asciende a]**
I become   **llego a ser**
I exist   **existo**
existence   **la existencia**
I have got/I have   **tengo**
it lies   **está situado**
I possess   **poseo**
possession   **la posesión**
present   **el presente**
I am present   **estoy presente**
I am present at   **estoy presente en**
I am situated   **estoy situado**

The town lies at a longitude of 32°.	**La ciudad está en la longitud de 32°.**
– Are you lost? – Yes. Can you tell me the quickest way to the post office?	**– ¿Se ha perdido usted?** **– Sí. ¿Me puede decir el camino más corto para ir al correos [a la oficina de correos]?**
– It's down there on the left.	**– Está allí abajo a la izquierda.**
How do you get to the other side?	**¿Cómo se va al otro lado?**
– Who's that? – It's me.	**– ¿Quién es? – Soy yo.**
– How many children are present? – There are 25. Five of them are at home.	**– ¿Cuántos niños asisten?** **– Hay 25. Cinco de ellos están en casa.**
– Is there any cake? Are there still any biscuits/cookies? – I am sorry, there is no cake, but there are some sandwiches.	**– ¿Hay torta/pastel? ¿Quedan galletas?** **– Lo siento, no hay pastel, pero sí hay unos bocadillos [emparedados/sándwiches].**
I have been to London. I was present at a concert.	**He estado en Londres. Fui a un concierto.**

2c Movement

I arrive	**llego**	I go out	**salgo, voy fuera**
I bring	**traigo**	I go round	**doy vueltas, doy la vuelta a**
by car	**en coche**		
I carry	**llevo**	I go up	**subo, voy arriba**
I climb	**escalo, subo**	I hike	**hago auto(e)stop**
I come	**voy, vengo**	I hurry	**me apresuro**
I come down	**bajo, voy abajo**	I hurry up	**me doy prisa**
I come in	**entro**	I jump	**salto**
I come out	**salgo**	I leave	**salgo**
I come up	**subo, voy arriba**	I leave (something)	**dejo (algo)**
I creep	**ando a gatas, [gateo]**	I lie down	**me echo, me acuesto**
I drive	**conduzco**	I march	**desfilo**
I drive on the right	**conduzco por la derecha**	I move	**me muevo, me cambio**
		on foot	**a pie**
I fall	**me caigo**	I pass	**paso**
I fall down	**me caigo**	I pass (in car)	**paso en coche, [rebaso en carro]**
I follow	**sigo**		
I get in	**subo en/a**	I pull	**tiro**
I get out	**bajo de, salgo de**	I push	**empujo**
I get up	**me levanto**	I put	**pongo**
I go	**voy**	I ride a horse	**monto a caballo**
I go down	**bajo, voy abajo**	I run	**corro**
I go for a walk	**voy a pasear**	I run away	**echo a correr**
I go in	**entro, voy dentro**	I rush	**voy de prisa**

Put the picnic in the car! Don't forget to bring your umbrella.	**Pon (la comida d)el picnic en el coche [el carro]! No te olvides de traer tu paraguas.**
I will take you as far as the river. Then you must get out and walk.	**Te llevaré hasta el río. Luego tendrás que bajar y continuar a pie.**
Keep to the left. Be careful not to fall into the river.	**Anda a la izquierda. Ten cuidado de no caerte al agua.**
We go down the hill, along the river, and then turn left towards the woods.	**Bajamos la cuesta, seguimos al lado del río, luego torcemos a la izquierda hacia el bosque.**
You pass a farm.	**Se pasa delante de una granja.**

➤ POSITION 2a; DIRECTIONS 2b; TRAVEL 19

I sit down **me siento**
I sit up **me levanto**
I slip **resbalo**
I stand **estoy de pie**
 I stand still **(me) estoy quieto**
 I stand up **estoy de pie**
I step **voy**
I stop **paro**
straight **derecho, seguido, recto**
 straight ahead **todo derecho, todo seguido, todo recto, [derecho]**
I stroll **paseo**
I take **cojo**
I turn **tuerzo**
 I turn left **tuerzo a la izquierda**
 I turn off **me desvío**
 I turn round **me vuelvo, doy la vuelta**
walk **el paseo**
I walk **ando, camino**
I wander **voy sin rumbo**
way **el camino**

Here and there

Come here! **¡Ven aquí!**

I go there **voy allí**
I rush there **voy de prisa allí**
I travel there **viajo allí**

Up and down

Stand up! **¡Levántate!**
I climb the mountain **subo la montaña**
I climb the stairs **subo las escaleras**
I climb the wall **subo por la pared**
I fall down **me caigo**
I lie down **me echo, me acuesto**
Do sit down! **¡Siéntate!, ¡Siéntese!**
I go down the path **bajo por el camino**

Round

I go round the town **me paseo por la ciudad**
I run round in the garden **corro alrededor del jardín**
I run around **corro alrededor**
I turn round **doy la vuelta**

– Where are you going?
– To town. Are you coming?

– No, I am going to my mother's.
– Which direction is that?
– I take the first road on the left, then straight ahead up to the market place, then I turn right.

– I will follow you as far as the market.
I am going by car but some of us will go on foot. John is going by bike.

– **¿Adónde vas/va usted?**
– **Al pueblo. ¿Vienes/Usted viene?**

– **No, voy a casa de mi madre.**
– **¿En qué dirección es esto?**
– **Tomo la primera calle a la izquierda, luego sigo todo recto hacia la plaza de mercado, luego tuerzo a la derecha.**
– **Te/le seguiré hasta el mercado.**
Voy en coche, pero algunos iremos a pie. John irá en bicicleta.

When? – expressions of time

3a Past, present & future

about **alrededor de**
after **después**
   after *(conj)* **después (de) que**
   afterwards **después, más tarde**
again **otra vez**
   again and again **una y otra vez**
ago **hace**
   a short time ago **hace poco tiempo**
already **ya**
always **siempre**
anniversary **el aniversario**
annual **anual**
as long as *(conj)* **siempre que, siempre cuando**
as soon as *(conj)* **tan pronto como**
at once **inmediatamente, ahora mismo**
before **antes (de)**
   before, beforehand **de antemano**
I begin **empiezo, comienzo**

beginning **el principio, el comienzo**
birthday **el cumpleaños**
brief **breve, corto**
briefly **brevemente**
by (next month) **al (mes próximo)**
calendar **el calendario, el almanaque**
centenary **el centenario**
century **el siglo**
   in the twentieth century **en el siglo veinte**
continuous **continuo**
daily **diariamente**
date **la fecha**
dawn **el amanecer**
   at dawn **al amanecer**
day **el día**
   by day **por día**
   every day **todos los días, cada día**
   one day (when) **un día (cuando)**
   the days of the week **los días**

– Last Friday the train was late and you didn't get there till a quarter to/ before three.
– I'll make it by three at the latest. If I'm late, you can have a coffee till I get there.

– I don't want to spend all afternoon drinking coffee. Then there will be no time left for shopping.

– El viernes pasado el tren llevaba un retraso y no llegaste antes de las tres menos cuarto.
– Llegaré a las tres como más tarde [a más tardar]. Si llego tarde, puedes tomar un café mientras esperas mi llegada.
– No quiero pasar toda la tarde bebiendo café. Luego no quedará tiempo para hacer las compras.

---

de la semana

decade **la década**

delay **el retraso, la posposición**
delayed **retrasado, aplazado**

during **durante**

early **temprano, pronto**
I am early **llego pronto**

end **el fin, el final**
I end (something) **termino, finalizo**
it ends **termina, finaliza**

ever **siempre**

every **todo, cada**
every time **todas las veces, cada vez**

exactly **exactamente**

fast **rápido, adelantado**
my watch is fast **mi reloj va adelantado**

finally **finalmente**

I finish **termino, finalizo**

first **el primero, primero**
at first **primero, al principio**

firstly **primeramente, en primer lugar**

for **para, a, por**

for a day (duration) **por (un) día**

for good/ever **para siempre, por siempre**

formerly **anteriormente**

fortnight/two weeks **la quincena**

frequent **frecuente**

frequently **frecuentemente**

from **de, desde**
as from (today) **de (hoy) en adelante**
from now on **de ahora en adelante, desde ahora**

I go on **continúo**

half **la mitad**
half **medio**
one and a half **uno y medio**

it happens **sucede, ocurre**

holiday/vacation **las vacaciones**

hurry **la prisa, [el afán]**
I hurry up **me apresuro, me doy prisa**
I am in a hurry **tengo prisa [afán]**

instant **el instante**

just **justo**
just now **justo ahora**

last/final **el último, el pasado**
last night **anoche**
last/previous **el último**
it lasts a long/short time **dura mucho/poco tiempo**

late **tarde**
I am late **llego tarde**
lately **últimamente**
later (on) **más tarde, después**

long **largo**

– You're sometimes late too.

– Only in winter or in bad weather.

– Last month I had to wait for twenty minutes.

Perhaps it would be better to meet another time. I'll call next week.

– A veces tu también llegas tarde.

– Sólo en invierno o con (el) mal tiempo.

– El mes pasado tuve que esperar veinte minutos.

Quizás sería mejor reunirnos en otra ocasión. Llamaré la semana que viene.

in the long term **a largo plazo**
many **muchos, muchas**
  many times **muchos días**
meanwhile **mientras tanto**
  in the meanwhile **mientras tanto**
middle **medio**
moment **el momento**
  at the moment **al momento**
  at this moment *(right now)* **en este momento**
  at that moment **en aquel momento**
  in a moment **en un momento**
month **el mes**
  monthly **mensualmente**
much **mucho/a**
never **nunca**
next *(adj)* **próximo**
  next *(adv)* **próximamente**
not till/until **no hasta**
now **ahora**
nowadays **hoy en día**
occasionally **a veces, ocasionalmente**
often **a menudo, con frecuencia**
on and off **de vez en cuando**
once **una vez**
  once upon a time **érase una vez, en tiempos de**
  once in a while **de vez en**

  cuando
  once a day **una vez al día**
one day **un día**
only **solo**
past **el pasado**
per (day) **por (día)**
present **el presente**
  present *(adj)* **presente, actual**
  presently **el el momento presente**
  at present **en este momento**
previous(ly) **anterior(mente)**
prompt **pronto, con prontitud, sin dilación**
  promptly at (two) **a (las dos) en punto**
rarely **raramente**
recent **reciente**
recently **recientemente**
I remain **me quedo**
right away **en seguida, ahora mismo**
Saint's day **el día del santo**
season **la estación**
  in season *(fruit)* **en sazón**
seldom **rara vez, raramente**
several **algunos, varios**
  several times **algunas veces, varias veces**
short **corto**
  (in the) short term **(a) corto**

– Hello, John, Peter here/speaking. Thank you for yesterday's call. Sorry I couldn't call then. I had only got back from London a quarter of an hour before.
After getting back I spent a long time with Anna; she thinks the project will take all month.

– **Hola, John, soy Peter. Gracias por haber llamado ayer. Siento que no pude llamar entonces. Sólo había llegado un cuarto de hora antes de Londres.**

Después de volver pasé mucho tiempo con Ana; ella cree que hará falta todo el mes para terminar el proyecto.

plazo
shortly **dentro de poco**
since **desde**
slow **lento**
my watch is slow **mi reloj va
retrasado [está atrasado]**
sometimes **algunas veces**
soon **pronto**
sooner or later **más tarde o
más temprano, antes o
después**
the sooner the better **cuanto
antes mejor**
I stay **me quedo**
still **todavía**
I stop (doing) **dejo (de hacer)**
suddenly **de repente**
sunrise **la salida del sol, el
amanecer**
sunset **la puesta del sol**
I take (an hour) **me lleva, [gasto]
(una hora)**
it takes (an hour) **lleva (una
hora)**
then (next) **luego, después**
then (at that time) **entonces**
thousand years **mil años**
till **hasta**
time (in general) **el tiempo**
time (occasion) **la vez**
at any time **en cualquier**

momento
at the same time **al mismo
tiempo**
from time to time **de vez en
cuando**
for a long time **durante mucho
tiempo**
in good time **a tiempo**
a long time ago **hace mucho
tiempo**
the whole time **todo el tiempo**
time zone **el huso horario**
twice **dos veces**
until **hasta**
usually **generalmente,
usualmente**
I wait **espero**
week **la semana**
weekly **semanalmente, por
semana**
weekday **el día de entre
semana, el día laboral**
weekend **el fin de semana**
when **cuando**
whenever **siempre que,
cuandoquiera que**
while (conj) **mientras**
year **el año**
yearly **anualmente**
yet **aún, todavía**
not yet **todavía**

We should start on the work at the beginning of June, before the summer holidays/vacations start. We can then get it done in good time.
– Hello Peter, John Brown here/speaking. I have been working on the project for a few days. Have you finished yours yet? Call me this afternoon. We must meet sometime.

Deberíamos empezar el trabajo a principios de junio, antes del comienzo de las vacaciones de verano. Entonces podremos terminarlo a tiempo.
– Hola Peter, soy John Brown. Llevo varios días trabajando en el proyecto. ¿Ya ha terminado el suyo? Llámeme esta tarde. Deberíamos reunirnos alguna vez.

3b The time, days & date

Time of day

a.m.   **de la mañana**
morning   **la mañana**
  in the morning(s)   **por la(s) mañana(s)**
noon   **el mediodía**
noon   **a mediodía**
afternoon   **la tarde**
  in the afternoon(s)   **por la(s) tarde(s)**
p.m.   **de la tarde**
evening   **la tarde, la noche**
  in the evening(s)   **por la(s) tarde(s), por la(s) noche(s)**
night   **la noche**
  at night   **por la noche**
midnight   **las doce de la noche, medianoche**
  at midnight   **a las doce de la noche, a medianoche**
today   **hoy**
  today week   **dentro de una semana**
tomorrow   **mañana**
  tomorrow morning   **mañana por la mañana**
  tomorrow afternoon   **mañana por la tarde**
  tomorrow evening   **mañana por la tarde, mañana por la noche**

  the day after tomorrow   **pasado mañana**
tonight   **esta noche**
yesterday   **ayer**
  yesterday afternoon   **ayer por la tarde**
  yesterday morning   **ayer por la mañana**
  yesterday evening   **ayer por la tarde, ayer por la noche**
  the day before yesterday   **anteayer**

Telling the time

second   **el segundo**
minute   **el minuto**
hour   **la hora**
  half an hour   **media hora**
  in an hour's time   **dentro de una hora**
  hourly   **cada hora**
quarter   **un cuarto**
  quarter of an hour   **un cuarto de hora**
  three quarters of an hour   **tres cuartos de hora**
  quarter past/after (two)   **(dos) y cuarto**
  quarter to/of (two)   **(dos) menos cuarto**

– What's the date today?

– The twenty-first of January.
– And what's the time, please?
– Ten past ten.
– What time does the film/movie start this evening?
– 20:00 hours.
– How long does it last?
– One and a half hours

– **¿A cuántos estamos? [¿Qué fecha es hoy?]**
– **Estamos a veintiuno de enero.**
– **¿Y qué hora es por favor?**
– **Son las diez y diez.**
– **¿A qué hora empieza la película esta tarde/noche?**
– **A las veinte horas.**
– **¿Cuánto dura?**
– **Dura una hora y media.**

---

half past (two)   **(dos) y media**
17:45   **las seis menos cuarto, las cinco cuarenta y cinco**
five past/after six   **las seis y cinco**
five to/of six   **las seis menos cinco**
12:00 noon   **las doce del mediodía, el mediodía**
12:00 midnight   **las doce de la noche**

The days of the week

Monday   **el lunes**
Tuesday   **el martes**
Wednesday   **el miércoles**
Thursday   **el jueves**
Friday   **el viernes**
Saturday   **el sábado**
Sunday   **el domingo**

The months*

January   **enero**
February   **febrero**
March   **marzo**
April   **abril**
May   **mayo**
June   **junio**
July   **julio**
August   **agosto**
September   **septiembre/setiembre**
October   **octubre**
November   **noviembre**
December   **diciembre**

The seasons

spring   **la primavera**
summer   **el verano**
autumn/fall   **el otoño**
winter   **el invierno**

The date

last Friday   **el viernes pasado**
on Tuesday   **el martes**
on Tuesdays   **los martes**
by Friday   **para el viernes**
the first of January   **el uno de enero, [el primero de enero]**
on the third of January   **el tres de enero**
in 2000   **en el año dos mil**
1st January/January 1st, 1994   **el uno de enero de 1994**
at the end of 1999   **a finales de 1999**
by the end of 1999   **para finales de 1999**
at the beginning (of July)   **a primeros de (julio)**
by the beginning (of July)   **para primeros de (julio)**
in December   **en diciembre**
in mid/the middle of January   **a mediados de enero**
at the end of March   **al final de marzo**
in spring   **en primavera**

– I am going shopping tomorrow morning. Would you like to come too?
– I'd prefer to go in the afternoon. And let's go on Tuesday. I always have such a lot to do on Mondays.
– All right, I'll leave home at two o'clock and meet you at half-past two at the station.

– **Voy de compras mañana por la mañana. ¿Te gustaría ir conmigo?**
– **Preferiría ir por la tarde. Y vayamos el martes. Siempre tengo mucho que hacer los lunes.**
– **Vale, saldré de casa a las dos y te veré a las dos y media en la estación.**

➤ All months in Spanish are masculine.

How much? – expressions of quantity

4a Length and shape

angle **el ángulo**	perpendicular **perpendicular**
area **el área, la superficie**	point **el punto**
big **grande**	room *(space)* **el espacio, el sitio**
centre/center **el centro**	round **redondo**
concave **cóncavo**	ruler **la regla**
convex **convexo**	shape **la forma, la figura**
curved **curvo**	short **corto**
deep **profundo, hondo**	size **el tamaño, la talla, la medida**
degree **el grado**	small **pequeño**
depth **la profundidad**	space **el espacio**
diagonal **diagonal**	straight **derecho**
distance **la distancia**	tall **alto**
I draw **dibujo**	thick **grueso, espeso**
height **la altura**	thin **fino, delgado**
high **alto**	wide **ancho**
horizontal **horizontal**	width **la anchura**
large **grande**	
length **la longitud**	*Shapes*
line **la línea**	circle **el círculo**
long **largo**	circular **circular**
low **bajo**	cube **el cubo**
it measures **mide**	cubic **cúbico**
narrow **estrecho**	cylinder **el cilindro**
parallel **paralelo**	hectare **la hectárea**

-- You need a straight ruler and pencil. Measure the space and then draw a plan.

Leave room for some vegetables. The distance from the house to the fence is 12 metres/meters. The garden is not wide enough for a pool.

– How high is the tree? – About 5 metres/meters.

– Necesita una regla y un lápiz. Mide el espacio, luego dibuja un plano.

Deja sitio para el huerto. La distancia entre la casa y la tapia es 12 metros. El jardín no es bastante ancho para un estanque.

– ¿Qué altura tiene el árbol? – Unos 5 metros.

pyramid **la pirámide**
rectangle **el rectángulo**
  rectangular **rectangular**
sphere **la esfera**
  spherical **esférico**
square **el cuadrado**
  square **cuadrado**
triangle **el triángulo**
  triangular **triangular**

Units of length

centimetre/centirmeter **el centímetro**
foot **el pie**
inch **la pulgada**
kilometre/kilometer **el kilómetro**
metre/meter **el metro**
mile **la milla**
millimetre/millimeter **el milímetro**
yard **la vara, la yarda**

Expressions of quantity

about **alrededor, aproximadamente**
almost **casi**
approximate **aproximado**
approximately **aproximadamente**
as much as **tanto como**
at least **al menos**
capacity **la capacidad, el volumen**

it contains **contiene**
cubic capacity **la capacidad cúbica**
it decreases **disminuye**
difference **la diferencia**
empty **vacío**
I empty **vacío**
enough **bastante, suficiente**
I fill **lleno**
full (of) **lleno (de)**
growth **el aumento**
hardly **difícilmente, casi**
increase **el aumento**
it increases **aumenta**
little **pequeño**
  a little **un poco**
a lot (of) **mucho (de)**
I measure **mido**
measuring tape **la cinta métrica, [el metro]**
more **más**
nearly **casi**
number **el número**
part **la parte**
quantity **la cantidad**
sufficient **suficiente**
too much **demasiado**
volume **el volumen**
whole **la totalidad, el todo**
  whole *(adj)* **todo**

The shed will be at an angle of about 40 degrees to the house, diagonally across from the gate.

El cobertizo estará a un ángulo de unos 40 grados con relación a la casa, en sentido diagonal con relación a la puerta.

The area of our garden is 100 square metres/meters. It is 10 metres/meters long and 10 wide.

La área de nuestro jardín es 100 metros cuadrados. Es largo de 10 metros y ancho de 10 metros.

We put a round pond in, only 80-100 centimetres/centimeters deep.

Introducimos un estanque redondo, de una profundidad de 80-100 centímetros.

4b Measuring

Expressions of volume

bag   **el saco, la bolsa**
bar   **la barra**
bottle   **la botella**
box   **la caja**
container   **el recipiente, [el contáiner]**
cup   **la copa, la taza**
gallon   **el galón**
glass   **el vaso**
liter/litre   **el litro**
   centilitre/centiliter   **el centilitro**

millilitre/millimeter   **el mililitro**
pack   **el paquete**
pair   **el par, la pareja**
piece   **la pieza**
   a piece of cake   **una porción de tarta**
pint   **la pinta**
portion   **la porción**
pot   **la olla**
sack   **el saco, [el costal]**
tube   **el tubo**

— How many centilitres/centileters are there in the bottle?
— 75, but you can also get it in litre/liter bottles.

— ¿Cuántos centílitros hay en la botella?
— Setenta y cinco, pero también se puede obtener en botellas de litro.

— Would you like a cup of tea? — No, I would prefer a glass of water.

— ¿Quiere una taza de té? – No, preferiría un vaso de agua.

Could I have two packets of tissues and a packet of aspirin please?

Deme dos paquetes de pañuelos de papel y un paquete de aspirina, por favor.

— How much wood do you want?
— Enough for the whole fence. I must not buy too much. Yes, that should be sufficient. Give me a bag of cement too.

— ¿Cuánta madera quiere?
— Lo suficiente para toda la valla. No debería comprar demasiado. Sí, esto será suficiente. Deme también un saco de cemento.

— How many cubic metres of concrete do you need? — About two.

— ¿Cuántos metros cúbicos de hormigón necesita? – Dos, más o menos.

Temperature

it boils **hierve**
I chill **enfrío**
cold **el frío**
   cold *(adj)* **frío**
cool **fresco**
   I cool it down **lo enfrío**
degree **el grado**
I freeze **congelo**
heat **el calor**
   I heat **caliento**
hot **caliente**
temperature **la temperatura**
I warm it (up) **lo caliento**
warmth **el calor**

Weight and density

dense **denso**
density **la densidad**
gramme/gram **el gramo**
heavy **pesado**
kilo **el kilo**
light **ligero**
mass **la masa**
ounce **la onza**
pound *(lb)* **la libra**
scales/balance **el peso, la balanza**
ton(ne) **la tonelada**
I weigh **peso**
weight **el peso**

It's so hot! What's the temperature? It must be nearly 30 degrees. I am too hot.

In winter it's cold here. We all freeze in this house and have to put the heating on in September.

When the temperature reaches zero we have to light two fires.

– Can you weigh the ingredients?
– How many grams of sugar do we need?
– I want a pound - that must be about 500 grammes/grams.
I need a little flour and a lot of sugar. Give me a piece of butter. About 100 grammes/grams. I will need several eggs.

– That's too little. We need even more cakes. Make a bit more.

¡Qué calor hace! ¿Cuál es la temperatura? Serán unos treinta grados. Tengo demasiado calor.

En el invierno hace frío aquí. Todos pasamos frío en esta casa y tenemos que poner la calefacción en setiembre. Cuando la temperatura baja a cero grados, tenemos que encender dos fuegos.

– Pesa los ingredientes.
– ¿Cuántos gramos de azúcar necesitamos?
– Quiero una libra - que serán unos quinientos gramos. Necesito un poco de harina y mucho azúcar. Póngame un trozo de mantequilla. Unos cien gramos. Necesitaré unos huevos.
– No basta así. Vamos a necesitar más pasteles aun. Haz un poco más.

➤ WEATHER 24d

4c Numbers

Cardinal numbers

zero	**cero**	twenty	**veinte**
one	**uno**	twenty-one	**veintiuno**
two	**dos**	twenty-two	**veintidós**
three	**tres**	twenty-nine	**veintinueve**
four	**cuatro**	thirty	**treinta**
five	**cinco**	thirty-one	**treinta y uno**
six	**seis**	forty	**cuarenta**
seven	**siete**	fifty	**cincuenta**
eight	**ocho**	sixty	**sesenta**
nine	**nueve**	seventy	**setenta**
ten	**diez**	eighty	**ochenta**
eleven	**once**	ninety	**noventa**
twelve	**doce**	a hundred	**cien**
thirteen	**trece**	a hundred and one	**ciento uno**
fourteen	**catorce**	two hundred	**doscientos**
fifteen	**quince**	a thousand	**mil**
sixteen	**dieciséis**	two thousand	**dos mil**
seventeen	**diecisiete**	million	**el millón**
eighteen	**dieciocho**	two million	**dos millones**
nineteen	**diecinueve**	milliard/billion *(US)*	**mil milliones**
		billion	**el billón**

Half of the house belongs to my brother. We divided it between us. However, he only pays a quarter of the costs as I let/rented my half out in summer.

La mitad de la casa pertenece a mi hermano. La dividimos entre los dos. Sin embargo, sólo paga la cuarta parte de los gastos, pues yo dejo mi mitad en alquiler durante el verano.

– What is the volume of water in the swimming pool?
– 10,000 gallons, that is about 45,000 litres/liters.

– ¿Cuánta agua hay en la piscina?
– Diez mil galones, es decir unos cuarenta y cinco mil litros.

Ordinal numbers

first   **el primero**
second   **el segundo**
third   **el tercero**
fourth   **el cuarto**
nineteenth   **el décimonoveno**
twentieth   **el vigésimo**
twenty-first   **el vigésimo primero**
hundredth   **el centésimo**

Nouns

one   **el uno**
  unit   **la unidad**
a pair/couple of   **un par (de)**
ten   **el diez**
  about ten (of)   **una decena (de)**
  tens   **las decenas**
dozen   **la docena**
about twenty   **una veintena (de)**
hundred   **el cien**
  hundreds of   **cientos de**
about a thousand   **un millar**
  thousands (of)   **millares/miles (de)**
million   **el millón**
  millions of   **millones de**

Writing numerals

1,000   **1.000**
1,500   **1.500**
1st   **1°**
2nd   **2°**
1.56   **1,56 (uno coma cincuenta y séis)**
.05   **,05 (coma cero cinco)**

Fractions

half   **la mitad, el medio**
  a half   **una mitad, un medio**
  one and a half   **uno y medio**
  two and a half   **dos y medio**
quarter   **el cuarto**
a quarter   **un cuarto**
three quarters   **tres cuartos**
third   **el tercio**
fifth   **el quinto**
five and five sixths   **cinco y cinco sextos**
tenth   **el décimo**
sixth   **el sexto**
hundredth   **la centésima**
thousandth   **el milésimo**
millionth   **el millonésimo**

– You can not all have half a bar of chocolate.
There is only enough for a quarter each.
And a quarter of a litre/liter of apple juice.
– I don't want a quarter, I want a half.

– **No todos podéis tener media tableta de chocolate.**
Sólo hay suficiente para una cuarta parte para cada uno.
Y un cuarto de litro de zumo de manzana.
– **No quiero una cuarta parte, quiero una mitad.**

4d Calculations

addition **la suma, la adición**	I divide by **divido entre**
I add **sumo, adiciono**	six divided by two **séis**
average **la media, el medio, el promedio**	**dividido entre/por dos**
I average out **saco la media**	it equals **es igual a**
on average **como media**	equation **la ecuación**
I calculate **calculo**	it is equivalent to **es equivalente a**
calculation **el cálculo**	I estimate **estimo**
calculator **la calculadora**	even **el par**
correct **corrijo**	figure **la cifra**
I count **cuento**	graph **el gráfico**
data **el dato, los datos**	is greater than **es mayor que**
piece of data **el dato**	is less than **es menor que**
decimal **el decimal**	maximum **el máximo**
decimal point **el punto decimal**	maximum **máximo**
diameter **el diámetro**	up to a maximum of **hasta un máximo de**
digit **el dígito, la cifra**	medium **la media**
two digit **de dos dígitos**	medium (adj) **medio**
I double **multiplico por dos, doblo**	minimum **el mínimo**
division **la división**	minimum (adj) **mínimo**
	minus **menos**

An inch is the same as 2.54 cm, and there are twelve inches in a foot, 36 in a yard. A mile is 1760 yards. A kilometre/kilometer is 1000 metres/meters.

Una pulgada equivale a 2,54 centímetros, y hay doce pulgadas en un pie, treinta y seis en una vara. Una milla tiene 1760 varas. Un kilómetro tiene 1000 metros.

What is 14 plus 8? It equals 22. Did you get the right result?

¿Cuántos son 14 más 8? Son 22. ¿Obtuviste el resultado correcto?

20 minus 5 is 15, 20 divided by 5 equals 4.

20 menos 5 son 15, 20 dividido por 5 son cuatro.

Work out 12 times 22. That is an easy sum.

Calcula 12 por 22. Es un cálculo fácil.

2 to the power of 3 is 8. Three squared equals 9.

2 a la potencia de 3 son 8 [2 al cubo son 8]. Tres al cuadrado son 9.

mistake/error **el error**
multiplication **la multiplicación**
   I multiply **multiplico**
   three times two **tres por dos**
negative **el negativo**
number **el número**
   cardinal/ordinal numbers **los números cardinales/ordinales**
numeral **el numeral**
odd **el impar**
percent **el por ciento**
   by 10% **el diez por ciento**
percentage **el porcentaje**
plus **más**
   two plus two **dos más dos**
positive **el positivo**
power **la potencia**
   to the power of five **a la quinta potencia**
problem **el problema**
quantity **la cantidad**
ratio **la proporción**
   a ratio of 100:1 **una**

   proporción de 100 a 1
result` **el resultado**
similar **similar**
solution **la solución**
   I solve **resuelvo**
square **el cuadrado**
square root **la raiz cuadrada**
   three squared **la raiz cúbica**
statistic **la estadística**
statistics **las estadísticas**
statistical **estadístico**
sum **la suma**
subtraction **la resta, la sustracción**
   I subtract **resto, sustraigo**
symbol **el símbolo**
I take away **resto**
total **el total**
   in total **en total**
I treble **triplico**
triple **el triple**
I work out **saco, calculo**
wrong **mal, equivocado**

– I estimate that we have about 500 visitors a year.
– What percentage of visitors are local? – 20% (percent).

Have you got any statistics about it?

A snail travels at an average speed of 0.041 kilometres/ kilometers per hour.

– In this game you add up your score over the week.
– What was the total score?
– I have a total of 500 points. To calculate the average you add up the totals and divide by the number of games.

– **Calculo que recibimos a unos 500 visitantes al año.**
– **¿Qué porcentaje de los visitantes son de esta misma región? – 20% (por ciento).**
– **¿Tiene estadísticas sobre ello?**

Un caracol viaja a una velocidad de 0,041 kilómetros por hora.

– **En este juego, se hace la puntuación total de la semana.**
– **¿Cuál fue la puntuación final?**
– **Tengo un total de 500 puntos. Para calcular el promedio, sumas los totales y lo divides por el número de juegos.**

What sort of? – descriptions & judgements

5a Describing people

appearance **la apariencia**	female **la mujer**
attractive **atractivo**	feminine **femenino**
average **medio**	figure **la figura, el tipo**
he is bald **es calvo**	fit **en forma**
beard **la barba**	I frown **frunzo el ceño**
bearded **con barba**	glasses **las gafas**
beautiful **guapo, bello**	good-looking **guapo**
beauty **la belleza**	I grow **crezco**
blond **rubio**	hair **el pelo, el cabello**
broad **ancho**	hairstyle **el peinado**
build **la constitución**	handsome **hermoso, bello, distinguido**
chic **chic, de moda**	
clean-shaven **afeitado**	heavy **pesado, grueso**
clumsy **torpe**	height **la altura**
complexion **la constitución**	large **grande**
curly **rizado, crespo**	I laugh **río, me río**
dark **oscuro, moreno**	laugh **la risa**
I describe **describo**	I am left-handed **soy zurdo**
description **la descripción**	light **claro**
different (from) **diferente de, distinto de**	long-sighted **hipermétrope**
	I look like **soy, mi apariencia es**
elegant **elegante**	I look well **soy guapo**
energy **la energía, el vigor**	male **el varón, el hombre**
expression **la expresión**	masculine **masculino**
fat **gordo**	moustache **el bigote**
feature **la facción, el rasgo**	neat **limpio, acicalado, pulcro**

adolescence **la adolescencia**	older/elder **mayor**
adolescent **el/la adolescente**	teenager **el adolescente**
age **la edad**	young **joven**
elderly **viejo, mayor, anciano**	young person **el joven, la persona joven**
grown up **el adulto**	
grown up **adulto**	young people **los jóvenes**
middle-aged **de mediana edad**	youth **la juventud**
old **viejo, mayor**	youthful **lleno de juventud**

neatness	**la limpieza**	I smile	**sonrío**
obese	**obeso**	smile	**la sonrisa**
overweight	**el sobrepeso, el exceso de peso**	spot	**el lunar, el grano**
		spotty	**con lunares, con granos**
part of body	**la parte del cuerpo**	stocky	**rechoncho, bajo pero fuerte**
paunch	**la barriga, la panza**		
physical	**físico**	strength	**la fuerza**
plump	**rechoncho**	striking	**impresionante, imponente**
pretty	**guapo, bonito**		
red-haired	**pelirrojo**	strong	**fuerte, robusto**
I am right-handed	**soy diestro**	tall	**alto**
I scowl	**pongo mal gesto, frunzo el ceño, hago mala cara**	thin	**delgado, flaco**
		tiny	**pequeño**
sex/gender	**el sexo, el género**	trendy	**moderno**
short	**bajo, corto**	ugliness	**la fealdad**
short-sighted	**miope**	ugly	**feo**
similar (to)	**parecido a, similar a**	walk	**el andar, el paso**
similarity	**la similaridad**	wavy	**ondulado**
size	**el tamaño, la talla**	I weigh	**peso**
slim/slender	**delgado, esbelto**	weight	**el peso**
small	**pequeño, bajo**		

– What's your uncle like? Can you describe him?

– He looks very like my father, but he wears glasses. Look, who's that tall fellow?

– That's my brother, with the beard. He's mad on keeping fit.

– What a pretty girl! Is that your cousin?

– Yes, she's blond with blue eyes. She's very slim, with a good figure and a beautiful smile.

– Little Ben now has dark hair and is about 1 metre/meter tall. He looks very well, but he's very thin.

– Yes, he only weighs 16 kilos.

– ¿Cómo es tu tío? ¿Puedes describirle?

– Se parece mucho a mi padre, pero lleva gafas. Mira, ¿quién es ese tipo alto?

– Es mi hermano con la barba. Es muy aficionado a mantenerse en forma.

– ¡Que chica más bonita! ¿Es tu prima?

– Sí, es rubia con ojos azules. Es muy esbelta, con un buen físico y una sonrisa hermosa.

– Ahora el pequeño Ben tiene el pelo moreno y mide un metro. Tiene buena cara, pero es muy delgado.

– Sí, sólo pesa 16 kilos.

5b The senses

bitter **amargo**
bright **claro, luminoso**
   bright *(harsh)* **brillante**
cold **el frío**
   cold **frío**
colour/color **el color**
colourful/colorful **lleno de color**
dark **oscuro**
darkness **la oscuridad**
delicious **delicioso**
disgusting **desagradable**
dull **apagado, sombrío**
I feel ... **siento**
   it feels **es**
I hear **oigo**
hot **caliente**
light *(colour/color)* **claro, pálido**
I listen **oigo, escucho**
I look **miro, veo**
   I look at *(something)* **miro a**
loud **alto, ruidoso**
noise **el ruido**
noisy **ruidoso**
odour/odor **el olor**
opaque **opaco**
perfume **el perfume**
perfumed **perfumado**

quiet **quieto, tranquilo, callado**
rough **rugoso, áspero**
salty **salado**
I see **veo**
sense **el sentido**
silence **el silencio**
silent **silencioso**
   I am silent **estoy silencioso,
   estoy en silencio**
smell **el olor**
   I smell **huelo**
   it smells (of) **huele a**
   smelly **oloroso, apestoso**
soft *(sound)* **bajo, flojo, suave**
   soft *(texture)* **suave**
sound **el sonido**
it sounds **suena**
   it sounds like **suena como**
sour **agrio**
sticky **pegajoso**
   it is sticky **es pegajoso**
sweet **dulce**
taste **el sabor**
I taste **saboreo**
it tastes (of) **sabe a**
tepid **tibio**
I touch **toco**

– What colour/color is your new
coat? – Well, it's sort of red.

– Dark or light red? – It is more
maroon.

The jam tastes of fruit but is very
bitter.

Don't touch that book, your hands
are all sticky.

– ¿De qué color es tu abrigo
nuevo? – Bueno, es una especie
de rojo.

– ¿Rojo oscuro o claro? – Es
más bien rojo oscuro.

La mermelada sabe a fruta, pero
está muy amarga.

No toques ese libro, tienes las
manos pegajosas.

transparent **transparente**
visible (in-) **(in)visible**
warm **caliente**
warmth **el calor**

Common parts of the body

arm **el brazo**
back **la espalda**
body **el cuerpo**
  part of the body **la parte del cuerpo**
chest **el pecho**
ear **la oreja**

eye **el ojo**
face **la cara**
hand **la mano**
head **la cabeza**
leg **la pierna**
mouth **la boca**
neck **el cuello**
neck (back of) **la nuca**
nose **la nariz**
shoulder **el hombro**
stomach **el estómago**
tooth **el diente**

Colours/Colors

beige **beige**
black **negro**
blue **azul**
brown **marrón, café**
brownish **amarronado**
cream **crema**
gold (metal) **el oro**
  gold (adj) **de oro, dorado**
green **verde**
grey/gray **gris**
maroon **rojo oscuro, marrón**
orange (fruit) **la naranja**

orange (adj) **anaranjado**
pink **rosa, rosado**
purple **purpúreo, [morado]**
red **rojo**
scarlet **escarlata** (invar)
silver (metal) **la plata**
  silver (adj) **plateado**
turquoise **la turquesa**
  turquoise (adj) **aturquesado**
violet **violeta** (invar)
white **blanco**
yellow **amarillo**

– What's in that bag? It feels hard.

– Let me feel - it's a bottle. What's in it?
– I don't know. It looks like orange juice.
– I'll taste it … It's disgusting. It tastes of oranges but it's too sweet.

– What a beautiful smell. – Yes, that's the flowers; they are so bright and colourful.

– ¿Qué hay en esta bolsa? Parece ser algo duro.

– Déjame palparlo - es una botella. ¿Qué tiene dentro?
– No sé. Se parece a zumo de naranja.
– Lo voy a probar … Es asqueroso. Sabe a naranjas, pero es demasiado dulce.

– ¡Qué olor más agradable! – Sí, son las flores; están tan llenas de colores vivos.

5c Describing things

appearance **la apariencia**	dirt **la suciedad**
big **grande**	dirty **sucio**
broad **ancho**	dry **seco**
broken **roto**	empty **vacío**
clean **limpio**	enormous **enorme**
closed **cerrado**	fashionable **de moda**
colour/color **el color**	fat **gordo**
coloured/colored **de color**	firm **firme**
colourful/colorful **de muchos**	flat **plano**
colores	flexible **flexible, elástico**
damp **húmedo**	fresh **fresco**
deep **hondo, profundo**	full (of) **lleno (de)**
depth **la hondura, la**	genuine/real **genuino, auténtico**
profundidad	hard **duro**

Ten questions

What's that thingummyjig? **¿Qué es ese chisme?, [¿Qué es esa cosa?]**

What's it for? **¿Para qué sirve?**
What do you use it for? **¿Para qué lo utilizas?**
Can you see it? **¿Lo ves?**
What's it like? **¿Cómo es?**

What does it look like? **¿A qué se parece?**
What does it sound like? **¿A qué suena?**
What does it smell of? **¿A qué huele?**
What colour/color is it? **¿De qué color es?**
What kind of thing is it? **¿Qué tipo de cosa es?**

– What's that over there?
– That thing there? It's a new kind of bottle opener.
– Does it work?
– Yes indeed. It's the best there is.

This is a genuine natural material, soft and thick. That is a synthetic material, it's smooth but the colours/colors are harsh.

– **¿Qué es aquello que está allí?**
– **¿Aquello allí? Es un nuevo tipo de abrebotellas.**
– **¿Funciona?**
– **Claro. Es el mejor que existe.**

Éste es un tejido genuinamente natural, blando y espeso. Aquél es un tejido sintético, es suave, pero los colores son chillones.

height **la altura**	shallow **poco profundo**
it looks like **parece**	shiny **brillante**
it matches **hace juego con**	short **corto**
kind **agradable**	shut **cerrado**
large **grande**	small **pequeño**
liquid **líquido**	smooth **liso**
little **pequeño**	soft *(texture)* **suave**
long **largo**	solid **sólido, compacto**
low **bajo**	soluble **soluble**
main **principal, importante**	sort **la clase, el tipo**
material **material**	spot **el lunar, la mota**
matter **la materia**	spotted **a lunares, moteado**
moist **mojado, húmedo**	stain **la mancha**
mouldy/moldy **mohoso, enmohecido**	stained **manchado**
	stripe **la raya**
narrow **estrecho**	striped **a rayas, rayado**
natural **natural**	subsidiary **secundario**
new **nuevo**	substance **la substancia**
open **abierto**	synthetic **sintético**
out of date **pasado de moda**	thick **espeso**
painted **pintado**	thing **la cosa, el objeto**
pale **pálido, claro**	thingummyjig **la cosa**
pattern **el diseño**	tint **el tinte**
patterned **modelado**	varied **variado**
plump **lleno, rechoncho**	water-proof **a prueba de agua**
resistant **resistente**	wet **mojado**
rotten **podrido**	wide **ancho**
shade **el tono, el matiz**	

– I'm looking for something big to stand on.	– **Busco algo grande en que levantarme.**
– Will anything do?	– **¿Bastará cualquier cosa?**
– Well, it must be something solid.	– **Bueno, tiene que ser algo sólido.**
– What about this?	– **¿Qué te parece esto?**
– Is there nothing bigger?	– **¿No hay nada más grande?**
– Stand on the chair.	– **Levántate en la silla.**
– It's too soft.	– **Es demasiado blando.**
– All the other chairs are too low.	– **Todas las demás sillas son demasiado bajas.**
– Both the cupboards are too high.	– **Ambos armarios están demasiado altos.**

5d Evaluating things

abnormal **anormal, raro**
I adore **adoro**
all right **muy bien, bueno**
it is all right **está bien**
appalling **espantoso, horroroso**
bad **malo**
beautiful **bonito**
better/best **mejor, el mejor**
cheap **barato**
correct **correcto**
it costs **cuesta**
delicious **delicioso**
I detest **detesto**
difficulty **la dificultad**
difficult/hard **difícil, duro**
disgusting **repugnante, asqueroso**
I dislike **no me gusta**

I enjoy **disfruto**
easy **fácil**
essential (in-) **(no) esencial**
excellent **excelente**
expensive **caro, costoso**
I fail **fallo, fracaso**
failure **el fallo, el fracaso**
false **falso**
fine **bueno, fino, delicado**
good **bueno**
good value **buen precio**
great/terrific **magnífico, estupendo, tremendo**
I hate **odio, detesto**
high **alto, bueno**
important (un-) **(no) importante**
incorrect **incorrecto**
interesting (un-) **(no) interesante**

a bit **un poco**
enough **bastante, suficiente**
extremely **extremamente**
fairly **bastante**
hardly ... at all **difícilmente**
litte **pequeño, poco**
  a little **un poco**
a lot **mucho**
much (better) **mucho mejor**

not at all **nada en absoluto**
particularly **particularmente, especialmente**
quite **bastante**
rather **muy, bastante**
really **realmente**
so **así, de esta manera**
too (good) **demasiado (bueno)**
very **muy**

How do you like our neighbour's garden/neighbor's yard? We do not like it at all.
I wish he would throw away that broken seat.
It is only plastic anyway. We always buy the best! Our garden furniture is made of wood.
And his lawn mower is out of order.

¿Qué te parece el jardín de nuestro vecino? A nosotros no nos gusta nada.
Me gustaría que tire [botara] aquella silla rota.
Sólo es de plástico. ¡Siempre compramos lo mejor! Nuestros muebles de jardín están hechos de madera.
Y su cortacésped no funciona.

I like **me gusta**
mediocre **mediocre**
necessary (un-) **(in)necesario**
normal **normal, común**
order **el orden**
   in order **en orden**
   out of order **sin orden**
out of date **fuera de fecha,**
caducado
ordinary **ordinario, normal,**
común
pleasant **agradable**
poor **pobre**
practical (im-) **(no) práctico**
I prefer **prefiero**
quality **la calidad**
   top quality **la mejor calidad, la**
alta calidad
   poor quality **la mala calidad, la**
baja calidad

right **bueno**
strange **extraño, raro**
I succeed **consigo**
success **el éxito, la consecución**
successful **exitoso**
true **verdadero**
I try **intento, pruebo**
ugly **feo**
unpleasant **desagradable**
unsuccessful **sin éxito, fracasado**
I use **uso, utilizo**
use **el uso, la utilización**
useful **útil**
well **bien**
worse/worst **peor, el peor**
I would rather **prefiero, preferiría**
wrong **equivocado**

He never puts it away, and now
he'll have to get it mended/fixed.
I fear he's not a very successful
gardener. His vegetables are a
complete failure.

Nunca la guarda, y ahora tendrá
que hacerla reparar.
Por desgracia no tiene mucho
éxito como jardinero. Sus
legumbres han fallado [se
perdieron] por completo.

I do like to keep the garden/yard
tidy/neat.
People always say our garden/
yard is the best in the road.

Me gusta mucho mantener el
jardín en buen estado.
La gente siempre dice que
nuestro jardín es el mejor de la
calle.

I tried to ring/call you yesterday,
but the telephones were out of
order.

Traté de llamarte ayer pero no
funcionaban los teléfonos.

– Would you like to try this wine?
– Thank you, it is quite delicious.

– ¿Te gustaría probar este vino?
– Gracias, está muy delicioso.

– Do you enjoy going to the
cinema/movies?
– Yes, I particularly enjoyed last
week's film/movie.

– ¿Te gusta ir al cine?

– Sí, me gustó sobre todo la
película de la semana pasada.

➤ EXPRESSING VIEWS 15b

5e Comparisons

Regular comparatives & superlatives*

easy **fácil**
easier **más fácil**
easiest **el más fácil**

Irregular comparatives and superlatives*

bad **malo**
worse **peor**
worst **el peor**

big **grande**
bigger **mayor, más grande**
biggest **el mayor, el más grande**
good **bueno**
better **mejor**
best **el mejor**
small **pequeño**
smaller **menor, más pequeño**
smallest **el menor, el más pequeño**

Look at the children! Peter, our eldest son, is now the tallest. He's best at football/soccer, too. That's what he enjoys best.

¡Mira a los niños! Pedro, nuestro hijo mayor, ya es el más alto. Es él que juega mejor al fútbol también. Es lo que a él le gusta más hacer.

John is now fairly large, almost as tall as Peter, and he really is too fat. He prefers to swim.

Juan ya es bastante grande, casi tan alto como Pedro, y la verdad es que es demasiado gordo. Prefiere nadar.

The smallish boy over there is David. He is quite small compared with the others, but on the other hand very confident. He behaves less well than his brother.

El chico pequeño que está allá es David. Es bastante pequeño en comparación con los demás, pero por otra parte es muy seguro de sí mismo. Se comporta menos bien que su hermano.

John has eaten the largest cake. He gets larger and larger.

Juan ha comido el pastel más grande. Se hace cada vez más grande.

5f Materials

acrylic	el acrílico	paper	el papel
brick	el ladrillo	plastic	el plástico
cashmere	la cachemira, el cachemir	polyester	el poliéster
		pottery	la cerámica
cement	el cemento	satin	el raso
china	la porcelana	silk	la seda
concrete	el hormigón	silky	sedoso
cotton	el algodón	silver	la plata
denim	el dril, la tela vaquera	steel	el acero
gas	el gas	steel (adj)	de acero, acerado
glass	el vidrio, el cristal	stone	la piedra
gold	el oro	stone (adj)	de piedra
iron	el hierro	terylene	el terilene
leather	la piel, el cuero	velvet	el terciopelo
linen	el lino, el lienzo, [el hilo]	viscose	la viscosa
metal	el metal	wood	la madera
mineral	el mineral	wooden	de madera
nylon	el nilón, el nailon	wool	la lana
oil	el aceite, el petróleo	woollen/woolen	de lana

Have you seen our latest products? They are just as cheap as the competition.

¿Ha visto usted nuestros últimos productos? Son tan baratos como los de la competencia.

We can not ask a higher price, as the greatest demand is for the cheaper product.

No podemos pedir un precio más alto, pues la demanda más grande es la del producto más barato.

Which dress would you like? Silk is softer than wool, but it costs a lot. Nylon is cheapest.

¿Qué vestido preferirías? La seda es más blanda que la lana, pero cuesta mucho dinero. El nilón es el más barato.

The most beautiful dress is the one made of cotton.

El vestido más bello es el que está hecho de algodón.

The colours/colors are brighter and I think the cut is better, although it is not as warm as the woollen/woolen dress.

Los colores son más vivos y creo que el corte es mejor, aunque no es tan cálido [abrigado] como el vestido de lana.

It is not at all expensive. I prefer it to the others.

De ninguna manera es caro. Lo prefiero a los demás.

► CLOTHING 9c; COMPOUNDS & ALLOYS, CHEMICAL ELEMENTS App.23b

The human mind & character

6a Human character

active **activo**
I adapt **me adapto**
amusing **divertido**
I annoy **molesto, importuno**
bad **malo**
bad-tempered **de mal temperamento/genio**
I behave **me comporto, me porto**
behaviour/behavior **la conducta, el comportamiento**
I boast **presumo, fanfarroneo**
calm **tranquilo, calmado**
care **cuidado**
careful **cuidadoso**
careless **descuidado**
character **el carácter**
characteristic **la característica**
characteristic (adj) **característico**
charming **encantador, atractivo**
cheerful **alegre**
clever **listo, despierto**
confident **seguro de sí mismo**
discipline **la disciplina, el orden**
dreadful **terrible, espantoso, horrible**

evil **el mal**
evil (adj) **maligno**
foolish **tonto**
forgetful **olvidadizo**
friendly (un-) **(poco) amistoso**
fussy **quisquilloso, exigente**
generous **generoso**
I get on with **me llevo bien con, [me entiendo con]**
gifted **con talento, dotado**
good **bueno**
good-tempered **amistoso, afable**
habit **la costumbre, el hábito**
hard-working **trabajador, laborioso**
I help **ayudo**
helpful **atento, servicial**
honest (dis-) **(des)honesto**
humour/humor **el humor, el estado de ánimo**
humorous **humorístico**
immorality **la inmoralidad**
innocent **inocente**
intelligence **la inteligencia**
intelligent **inteligente**
kind (un-) **(poco) amable**

Don't be so suspicious. Please trust me.

No seas tan desconfiado. Por favor, fíate de mí [confía en mí].

Our neighbour/neighbor is a lazy fellow, but very gifted. He has a good sense of humour but is very boastful.

Nuestro vecino es un tipo perezoso, pero tiene mucho talento. Tiene un buen sentido de humor, pero es muy presumido.

His wife is very pleasant and helpful.

Su esposa es muy simpática y amable.

The children are lively characters. They never obey their mother.

Estos niños son muy enérgicos. Nunca le obedecen a su madre.

kindness la amabilidad
lazy perezoso, holgazán
laziness la pereza, la
  holgazanería
lively animado, alegre, vivo
mad loco
manners los modales, las maneras
mental(ly) mental(mente)
moral (im-) (in)moral
morality la moralidad
nervous nervioso, agitado
nice agradable, bonito
I obey (dis-) (des)obedezco
optimistic optimista
patient (im-) (im)paciente
personality la personalidad
pessimistic pesimista
pleasant agradable, placentero
polite (im-) (mal) educado,
  (des)cortés
popular popular
quality la calidad
reasonable (un-) (ir)razonable
respect el respeto
I respect respeto
rude grosero, descortés
sad triste
self-confident seguro de sí mismo
self-esteem la autoestima
sense el sentido
  common sense el sentido
  común

good sense el buen sentido
sensible sensato, prudente
serious serio, formal
shy tímido, retraído
skill la habilidad
skilful habilidoso
sociable (un-) (in)sociable
strange extraño, raro
stupid tonto, estúpido
stupidity la estupidez
suspicious suspicaz, desconfiado
sympathetic comprensivo,
  compasivo
sympathy la simpatía, la
  solidaridad, la comprensión
tactful discreto, con tacto
tactless indiscreto, sin tacto
talented con talento, dotado
temperament el temperamento, el
  carácter
temperamental temperamental,
  con mucho temperamento
I trust confío, me fío de
trusting confiado
warm cálido, efusivo
well-known conocido, sabido
wise prudente, cauteloso
wit el ingenio, la agudeza mental
witty ingenioso, agudo,
  ocurrente

The pupils here are hard-working
and well-behaved.
We encourage self-confidence and
discipline.
Bad behaviour/behavior and
laziness are punished.

Los alumnos de aquí son muy
trabajadores y formales.
Fomentamos la confianza en sí
mismo y la disciplina.
Castigamos a los que se
comportan mal y a los
perezosos.

Mr B is a serious person, but
rather pessimistic.

El señor B es un hombre muy
serio, pero bastante pesimista.

➤ THOUGHT PROCESSES 6c; EXPRESSING VIEWS 6d

6b Feelings & emotions

I am afraid (of) **tengo miedo (de)**
I am amazed (at) **estoy asombrado**
amazement **el asombro, la sorpresa, la estupefacción**
I amuse **divierto, entretengo**
   I am amused by **me divierte, me hace gracia**
amusement **la diversión**
anger **la furia, la ira, la cólera**
angry **enfadado, furioso**
I am annoyed (at/about) **estoy molesto (por/con)**
anxiety **la ansiedad**
anxious **ansioso**
I approve (of) **apruebo, tengo buen concepto (de)**
I am ashamed (of) **estoy avergonzado (de)**
I am bored **estoy aburrido**
boredom **el aburrimiento**
content (with) **contento (con), satisfecho (de)**
cross (with) **enfadado (con)**
delighted (about) **encantado (con)**
I dislike **no me gusta**

dissatisfaction **el descontento, la insatisfacción**
dissatisfied (with) **descontento (con), insatisfecho (de)**
embarrassed (about) **desconcertado (con), avergonzado (por)**
embarrassment **el desconcierto, la turbación, la vergüenza**
emotion **la emoción**
emotional(ly) **emocional(mente)**
I enjoy **disfruto**
envy **la envidia**
envious (of) **envidioso (de)**
fear **el miedo**
I feel **siento**
I forgive **perdono**
forgiveness **el perdón**
I am frightened (of) **estoy asustado (de), tengo miedo (a)**
furious (about) **furioso (acerca de)**
fussy **quisquilloso, exigente**
grateful (to) **agradecido (a)**
gratitude **la gratitud**
guilty **culpable**

I like our neighbour/neighbor a lot but worry about his wife. She cares for her old mother, who has not adapted to life in town. She is often in a bad temper and very fussy.

Me gusta mucho nuestro vecino, pero me preocupa su esposa. Cuida a su madre anciana que no ha adaptado a la vida de la ciudad. Muchas veces tiene [está de mal] genio y es muy quisquillosa.

– I am really ashamed of my behaviour/behavior yesterday. I was so upset and worried.
– It really doesn't matter. I am thankful that you feel better.

**– De verdad estoy avergonzado de mi comportamiento de ayer. Quedé tan trastornado y preocupado.
– La verdad es que no importa. Estoy agradecido de que te sientas mejor.**

happiness **la alegría, la felicidad**
happy (about) **contento (con)**
hate **el odio**
I hate **odio, detesto**
I have a grudge against him **le tengo rencor, le tengo inquina**
hope **la esperanza**
I hope **espero**
hopeful **optimista, esperanzado**
idealism **el idealismo**
indifference **la indiferencia**
indifferent (to) **indiferente (a)**
  I am indifferent (to) **soy indiferente (a)**
interest **el interés**
I am interested (in) **me interesa, estoy interesado (en)**
jealous **celoso**
jealousy **los celos**
joy **la alegría, el júbilo, el gozo**
joyful **alegre, jubiloso**
I like **me gusta**
  I would like **quisiera**
love **el amor**
I love **amo**
miserable (about) **triste (por)**
misery **el sufrimiento, la tristeza, la aflicción**

mood **el humor, el estado de ánimo**
  in a good/bad mood **de buen humor, de mal humor**
I'm pleased/glad that **estoy contento/satisfecho que**
I prefer **prefiero**
I regret **me arrepiento de, lamento**
satisfaction **la satisfacción**
satisfied (with) **satisfecho (de)**
surprise **la sorpresa**
I am surprised (at) **estoy sorprendido (de)**
thankful **agradecido**
unhappy **infeliz, desdichado**
unhappiness **la infelicidad, la desdicha**
I am upset (about) **desconcertado, perturbado, molesto (por)**
I wonder (at) **me pregunto**
  I wonder if **me pregunto si**
worried (about) **preocupado (por)**
worry **la preocupación**
I worry (about) **me preocupo (por)**
  it worries me **me preocupa**

I am so glad you are not angry with me.

Me alegro mucho de/[Me alegra] que no estés enfadado conmigo.

We are very fond of our uncle. He has many good qualities. However, he is often somewhat temperamental. He hates it when we thank him. It makes him embarrassed.

Le tenemos mucho cariño a nuestro tío. Tiene muchas buenas cualidades. Sin embargo, a menudo es algo caprichoso. Lo odia cuando le expresamos nuestra gratitud. Le hace sentirse desconcertado.

The boss is in a bad mood. He is cross with his secretary. She is bored with the work and indifferent to his annoyance.

El jefe está de mal humor. Está enfadado con su secretaria. A ella le aburre su trabajo, y no le importa nada su enojo.

6c Thought processes

against **en contra de**
  I am against it **estoy en contra de ello**
I analyze **analizo, estudio**
analysis **el análisis, el estudio**
I assume **asumo, me hago cargo de**
assuming that ... **asumiendo que, suponiendo que**
attention **la atención**
aware of (un-) **enterado de, (in)consciente de**
I base **baso**
basic **básico**
basically **básicamente**
basis **la base**
belief **la creencia**
I believe **creo, pienso**
  I believe in **creo en**
certainty **la seguridad, la certeza**
certain, sure **cierto, seguro**
coherent (in-) **(in)coherente**
complex **el complejo**
  inferiority complex **el complejo de inferioridad**
I comprehend **entiendo**
comprehensible **comprensible**
I concentrate **concentro**
  I concentrate on **me concentro en**
I conclude (that) **concluyo (que)**
conscience **la conciencia**
  with a clear conscience **con la conciencia limpia**
I consider ... (to be) **considero**
consideration **la consideración**
  I take into consideration **tengo en consideración/cuenta, tomo en consideración**
  taking everything into consideration **considerando todo**
I contemplate **pienso**
context **el contexto**

on the contrary **por el contrario**
controversial **controvertido, conflictivo**
I decide **decido**
decision **la decisión**
I deduce **deduzco que**
I delude myself **me engaño**
delusion **el engaño, la ilusión**
I determine **determino**
I disbelieve **no creo**
I distinguish **distingo**
doubt **la duda**
I doubt **dudo**
doubtful **dudoso**
doubtless/without a doubt **sin duda**
exception **la excepción**
evidence **la evidencia**
evidently **evidentemente**
fact **el hecho**
  in fact **de hecho**
false **falso**
fantasy **la fantasía**
fiction **la ficción**
for **por, para**
  I am for it **estoy por ello, [estoy a favor de ello]**
I forbid **prohíbo**
I forget **olvido, no me acuerdo de**
genius (for) **el genio (para)**
I grasp **comprendo**
hypothesis **la hipótesis**
I imagine **imagino**
imagination **la imaginación**
implication **la implicación**
interesting **interesante**
I invent **invento**
invention **el invento, la invención**
issue **el asunto, la materia**
I judge **juzgo**
judgement **el juicio**
justice **la justicia**
I justify **justifico**
I know **sé, conozco**

knowledge **el conocimiento, el saber**

logic **la lógica**

logical **lógico**

I go mad **me vuelvo loco**

madness **la locura**

meaning **el sentido**

it means **quiere decir**

I meditate (on) **medito**

memory **la memoria**

metaphysics **la metafísica**

mind **la mente, la inteligencia**

a great mind **el sabio**

I misunderstand **no entiendo**

misunderstanding **el malentendido**

motive **el motivo**

philosophy **la filosofía**

point of view **el punto de vista**

I ponder **reflexiono, medito**

premise **la premisa**

I presume **presumo, supongo**

principle **el principio**

in/on principle **en principio**

problem **el problema**

proof **la prueba**

I prove **pruebo**

psychology **la psicología**

psychoanalysis **el psicoanálisis**

rational (ir-) *(thinking)* **(ir)racional, (i)lógico**

reality **la realidad**

I realize **me doy cuenta**

I reason **razono**

I reason *(conclude)* **concluyo**

reason *(faculty)* **la razón**

I recognize **reconozco**

I reflect **reflexiono**

relevant **pertinente, conexo, relacionado**

I remember **me acuerdo**

right **correcto, verdadero**

I am right **tengo razón**

it is right **es verdad, está bien**

I see **veo**

I solve **resuelvo**

solution **la solución**

I speculate **especuio**

subconscious **el subconsciente**

I suppose **supongo**

theoretical **teórico**

theory **la teoría**

in theory **en teoría**

I think **pienso, creo**

thought **el pensamiento**

true **verdadero**

truth **la verdad**

I understand **entiendo, comprendo**

understanding **el entendimiento, la comprensión**

valid (in-) **(in)válido**

view **la opinión**

in my view **en mi opinión**

wrong **equivocado**

I am wrong **estoy equivocado**

it is wrong **está equivocado**

He is partly right about the reasons for our difficulties, but there is probably much more behind it.

Even if he is right, there is virtually nothing we can do about it.

En parte tiene razón cuando se refiere a las causas de nuestras dificultades, pero habrá otras razones que no son tan obvias.

Aun si tiene razón, no hay casi nada que podamos hacer para remediarlo.

6d Expressing views

I accept **acepto**
I agree (with/about) **estoy de acuerdo (con/sobre)**
I answer **contesto, respondo**
answer **la respuesta**
I argue **arguyo, discuto**
argument **el argumento, la discusión**
I ask (a question) **pregunto**
I contradict **contradigo**
I criticize **critico**
I define **defino**
definition **la definición**
I deny **niego**
I describe **describo**
description **la descripción**
I disagree (with/about) **no estoy de acuerdo (con/sobre)**
I discuss **discuto**
discussion **la discusión**
I maintain **mantengo, [sostengo]**
I mean **quiero decir**
opinion **la opinión**

in my opinion **en mi opinión, a mi modo de ver**
question **la cuestión, el caso**
a thorny question **una cuestión espinosa**
it is a question of **es una cuestión de**
I question **me cuestiono**
I say **digo**
I state **afirmo**
statement **la afirmación**
suggestion **la sugerencia**
I suggest **sugiero**
I summarize **resumo**
summary **el sumario, el resumen**
I think (of/about) **pienso (en)**
thought **el pensamiento**

Giving examples

as is known **como es sabido**
etc./and so on **y así sucesivamente**
example **el ejemplo**

– In my opinion he did not consider the basic problem. I would have liked to ask more questions.
– In principle I agree with his views. On the one hand he proved the need for new housing. On the other hand he discussed the problems of finding a site.

– I suggest we try to analyze the problem carefully. Then we shall be able to judge the situation and come to a sound conclusion.

– **En mi opinión no consideró el problema básico. Querría haber preguntado algo más.**
– **En principio estoy de acuerdo con sus opiniones. Por una parte, ha demostrado la necesidad de construir casas nuevas. Por otra parte habló de los problemas de encontrar un solar [lote] apropiado.**
– **Sugiero que tratemos de analizar el problema con cuidado. Luego podremos juzgar la situación y llegar a una conclusión razonable.**

for example **por ejemplo**
i.e. **a saber**
namely **es decir**
I quote **cito**
such as **como**

Comparing and contrasting

advantage **la ventaja**
I compare **comparo**
comparison **la comparación**
 in comparison with **en comparación con**
it contrasts with **contrasta con**
contrast **el contraste**
 in contrast **en contraste**
I differ **difiero**
difference **la diferencia**
different (from) **diferente de, distinto de**
disadvantage **la desventaja**
dissimilar **distinto**
I distinguish **distingo**
pros and cons **los pros y los contras**
relatively **relativamente**

same **el mismo**
similar **similar, igual**

Expressing reservations

even if **aun cuando**
even so **aun así**
to some extent **en alguna medida**
at first sight **a primera vista**
hardly **con dificultad, difícilmente**
in general **en general**
in the main **en general, en su mayoría**
in part/partly **en parte**
perhaps **quizás**
presumably **posiblemente**
probably **probablemente**
relatively **relativamente**
reservation **la reserva, [la reservación]**
unfortunately **desafortunadamente**
virtually **virtualmente**
in a way **de algún modo**

---

beginning **el principio, el comienzo**
from the beginning **desde el principio, desde el comienzo**
I am brief **soy breve, soy lacónico**
 in brief **en resumen**
I conclude **concluyo**
conclusion **la conclusión**
 in conclusion **en conclusión**
final **final**
finally **finalmente**
first **el primer, el primero**
firstly **en primer lugar**
furthermore **más aun**
on the one hand **por una parte, de una parte**

on the other hand **por otra parte**
initially **inicialmente**
last **el último**
lastly **últimamente**
 at last **por fin**
next **el próximo**
place **lugar**
 in the first place **en primer lugar**
 in the second place **en segundo lugar**
secondly **en segundo lugar**
in short **en breve, próximamente**
I sum up **resumo**

THE HUMAN MIND & CHARACTER

Arguing a point

admittedly **se reconoce que, es verdad que, [se sabe que]**

all the same **de cualquier manera**

although **aunque**

anyway **de todas formas, de cualquier modo**

apart from **aparte de**

as for **en cuanto a, en lo que concierne a, en lo que se refiere a**

as I see it **como yo lo veo**

as well **también**

despite this **a pesar de esto**

in effect **en efecto**

however **sin embargo**

incidentally **incidentalmente**

instead **en cambio**

instead of **en vez de, en lugar de**

just as important **tan importante**

likewise **asimismo, además**

no matter whether **sin que importe que**

that may be so **puede ser así**

nevertheless **sin embargo, no obstante**

otherwise **de otra manera**

in reality **en realidad**

in many respects **en muchos respectos**

in return **en cambio**

as a rule **como regla (general)**

so to speak **para decirlo así**

in spite of **a pesar de**

still, … **aun así**

to tell the truth **para decir la verdad, [para ser franco]**

whereas **mientras, visto que**

on the whole **en general, por regla general**

Cause & effect

all the more (because) **tanto más (porque)**

as **como**

because **porque**

cause **la causa**

consequence **la consecuencia**

consequently **consecuentemente, por consecuencia**

effect **el efecto**

it follows that **se deduce que**

how? **¿cómo?**

if **si**

– How did he break his leg?
– When he fetched the ladder he did not notice it was broken. So he fell off it.
– Why did he want the ladder?

– Because he wanted to paint the house.

– What are the reasons for his behaviour/behavior?
– Maybe he is cross with me and that is why he went away.

– **¿Cómo se rompió la pierna?**
– **Al ir a buscar una escalera, no se fijó en que estaba roto. Por lo tanto se cayó de ella.**
– **¿Por qué necesitaba la escalera?**

– **Porque quería pintar la casa.**

– **¿Cuáles son las causas de su comportamiento?**
– **A lo mejor está enfadado conmigo y por eso se fue.**

reason **la razón**
for this reason **por esta razón**
result **el resultado, la consecuencia**
as a result **como resultado**
provided that **suponiendo que**
since **desde que, en vista de que**
so long as **con tal que**
therefore, so **por lo tanto**
thus **de este modo, así es que**
whether **si**
why? **¿por qué?**

Emphasizing

above all **sobre todo**
in addition **además**
all the more **tanto más**
also **también**
certainly **desde luego, por supuesto, naturalmente**
clearly **claramente**
under no circumstances **bajo ninguna circunstancia**
completely **completamente**
especially **especialmente**
even (more) **aun**
without exception **sin excepción**

I emphasize **enfatizo**
extremely **extremamente**
far and away **con mucho**
fortunately **afortunadamente**
honestly **honestamente, honradamente**
just when **solo cuando**
mainly **principalmente**
moreover **más aun**
naturally **naturalmente**
not at all **para nada, de ninguna manera**
not in the least **en lo más mínimo**
both ... and **tanto ... como**
obviously **obviamente**
in particular **en particular**
particularly **particularmente**
in every respect **en todos los respectos**
I stress **acentúo**
thanks to **gracias a**
undeniably **innegablemente**
very **muy**
and what is more **y lo que es más**

Honestly I'm extremely angry with him. Thanks to his carelessness we missed the plane.

De verdad, estoy muy enfadada con él. Gracias a su descuido perdimos el avión.

Fortunately there was another, but we got to Chicago completely exhausted.

Fortunadamente hubo otro, pero llegamos completamente agotados a Chicago.

And what is more, he clearly didn't care at all.

Y lo que es más, no le preocupaba a él de ninguna manera.

Obviously I shall tell his firm exactly what I think of him. Under no circumstances will I employ him again.

Claro informaré a su compañía lo que pienso de él. No le emplearé otra vez bajo ninguno circunstancia.

Human life & relationships

7a Family & friends

Friendship

acquaintance **el conocido**
boyfriend **el amigo, el novio**
chum/pal **el compañero, el compinche**
classmate **el compañero de clase**
companion **el compañero**
friend (close) **el íntimo**
friend **el amigo**
friendship **la amistad**
gang **la pandilla, la cuadrilla**
we get on well together **nos llevamos bien**
we get together **nos reunimos**
I get to know **llego a conocer ..., concozco**
girl friend **la amiga, la novia**
I introduce **presento a ...**
mate/buddy **el compañero, el camarada, [el compinche]**
penfriend/pen pal **el amigo por correspondencia**
relationship **la relación**
school-friend/pal **el amigo de clase**

The family and relatives

adopted **adoptivo**
ancestor **el antepasado**
aunt **la tía**
baby **el bebé, el nene, la nena, [el/la guagua]**
brother **el hermano**
brother-in-law **el cuñado, el hermano político**
brothers and sisters **los hermanos**
children **los niños, los hijos**
close relative **el pariente cercano**
common-law husband **el marido en una reunión consensual**
common-law wife **la mujer en una reunión consensual**
cousin **el primo**
dad **el papá, el papaíto, [el papito]**
daughter **la hija**
daughter-in-law **la nuera, la hija política**
distant relative **el pariente lejano**
elder **mayor**
family **la familia**
family-tree **el árbol genealógico**

We are good friends. We get on well together. We do a lot together.

Somos buenos amigos. Nos llevamos bien. Hacemos muchas cosas juntas.

We are more open with one another. We settle conflicts.

Somos más sinceros el uno con el otro. Resolvemos los conflictos.

father   **el padre**
father-in-law   **el suegro, el padre político**
fiance(e)   **el novio, la novia, el prometido, la prometida**
forbear   **el antepasado**
foster *(adj)*   **adoptivo**
foster mother   **la madre adoptiva**
genealogy   **la genealogía**
godchild/son   **el ahijado**
goddaughter   **la ahijada**
godfather   **el padrino**
godmother   **la madrina**
grandad/pa   **el abuelito**
grandchildren   **los nietos**
granddaughter   **la nieta**
grandfather   **el abuelo**
grandma/granny   **la abuelita**
grandmother   **la abuela**
grandparents   **los abuelos**
grandson   **el nieto**
great-aunt   **la tía abuela**
great grandchild   **el bisnieto**
great-grandfather   **el bisabuelo**
great-grandmother   **la bisabuela**
great-nephew   **el sobrinonieto**
great-niece   **la sobrinanieta**
great-uncle   **el tío abuelo**
guardian   **el tutor, la tutora**
half-brother   **el medio hermano, el hermanastro**
half-sister   **la media hermana, la hermanastra**

husband   **el marido**
mother   **la madre**
mother-in-law   **la suegra, la madre política**
mum/mom   **la mamá**
nephew   **el sobrino**
niece   **la sobrina**
only (child)   **(el hijo) único**
parents   **los padres**
partner   **el cónyuge, la pareja, el compañero**
related   **emparentado**
relation   **el pariente**
relationship   **el parentesco, la parentela, el trato, la relación**
relative   **el pariente**
second cousin   **el primo segundo**
sister   **la hermana**
son   **el hijo**
son-in-law   **el yerno, el hijo político**
spouse   **el cónyuge**
stepbrother   **el hermanastro**
stepdaughter   **la hijastra**
stepfather   **el padrastro**
stepmother   **la madrastra**
stepsister   **la hermanastra**
stepson   **el hijastro**
twin brother   **el (hermano) gemelo**
twin sister   **la (hermana) gemela**
uncle   **el tío**
wife   **la mujer, la esposa**
younger   **menor**

I come from a large family. We just don't get on well.	**Vengo de una familia grande. Es que no nos llevamos bien.**
There are family problems.	**Hay problemas familiares.**
It runs in the family.	**Viene de familia.**
She's very difficult to get on with. I fell out with her.	**Es muy difícil llevarse bien con ella. Me reñí con ella.**

➤ LOVE, MARRIAGE, CHILDREN 7b; GROWING UP, DEATH 7c

7b Love & children

Love & marriage

affair **la aventura amorosa, el amorío**
bachelor **el soltero**
best man **el padrino de boda**
betrothal **el noviazgo, los desposorios**
betrothed **prometido**
bride **la novia**
bridegroom **el novio**
bridesmaid **la dama de honor**
couple **la pareja**
   married couple **el matrimonio**
I court **cortejo, hago la corte a ...**
courtship **el cortejo, el noviazgo**
divorce **el divorcio**
divorced **divorciado**
divorcee **el divorciado, la divorciada**
engaged **prometido**
engagement **el compromiso, el noviazgo**
I fall for **me enamoro de**
I fall in love (with) **me enamoro (de)**
I get divorced (from) **me divorcio (de)**

I get engaged (to) **me prometo, [me compremeto] (con)**
I get married (to) **me caso (con)**
I go out with **salgo con**
honeymoon **la luna de miel**
lover **el amante, la amante, el querido, la querida**
marriage/matrimony **el matrimonio**
married **casado**
I marry **me caso con**
mistress **la querida, la amante**
newly-married couple **los recién casados**
I separate from **me separo de**
separated **separado**
separation **la separación**
I have sex (with) **tengo relaciones sexuales (con)**
unmarried **soltero**
unmarried mother **la madre soltera**
wedding **la boda, las bodas, el casamiento**
widow **la viuda**
widower **el viudo**

We are madly in love. It was love at first sight.

Estamos enamorados perdidamente. Fue un flechazo [Fue amor a primera vista].

Are you married?

¿Estás casado?

She doesn't understand me. She is always nagging.

No me entiende. Siempre me importuna con sus quejas.

We have nothing to say to each other.

Ya no tenemos nada que decirnos.

Our relationship is breaking up.

Nuestras relaciones se están rompiendo.

Birth & children

abortion   **el aborto**

I have an abortion   **me hago un aborto**

I adopt   **adopto**

adoption   **la adopción**

au pair   **la chica au pair, [la niñera]**

baby   **el bebé, el nene/la nena, [el/la guagua]**

baby food   **la comida para niños**

babysitter   **el canguro, la niñera**

baptism   **el bautizo, el bautismo**

bib   **el babero, el babador**

birth   **el nacimiento, el parto**

birth-rate   **(la tasa de) natalidad**

birthday   **el cumpleaños**

I was born   **nací**

boy   **el niño, el muchacho, el chico**

I breast feed   **crío a los pechos, amamanto, doy el pecho**

I bring up a child   **crío/educo a un niño**

caesarian operation   **la operación cesárea**

child, children   **el niño, los niños**

child-minder   **la niñera**

childhood   **la niñez, la infancia**

christening   **el bautizo, el bautismo**

condom   **el condón**

contraception   **la contracepción, [la anticoncepción]**

contraction   **la contracción**

cot/crib   **la cuna**

I deliver (a baby)   **asisto en el nacimiento, parto**

dummy/teat   **el chupete**

I am expecting a baby   **estoy encinta/embarazada**

feeding bottle   **el biberón**

fertile (in-)   **(in)fecundo (estéril)**

fertility   **la fecundidad**

foetus   **el feto**

I foster   **crío**

fostering/fosterage   **el acogimiento familiar**

I get pregnant   **me quedo embarazada**

I give birth   **doy a luz**

girl   **la niña, la muchacha, la chica**

incubator   **la incubadora**

infancy   **la infancia**

infant   **el niño, la criatura**

infantile   **infantil**

I am in labour   **estoy de parto**

lad   **el joven, el muchacho, el chico, el mozo, el chaval, el zagal**

lass   **la joven, la muchacha, la chica, la moza, la chavala, la zagala**

live birth   **el nacimiento vivo**

I have a miscarriage   **malparo, aborto**

nanny   **la niñera**

nappy/diaper   **el pañal**

new-born child   **el (bebé) recién nacido**

orphan   **el huérfano**

period   **el período, la regla**

pill   **la píldora**

pram/perambulator   **el cochecito de niño**

pregnant   **encinta, embarazada**

saints-day   **el santo, la fiesta del santo**

sibling   **el hermano, la hermana**

still birth   **el nacimiento de un niño muerto**

still born   **nacido muerto, mortinato**

I take after   **salgo a, me parezco a**

toddler   **el pequeñito (que da sus primeros pasos)**

triplets   **los trillizos**

twin   **gemelo**

7c Life & death

Growing up

adolescent **adolescente**
adult **el adulto, el mayor**
  adult *(adj)* **adulto, mayor**
age **la edad**
aged **viejo, anciano**
centenarian **el centenario**
he comes from **es de**
I come of age **llegar a la mayoría de edad**
elderly **de edad, mayor, anciano, viejo**
eldest **el/la mayor**
female **la hembra**
  female *(adj)* **femenina**
foreigner **el extranjero**
generation **la generación**
generation gap **la barrera generacional**
life **la vida**
life insurance **el seguro de vida**
I look my age **represento los años que tengo**
male **el macho, el varón**
  male *(adj)* **masculino, macho**
man **el hombre**
manhood **la virilidad, la masculinidad**

manly **varonil, viril, masculino**
mature **maduro**
maturity **la madurez**
menopause **la menopausia**
middle age **de mediana edad**
name **el nombre**
nickname **el apodo, el mote**
octogenarian **el octagenario**
old **viejo, anciano**
old age **la vejez**
old man, woman **el viejo, la vieja, el anciano, la anciana**
old people's home **el asilo de ancianos**
pension **la pensión**
pensioner **el jubilado, la jubilada, el pensionado, la pensionada, el/la pensionista**
people **la gente**
permissive society **la sociedad permisiva**
person **la persona**
present **el regalo**
I prosper **prospero**
responsible **responsable**
retired **jubilado**
single **soltero**
spinster **la soltera**

He respects his elders.	**Respeta a sus mayores.**
I learn from my own experience.	**Aprendo por mi propia experiencia.**
– How old are you?	**– ¿Cuántos años tienes?**
– I'm twenty-five.	**– Tengo veintecinco años.**

stranger **el forastero**
surname **el apellido**
under age **menor de edad**
woman **la mujer**
womanhood **la feminidad**
young **joven**
young person **el/la joven**
younger **más joven**
youngest **el/la más joven**
youth **la juventud**
youth *(persons)* **el/la joven**

Death

afterlife **la vida futura**
angel **el ángel**
ashes **las cenizas**
autopsy **la autopsia, [la necropsia]**
body **el cadáver**
burial **el entierro**
I bury **entierro**
corpse **el cadáver**
he is cremated **es incinerado**
cremation **la incineración, la cremación**
crematorium/crematory **el horno crematorio**
dead **muerto**
death **la muerte**
death certificate **la partida de defunción**
he dies **muere**
epitaph **el epitafio**
eulogy **el elogio, el encomio**
funeral **el entierro, los funerales**
he goes to heaven **sube al cielo**
grave **la sepultura**
gravestone/tombstone **la lápida**
graveyard/cemetery **el cementerio**
heaven **el cielo**
hell **el infierno**
I inherit **heredo**
inheritance **la herencia**
last rites **las exequias**
he lies in state **está expuesto en capilla ardiente**
mortuary **el depósito de cadávares**
I mourn **estoy de luto**
mourning **la lamentación, el luto**
I am in mourning for **llevo luto por**
neo-natal death rate **la (tasa de) mortalidad neonatal**
obituary **la necrología**
he passes away **fallece**
remains **los restos**
tomb **la tumba**
undertaker **el director de pompas fúnebres**
will **el testamento**

The baby was born in the early hours of the morning but died an hour later.

El nene nació por la madrugada pero murió una hora después.

Daily life

8a The house

amenities **las comodidades, las conveniencias**
apartment **el piso, el apartamento**
block of flats/apartment house **el bloque de pisos, [el edificio de apartamentos]**
(of) brick **de ladrillo**
I build **construyo**
building **el edificio**
building plot **el solar (para construcción), [el lote]**
building site **el solar (para construcción), la obra**
bungalow **el chalet, el bungalow**
caretaker **el conserje, el portero, el vigilante**
chalet **el chalet, el chalé**
council flat **el piso de protección oficial, [el apartamento estatal]**
council house **la casa protegida**
detached house **la casa independiente, el chalet**
flat/apartment **el piso, el apartamento**

furnished flat/apartment house **el piso/apartamento amueblado**
furnished house **la casa amueblada**
freehold **propiedad absoluta**
I have an extension built **hago construir un ensanche**
house **la casa**
housing **la vivenda**
landlord **el propietario, el dueño**
leasehold/lease **el arrendamiento**
leasehold property **el inmueble arrendado**
lodger/roomer **el huésped**
I modernize **modernizo**
mortgage **la hipoteca**
mortgage rate **el tipo de interés hipotecario**
I move (house) **me mudo (de casa)**
I occupy **ocupo**
I own **poseo**
owner-occupied flat/apartment **el piso/apartamento ocupado por**

The whole house needs painting before we sell it. We are buying a new detached house.

Tenemos que pintar la casa entera antes de venderla. Compramos un nuevo chalet.

We are having a house built.

Hacemos construir una casa.

I live in a rented, furnished apartment.

Vivo en un apartamento amueblado, alquilado.

Her penthouse is for rent.

Su ático está disponible para alquilar.

el propietario
owner-occupied house   la casa
   ocupada por el propietario
penthouse   el ático, la casa de
   azotea
partly furnished   amueblado en
   parte
prefabricated house   la casa
   prefabricada
premises   el local, la propiedad
refuse/garbage collection   la
   recolección de basuras
rent   el alquiler, el arriendo
I rent   alquilo
semi-detached house   la casa
   semi-separada
sewage disposal   la depuración de
   aguas residuales
(of) stone   de piedra
street light   el farol
I take out a mortgage   obtengo
   una hipoteca
tenancy   el inquilinato, la
   ocupación
tenant   el inquilino, el
   arrendatario
unfurnished   sin muebles
unfurnished flat/apartment   el
   piso/apartamento
   desamueblado

Rooms

attic   el ático, el desván, la
   buhardilla
basement   el sótano
back-door   la puerta trasera
bathroom   el cuarto de baño
bedroom   el dormitorio
breakfast room   la habitación del
   desayuno
cellar   el sótano, la bodega
corridor   el pasillo, el corredor
dining-room   el comedor
hall(way)   el hall, el vestíbulo
landing   el descanso, el rellano
kitchen   la cocina
lavatory/bathroom   el retrete, el
   lavabo, el inodoro, el
   excusado, [el baño]
living room   el cuarto de estar, el
   living, el salón
loft   el desván
lounge   el cuarto de estar, el
   living, el salón
shower room   la ducha
sitting-room/living room   el cuarto
   de estar, el living, el salón
study   el despacho, el estudio
utility room   la trascocina
verandah   la veranda, la terraza,
   la galería
W.C.   el retrete, el lavabo, el
   inodoro, el excusado, [el baño]

My tenancy has two weeks to run. | **Quedan dos semanas de mi arrendamiento.**

We moved house two years ago. | **Mudamos de casa hace dos años.**

The house has a fairly pleasant view: it grows on you after a while! | **La casa tiene un panorama bastante agradable: después de un rato le gusta a uno cada vez más.**

8b The household

aerial **la antena**
back-door **la puerta trasera**
balcony **el balcón**
blind **la persiana**
boiler **la caldera, el calentador**
burglar alarm **la alarma antirrobo**
carpet **la moqueta, la alfombra**
ceiling **el techo**
chimney/smokestack **la chimenea**
central heating **la calefacción**
clean **limpio**
comfortable **cómodo**
cosy **cómodo, acogedor**
curtain **la cortina**
desk **el escritorio, la mesa de trabajo**
dirty **sucio**
door **la puerta**
door-handle **el tirador (de puerta), el puño, [el porno]**
door-knob **el tirador (de puerta), el pomo (de puerta)**
door-mat **el felpudo, la estera, la alfombrilla, [el tapete]**
downstairs **abajo, en el piso de abajo**
dustbin/trash-can **el cubo de basura, [el balde], [la caneca]**
electric **eléctrico**
electric plug **el enchufe,**
electric socket **el enchufe, la toma (de electricidad), el toma-corriente**

electricity **la electricidad, la luz**
en-suite **con baño adjunto**
fire alarm **la alarma de incendio**
fire extinguisher **el extintor de incendio**
fireplace **el hogar, la chimenea**
flex/extension cord **el cable, el cordón (de la luz)**
floor **el suelo**
floor *(storey/story)* **el piso, la planta**
front door **la puerta principal, la puerta de entrada**
furnished **amueblado**
furniture **los muebles**
  item of furniture **el mueble**
garage **el garaje, la cochera**
gas **el gas**
glass *(material)* **el vidrio, el cristal**
ground floor **la planta baja, [el primer piso]**
handle **el puño**
  (on jug, etc.) **el asa *(f)*, el asidero**
  (drawer, etc.) **el tirador, la manija**
hearth **el hogar, la chimenea**
included **incluido**
key **la llave**
keyhole **el ojo de la cerradura**
lamp **la lámpara**
lampshade **la pantalla de lámpara**
letterbox **el buzón**

The bed has not been changed.

La cama no ha sido cambiada.

I have just bought a compact-disc/disk player.

Acabo de comprar un reproductor de discos compactos.

lever   la palanca
lift/elevator   el ascensor
light bulb   la bombilla
light   la luz
light-switch   el interruptor, el
   conmutor
lock   la cerradura
it looks onto   da a
mantelpiece   el manto (de
   chimenea), la repisa de
   chimenea
mat   la estera, la esterilla
mezzanine floor   el entresuelo
modern   moderno
new   nuevo
nice   bonito, ameno
off *(switches, electrical apparatus)*
   desconectado, desenchufado,
   apagado
   off *(tap)*   cerrado
old   viejo
on *(switches, electrical apparatus)*
   conectado, enchufado,
   encendido, puesto
   on *(tap)*   abierto
on the first floor   en el primer piso
own   propio
passage   el pasillo
radiator   el radiador
rent   el alquiler, el arriendo
roof   el tejado, el techo
room   la habitación, el cuarto
shelf   el estante, la tabla, el
   anaquel, [la repisa]
shutters   la contraventana

situation   la situación, el
   emplazamiento
skirting board/baseboard   el
   rodapié, la cenefa
skylight   el tragaluz, la claraboya
small   pequeño
spacious   espacioso, amplio
staircase   la escalera
stairs   la escalera
step   el peldaño, el escalón, la
   grada
terrace   la terraza
tile *(floor)*   la baldosa
   roof tile   la teja
toilet   el retrete, el inodoro, el
   lavabo, el wáter, el excusado,
   [el baño]
upper floor   el piso superior, el
   piso de arriba
upstairs   arriba
view   la vista, el panorama
wall   el muro
   inside wall   la pared
   partition wall   el tabique
   garden wall   la tapia
waste paper basket/litter bin   la
   papelera
water   el agua *(f)*
window   la ventana
window-sill   el alféizar, el
   antepecho
wire   el alambre
wiring   el alambrado
wood   la madera*Lounge*

The washing machine doesn't
work! Can you repair it?

Come into the dining-room.

¡La lavadora no funciona!
¿Puede usted repararla?

Pase al comedor.

8c Furnishings

Lounge

armchair   la butaca, la silla
ashtray   el cenicero
bookshelf   el estante, la estantería
bookcase   la librería, el estante
bureau   el escritorio
coffee table   la mesita baja
cupboard/closet   el armario
cushion   el cojín
easy chair   la butaca, la silla
ornament   el adorno, el ornamento
picture   el cuadro, la pintura
   picture *(portrait)*   el retrato
photo   la foto
poster   el cartel, el póster
rocking-chair   la mecedora
rug   el tapete, la alfombrilla
settee/sofa   el sofá

Kitchen

bottle-opener   el abre-botellas
bowl   el plato, el tazón
clothes line   la cuerda de tendedero, la tendedera
clothes peg   la pinza
coffee machine   la máquina de café, la cafetera
coffee pot   la cafetera
colander   el colador, el escurridor
cooker/stove   la cocina
crockery   la vajilla, los platos
cup   la taza
cupboard   el armario
   wall-cupboard   la alacena
cutlery   los cubiertos, la cuchillería
deepfreeze   el (ultra)congelador
dish   el plato
dishcloth   el trapo de fregar, el paño de cocina, el limpión
draining-board   el escurreplatos, la escurridera, el escurridor
fork   el tenedor

frying-pan   la sartén
gas cooker/stove   la cocina/estufa de gas
glass   el vaso, la copa, la copita
knife   el cuchillo
oven   el horno
plate   el plato
rubbish bin/garbage can   el cubo [la caneca] de la basura, el basurero
saucepan   la cacerola, el cazo
saucer   el platillo
scouring pad   el estropajo
sink   el fregadero, la pila
sink unit   el lavadero, el fregadero
spoon   la cuchara
tap/faucet   el grifo, [la llave]
teapot   la tetera
tea-towel   el paño de cocina, [el trapo de cocina]
tray   la bandeja
washing powder   el jabón en polvo
washing-up/washing liquid   el detergente líquido, el lavavajillas

Dining-room

candle   la vela
candlestick   el candelero
chair   la silla
chandeliers   la araña, el candelero
dresser   el aparador, la rinconera
serviette   la servilleta
sideboard   el aparador
table   la mesa
table cloth   el mantel
table mat   el salvaplatos, el salvamanteles
table napkin/serviette   la servilleta

Bedroom

alarm clock   el despertador
bed   la cama

bunk bed **la litera, la cama camarote**
double bed **la cama doble**
bedclothes **la ropa de cama**
bedding **la ropa de cama**
bedside table **la mesa de noche**
bedspread **el sobrecama, el cubertor, el cubrecama**
blanket **la manta, la cobija**
chest of drawers **la cómoda**
dressing table **el tocador**
duvet **el edredón, la colcha**
mattress **el colchón**
pillow **la almohada**
quilt **la colcha, el edredón**
sheet **la sábana**
wardrobe **la guardarropa, el armario (ropero)**

Bathroom

bath **el baño, la bañera**
bath-mat **la estera de baño**
bidet **el bidet, el bidé**
clothes brush **el cepillo de la ropa**
flannel **la manopla, el paño**
(hand)basin **el lavabo, [el lavamanos]**
laundry basket **el cesto de la ropa sucia**
mirror **el espejo**
nail-brush **el cepillo para las uñas**
plug **el tapón**
scales **la balanza**
shampoo **el champú**
shower **la ducha**
sink **el lavabo**
soap **el jabón**
tap/faucet **el grifo, [la llave]**
toilet **el retrete, el inodoro, el lavabo, el excusado, el wáter**
toilet paper **el papel higiénico**
toothbrush **el cepillo de dientes**
toothpaste **la pasta dentífrica**
towel **la toalla**
towel rail **el toallero**
washbasin **el lavabo, la jofaína, la**

palangana, [el lavamanos]

Electrical goods

cassette player **el casete, el cassette, el tocacintas**
cassette recorder **la grabadora de cassette**
compact-disc player **el reproductor de discos compactos**
dishwasher **el lavaplatos, el lavavajillas**
electric appliance **el (aparato) electrodoméstico**
electric cooker/stove **la cocina/estufa eléctrica**
electric razor/shaver **la afeitadora (eléctrica), la rasuradora.**
freezer **el (ultra)congelador, [la congeladora]**
fridge/refrigerator **la nevera, el frigo, [la refrigeradora]**
hi-fi **el equipo de hi-fi/de alta fidelidad, [el equipo de sonido]**
iron **la plancha, el planchador**
microwave oven **el horno de microonda, el microondas**
mixer **la batidora, la mezcladora, la licuadora**
record player **el tocadiscos**
refrigerator **la nevera, el frigo, [la refrigeradora]**
spin-drier **el secador centrífugo**
stereo system **el estéreo, [el equipo de sonido]**
tape player **el casete**
tape recorder **la grabadora**
trouser press **la prensa para pantalones**
tumble-drier **la secadora**
TV set **el televisor**
television (TV) **la televisión**
vacuum cleaner **la aspiradora**
video recorder **la videograbadora**
walkman® **el Walkman®**
washing machine **la lavadora**

➤ TOILETRIES 9b; PLANTS 24c; VEGETABLES & FRUIT 10c; TOOLS App.8c

8d Daily routine

bath   el baño, [la tina]
bed   la cama
breakfast   el desayuno
clean   limpio
daily routine   la rutina diaria
dinner   la cena
dressed   vestido
evening meal   la cena
home   la casa, el hogar
  at home   en casa
housekeeper/maid   el ama (f) de
  casa
housework   los quehaceres
  domésticos (pl)
lunch   el almuerzo, la comida
rubbish/garbage   la basura, los
  desperdicios (pl), los desechos
  (pl)
school   la escuela
shop   la tienda
shower   la ducha
sleep   el sueño
spare time   el tiempo libre, las
  horas libres
supper   la cena
tea   el té, la merienda
time (commodity)   el tiempo
  time (of day)   la hora
undressed   desnudo, desvestido
vacuum cleaner   la aspiradora
washing   el lavado, el lavar
  dirty washing   ropa sucia, ropa
  por lavar

washing (hung to dry)   el
  tendido, la colada
washing up/dish washing (act)   el
  fregado, el fregar, [el lavado de
  platos]
  dishes (to be washed)   los
  platos para lavar
work   el trabajo

Actions

I bath   me baño
I break   rompo
I bring   traigo
I build   construyo
I buy   compro
I carry   llevo
I change (clothes)   me cambio (de
  ropa)
I chat   charlo
I clean   limpio
I clear away   quito (los platos, la
  mesa)
I clear the table   quito la mesa
I cook   cocino
I close   cierro
I darn   zurzo
I dig   cavo, cultivo
I do   hago
I drink   bebo
I drop   dejo caer
I dry up   seco (los platos)
I dust   quito (el polvo), limpio
I eat   como

We usually get up at 7 o'clock and have breakfast at eight.

Solemos levantarnos a las siete y desayunamos a las ocho.

Who is going to wash up/wash the dishes?

¿Quién va a lavar los platos?

I'll do the drying up.

Voy a secar los platos.

Sweep up that mess right now!

¡Barre este revoltijo ahora mismo!

I empty **vacío**
I fasten **abrocho**
I fill **lleno**
I get dressed **me visto**
I get undressed **me desnudo**
I get up **me levanto**
I go to bed **me acuesto**
I go to sleep **me duermo**
I go to the toilet **voy al lavabo/baño/wáter**
I have a bath **tomo un baño**
I have breakfast **desayuno**
I have lunch **como, almuerzo**
I have tea **meriendo**
I heat **caliento**
I hire/rent **alquilo**
I hire/rent out **alquilo**
I iron/press **plancho**
I knit **hago punto, [tejo]**
I lay the table **pongo la mesa**
I let (allow) **dejo**
I live **vivo**
I lock **cierro con llave**
I make **hago**
I polish **limpio, saco brillo a ...**
I prepare **preparo**
I press (button) **aprieto, pulso**
I put on (clothes) **me pongo**
  I put on (radio, TV) **pongo, conecto, enchufo, enciendo**
I rest **descanso**
I ring/call (telephone) **llamo por teléfono**
  (doorbell) **toco el timbre**
I scrub **friego**

I sew **coso**
I shine **saco brillo a, limpio**
I shop **hago las compras**
I shower **me ducho**
I sit down **me siento**
I sit **me siento, me quedo sentado, estoy sentado**
I sleep **duermo**
I speak **hablo**
I stand **estoy de pie**
I stand up **me levanto**
I start **empiezo, comienzo**
I stop **(me) paro**
I sweep **barro**
I switch/turn off **apago, desenchufo, desconecto**
I switch/turn on **pongo, enchufo, enciendo**
I take off (clothes) **me quito**
I take **cojo**
I throw away **tiro, echo, [boto]**
I tidy/straighten up **arreglo, pongo en orden, limpio**
I tie **ato, lío**
I trim **arreglo, ajusto**
I unblock **desatasco**
I use **utilizo, uso**
I wake up **me despierto**
I wallpaper **empapelo**
I wash up/wash dishes **lavo los platos**
I wash **(me) lavo**
I watch TV **veo la televisión**
I water **riego**
I wear **llevo**

The table has not been cleared!

¡Aún no se ha quitado la mesa!

She does the dusting and cleaning for us on Fridays.

Los viernes quita el polvo y hace la limpieza en nuestra casa.

My husband cooks on Saturdays. Dinner will be at nine p.m.

Mi marido cocina los sábados. La cena será a las nueve.

➤ GARDENING 24c

Shopping

9a General terms

article **el artículo**
assistant **el dependiente, la dependienta**
automatic door **la puerta automática**
bargain **la ganga, el artículo de ocasión**
business **el comercio, la empresa**
cash desk/register **la caja**
cash machine **la caja electrónica**
change *(money)* **la moneda suelta, el suelto, el vuelto**
cheap **barato**
check-out **la caja**
choice **la elección, la selección**
closed **cerrado**
coin **la moneda**
contents **los contenidos**
costly **costoso, caro**
credit **el crédito**
credit card **la tarjeta de crédito**
customer information **el servicio de información para clientes**
customer service **el servicio de asistencia posventa**
day off/closed **cerrado (por vacaciones)**
dear **caro, costoso**

department **el departamento, la sección**
discount **la rebaja**
entrance **la entrada**
escalator **la escalera mecánica**
exit **la salida**
expensive **caro, costoso**
fashion **la moda**
fire door **la puerta contra/de incendios**
fire exit **la salida de incendios**
fitting room **el probador, el vestidor**
free **gratis**
free gift **el regalo (gratuito)**
it is good value **bien vale lo que pagué**
handbag **el bolso, la bolsa, [la cartera]**
instructions for use **el modo de empleo**
item **el artículo**
lift/elevator **el ascensor**
mail-order **las ventas por correo**
manager **el director, el gerente**
manageress **la directora/gerente**
market **el mercado**
money **el dinero**

Expressions you hear

Anything else?/Is that all?	¿Algo más/Es todo?
Can I help you?	¿En qué puedo servirle?
Do you want anything in particular?	¿Desea algo en concreto?
What would you like?	¿Qué desea usted?
Who's next?	¿Quién sigue?
Whole or sliced?	¿Entero o en trozos?

---

note *(money)* **el billete**
open **abierto**
opening hours **las horas de abrir**
packet **el paquete**
pocket **el bolsillo**
pound *(weight)* **la libra**
PULL **tirad, tire, hale**
purse **el monedero**
PUSH **empujad, empuje**
quality **la calidad**
real/genuine **verdadero, genuino, auténtico**
receipt **el recibo**
reduction **la reducción**
refund **el reembolso, la devolución**
sale **las rebajas, la liquidación, el saldo, [la promoción]**
security guard/store detective **el guarda jurado**
self-service **autoservicio**
shop-assistant/sales person **el dependiente, el vendedor**
shop-keeper **el tendero/la tendera**
shop-lifter **la mechera, el ratero de tiendas**
shopping **las compras**
I go shopping **voy de compras**
shopping basket **la cesta de compras**
shopping list **la lista de compras**
shopping trolley **el carrito de la compra**
shut **cerrado**
slice **el trozo, la tajada**
special offer **la oferta especial**

stairs **la escalera**
summer sale **las rebajas de(l) verano, [la promoción]**
till **la caja registradora**
trader **el comerciante, el traficante, el vendedor**
travellers cheque/check **el cheque de viaje/de viajero**
wallet **la cartera, [la billetera]**
way in **la entrada**
way out **la salida**

Actions

I change **cambio**
I choose **escojo, elijo**
I decide **decido**
I exchange **cambio**
I have on/wear **llevo, [me pongo]**
I order **pido, encargo**
I pay **pago**
I put on **me pongo**
I queue/line **hago cola**
I select **elijo, selecciono, escojo**
I sell **vendo**
I serve **sirvo**
I shop **hago las compras**
I shop-lift **hurto/robo en tiendas**
I show **(de)muestro, enseño**
I spend *(money)* **gasto**
I steal **robo**
I take off **me quito**
I try on **(me) pruebo, [me mido]**
I wait **espero**
I wear **llevo, me pongo**
I weigh **peso**
I wrap up **envuelvo**

Is there a dairy around here?	**¿Hay una lechería por aquí?**
Where is the nearest baker's?	**¿Dónde está la panadería más cercana?**
Can I pay by cheque/check?	**¿Puedo pagar por cheque?**

9b Household goods & toiletries

Toiletries

after-shave   la loción para después del afeitado
anti-perspirant   el antiperspirante
brush   el cepillo
comb   el peine, la peinilla
condom   el condón, el preservativo
cotton wool   el algodón, el hidrófilo
deodorant   el desodorante
dental floss   el hilo de higiene dental
eyeliner   el lápiz de ojos
face cream   la crema de belleza
glasses   las gafas
hairbrush   el cepillo para el pelo
lipstick   la barra de labios, el lápiz labial, el colorete
make-up   el maquillaje, los cosméticos
nail-file   la lima para las uñas
paper handkerchief   el pañuelo de papel
perfume   el perfume
razor   la afeitadora, la maquinilla de afeitar
razor blade   la hoja de afeitar, la cuchilla de afeitar
sanitary towel   el paño higiénico, la compresa (higiénica), [la toalla higiénica]
shampoo   el champú
soap   el jabón
spray   el aerosol, el atomizador
sunglasses   las gafas de sol
suntan lotion   el bronceador
talcum powder   (los polvos de) talco
tampon   el tampón, el tapón
tissues   los pañuelos de papel
toilet water   el agua *(f)* de colonia, la colonia
toilet-paper   el papel higiénico

toothpaste   la crema dental, la pasta dentífrica
toothbrush   el cepillo de dientes
tweezers   las pinzas

Household items

bottle   la botella
bowl   la fuente, la escudilla, el tazón
cling-film/cellophane wrapping   el plástico para envolver
clothes-peg   la pinza
cup   la taza
dish   el plato, la fuente
foil/aluminum foil   el aluminio doméstico, el papel de aluminio
fork   el tenedor
glass   el vaso
jar   el tarro, el pote, el frasco, la jarra, el bote
jug   el jarro, la jarra
kitchen roll   el rollo de cocina
knife   el cuchillo
matches   los fósforos, las cerillas
paper napkin/serviette   la servilleta de papel
paper towel   la toallita de papel
plate   el plato
pot   la olla, la cacerola, la cazuela, el cazo
saucer   el platillo
scouring pads   el estropajo
spoon   la cuchara
string   la cuerda, el cordel
washing/wash powder   el jabón en polvo
washing-up/dishwashing liquid   el detergente líquido, el lavavajillas

Basic foodstuffs

bacon   **el tocino, el bacón**
beans   **las habas, las judías**
beef   **la carne de vaca**
beer   **la cerveza**
biscuits   **las galletas, los bizcochos**
bread   **el pan**
butter   **la mantequilla**
cakes   **los pasteles**
carrots   **las zanahorias**
cereals   **los cereales**
chocolate spread   **la pasta de chocolate**
cola   **la cola**
coffee   **el café**
custard   **las natillas, la crema instantánea (en polvos)**
fish   **el pescado**
fruit   **la fruta**
ham   **el jamón**
jam   **la confitura, la mermelada**
juice   **el zumo, el jugo**
lemonade   **la limonada, la gaseosa**
loaf   **el pan, la barra de pan**
macaroni   **los macarrones**
margarine   **la margarina**
marmalade   **la mermelada**
mayonnaise   **la mayonesa**
meat   **la carne**

milk   **la leche**
mustard   **la mostaza**
oil   **el aceite**
olive-oil   **el aceite de oliva**
pasta   **las pastas alimenticias**
pate   **el paté, el pastel (de carne)**
peanut-butter   **la manteca de cacahuete, [la mantequilla de maní]**
peas   **los guisantes, [las alverjas]**
pepper   **la pimienta**
peppers   **los pimientos**
pork   **el cerdo, la carne de cerdo**
potatoes   **las patatas, [las papas]**
pudding   **el púding, el postre**
salt   **la sal**
sardines   **las sardinas**
sauce   **la salsa**
sausage   **la salchicha, el embutido**
soup   **la sopa**
spaghetti   **los espaguetis, los fideos**
sugar   **el azúcar**
tea   **el té**
tea bag   **la bolsita de té**
tortilla   **la tortilla, [el taco]**
vegetables   **las legumbres, las verduras, los vegetales**
vinegar   **el vinagre**
wine   **el vino**

Expressions of quantity

a bar of ...   **una pastilla de ...**
a bottle of ...   **una botella de ...**
a box of ...   **una caja de ...**
a hundred gram(me)s of ...   **cien gramos de ...**
a kilo of ...   **un kilo de ...**
a litre/liter of   **un litro de ...**

a packet of ...   **un paquete de ...**
a slice of ...   **un trozo de ..., una tajada de ...**
a tin/can of ...   **una lata de ...**
half a pound of ...   **media libra de ...**

9c Clothing

anorak/parka **el anorak/anorac, el chubasquero**
artificial **artificial**
beautiful **hermoso**
belt **el cinturón**
big **grande**
bikini **el bikini**
blouse **la blusa**
boot **la bota**
bra **el sostén**
brand new **flamante, completamente nuevo**
cagoule **el canguro, el chubasquero**
cap **el gorro, la gorra**
cardigan **la rebeca, el cardigán**
checked **a cuadros**
clothes **la ropa, los vestidos**
clothing **la ropa, los vestidos**
coat **el abrigo, [el saco]**
colour/color-fast **no desteñible**
colourful/colorful **vivo, animado**
corduroy **la pana**

cravate **la corbata de fantasía, el fular, el foulard**
dress **el vestido**
elegant **elegante**
embroidered **bordado, recamado**
fashionable **de moda**
glove **el guante**
handkerchief **el pañuelo**
hat **el sombrero**
high-heeled **de tacones altos**
in the latest fashion **a la última moda**
jacket **la chaqueta, la americana**
jeans **el/los vaqueros, el/los tejanos**
jersey **el jersey, el suéter**
jewellery/jewelry **las joyas, las alhajas**
jumper **el jersey, suéter**
knitted **de punto, [tejido]**
knitwear **los géneros de punto**
ladies' wear **la ropa de señora**
lingerie **la lencería**

Expressions in clothes shops/stores

Can I try it on? **¿Puedo probarlo?**
Do you have the same in red?
  ¿Tiene usted uno/a parecido/a en rojo?
I like it. **Me gusta.**
I take/wear size (clothes) **Llevo el ..., [Me llevo una talla ...]**
I take/wear size (shoes) **Calzo el ...**
I would like a ... **Quiero un/una ...**
I would like to change ... **Quisiera cambiar ...**
I would rather have ... **Preferiría ...**
I'll take it. **Me lo/la llevo.**
I'll take the big one. **Me llevo el/la grande.**

I'd like it two sizes bigger. **Lo quisiera 2 números más grande.**
I'm next. **Me toca a mí.**
It suits me. **Me va bien, Me sienta bien.**
That's not quite right. **No es del todo correcto./ Eso no está del todo bien.**
They don't go together. **No armonizan., No hacen juego.**
What colour/color? **¿De qué color?**
What's it made of? **¿De qué está hecho?**
Will it shrink? **¿[Se] encogerá?**

long **largo**
long-sleeved **con mangas largas**
loose **suelto**
loud/brash **chillón, charro, cursi**
low-heeled **de tacones bajos**
man-made fibre/fiber **las fibras sintéticas**
matching **acompañado, a tono, que hace juego con**
men's wear **la ropa de caballero**
non-iron **de no planchar, que no necesita planchado**
pair **el par**
panties **las bragas, la braga, las braguitas, [los pantys]**
pants **los calzoncillos, los pantalones**
plain **sencillo, llano, sin adornos**
printed **impreso, estampado**
pure **puro**
pyjamas **el pijama, la pijama**
raincoat **el impermeable, la gabardina**
sandal **la sandalia, la alpargata**
scarf **la bufanda**
shirt **la camisa**
shoe **el zapato**
shoe-lace **el lazo, el cordón**
short-sleeved **con mangas cortas**
sinthetic **sintético**
size **el tamaño, la talla, el número**
skirt **la falda**
slip **las enaguas, la combinación**
small **pequeño**
smart **elegante, pulcro**
sneakers **los zapatos de lona/deportivos, las zapatillas**
sock **el calcetín, [la media]**
soft **blando**
stocking **la media**
striped **listado, rayado, a rayas**
suit **el traje**
sweater **el suéter, el jersey**
sweatshirt **la sudadera**
swimming trunks **el bañador, [el traje de baño]**
swimsuit/bathing suit **el traje de baño, el bañador**
tie **la corbata**
tight **estrecho, apretado, ajustado, ceñido**
tights **el panti, las medias**
too big/small **demasiado grande/pequeño**
towelling **la felpa**
trainers **las zapatillas de deporte**
trousers **el pantalón, los pantalones**
T-shirt **la camiseta, el niki, [la playera], [la remera]**
ugly **feo**
umbrella **el paraguas**
underpants **los calzoncillos**
underwear **la ropa interior**
unfashionable **fuera de moda, pasado de moda** velvet **el terciopelo**
vest/undershirt **la camiseta**
waistcoat/vest **el chaleco**

Alterations & repairs

I alter **arreglo**
buckle **la hebilla**
button **el botón**
heel **el tacón**
hem **el dobladillo**
hole **el roto**
I knit **tricoto**
knitting needle **la aguja de hacer calceta**
material **el tejido**
I mend/repair **remendo, [zurco]**
patch **el remiendo**
pin **el alfiler**
pocket **el bolsillo, [la bolsa]**
I sew **coso**
stain **la mancha**
tailor **el sastre**
tailored **hecho por sastre**
thread **el hilo**
zip **la cremallera**

Food & drink

10a Drinks & meals

Drinks

alcoholic **alcohólico**
aperitif **el aperitivo**
beer **la cerveza**
brandy **el brandy, el coñac**
champagne **el champán**
(drinking) chocolate **el chocolate (para beber)**
cider **la sidra**
cocktail **el cóctel**
coffee **el café**
cola **la cola**
draught beer **la cerveza al grifo**
drink **la bebida**
dry **seco**
(fruit) juice **el zumo/[el jugo] (de fruta)**
lemonade **la limonada**
low-alcohol **de baja graduación de alcohol**
orange/lemon squash **la naranjada/la limonada**
milk **la leche**
milk-shake **el batido, [la malteada]**
mineral water **el agua** (f) **mineral**
non-alcoholic **sin alcohol**
sherry **el vino de jerez, el jerez**

sparkling **espumoso**
spirits **los licores, las bebidas alcohólicas**
sweet **dulce**
tea **el té**
water **el agua**
still water **el agua sin gas**
with ice **con hielo**
whisky **el whisky**
wine **el vino**

Drinking out

bar **el bar**
barman **el barman**
beer hall **la cervecería**
bottle **la botella**
cafe **el café**
coffee bar/shop **la cafetería**
cellar **la bodega**
counter/bar **la barra**
cup **la taza, la copa**
I drink **bebo**
glass **el vaso**
pub **el pub, la taberna**
public-house **la taberna**
refreshments **los refrescos**
sip **el sorbo**
straw **la pajita**

cafeteria **la cafetería**
canteen **la cantina**
stall **el puesto**
ice-cream parlour/parlor **la heladería**
pizza parlour/parlor **la pizzería**
restaurant **el restaurante**
self-service **el autoservicio, el**

self-service
snack-bar **el bar de aperitivos, el snack-bar**
take-away **para llevar**
take-away restaurant **el restaurante con comida para llevar**

teaspoon **la cuchara de café**
wine cellar **la bodega**
wine glass **el vaso de vino**
wine-tasting **el catamiento de vino**

Meals

appetizer/starter **el entremés, la entrada**
breakfast **el desayuno**
course **el plato**
dessert **el postre**
I dine **ceno**
dinner **la cena**
I eat **como**
I have a snack **tomo un aperitivo, tomo una tapa**
I have breakfast **desayuno**
I have dinner **ceno**
I have lunch **como, almuerzo**
lunch **la comida, el almuerzo**
main **principal**
meal **la comida**
snack **el aperitivo, la tapa, el refrigerio**
supper **la cena**

Eating out

I add up the bill **hago la cuenta**
bill/check **la cuenta**
bowl **el cuenco, la fuente**
charge **el precio**
cheap **barato**
I choose **elijo, escojo**

it costs **cuesta**
I decide **decido**
expensive **caro**
first course **el primer plato**
fixed price **el precio fijo**
fork **el tenedor**
inclusive **incluido, inclusive**
knife **el cuchillo**
main course **el plato principal**
menu **el menú**
menu of day **el menú del día**
napkin **la servilleta**
I order **pido**
order **el pedido**
place-setting **la colocación de la mesa**
plate **el plato**
portion **la porción**
reservation **la reserva**
I serve **sirvo**
service **el servicio**
set menu **el menú prefijado**
side-dish **el plato adicional**
spoon **la cuchara**
table **la mesa**
tablecloth **el mantel**
tip/gratuity **la propina**
I tip **doy propina**
toothpick **el palillo de dientes**
tourist menu **el menú turístico**
tray **la bandeja**
waiter **el camarero**
waitress **la camarera**
wine list **la lista de vinos**

Can you tell me where the nearest cafe is, please?

¿Me puede decir dónde está el café más cercano, por favor?

Where can we get a drink around here?

¿Dónde podemos tomar algo por aquí?

I'd like a chocolate milk-shake, please.

Un batido [Una malteada] de chocolate, por favor.

➤ VEGETABLES, FRUIT, DESSERT 10c; COOKING & EATING 10d

10b Fish & meat

Fish & seafood

anchovy	**la anchoa**
clam	**la almeja**
cockles	**los berberechos**
cod	**el bacalao**
crab	**el cangrejo**
crayfish	**el cangrejo de río**
eel	**la anguila**
fish	**el pescado**
hake	**la merluza**
herring	**el arenque**
langouste	**la langosta, el bogavante**
lobster	**la langosta**
mussels	**el mejillón**
octopus	**el pulpo**
oyster	**la ostra**
plaice	**la patija**
prawn	**la gamba, [el camarón]**
salmon	**el salmón**
sardine	**la sardina**
scallop	**la venera**
scampi	**las gambas, los langostinos**
seafood	**el marisco**
shell	**el caparazón**
shellfish	**el crustáceo, los mariscos**
shrimp	**el camarón, el langostino**
snails	**los caracoles**
sole	**el lenguado**
squid	**el calamar**
swordfish	**el pez espada**
trout	**la trucha**
tuna	**el atún**
whitebait	**el chanquete**

Is this fish fresh?	**¿Es fresco este pescado?**
I'd rather have tuna than crab.	**Prefiero comer atún a cambio de cangrejo.**
Would you prefer cod or sole?	**¿Prefiere usted bacalao o lenguado?**
– Shall we try the chicken?	**– ¿Probamos el pollo?**
– I'd like a pork chop.	**– Me gustaría tomar una chuleta de cerdo.**
Can we both have steak, one rare and one well cooked?	**¿Nos trae dos filetes de vaca, uno poco hecho y el otro muy hecho?**
I'll have a rare steak with chips/fries and salad, please.	**Quisiera el biftec poco hecho con patatas [papas] fritas y una ensalada, por favor.**
I want a tomato salad. Does it have garlic in it?	**Quiero una ensalada de tomate. ¿Tiene ajo?**

Meat & meat products

bacon **el tocino, la panceta**
beef **la carne de vaca**
beefburger **la hamburguesa**
bolognese **boloñesa**
casserole **la cazuela, [la cacerola]**
chop **la chuleta**
cutlet **la chuleta**
escalope **el escalope**
ham **el jamón**
hamburger **la hamburguesa**
hot-dog **el perrito caliente**
kid **el cabrito**
kidney **los riñones**
lamb **el cordero**
liver **el hígado**
meat **la carne**
meat-balls **las albóndigas**
minced meat **la carne picada**
mixed grill **la parrilada mixta**
mutton **la carne de cordero**
pâté **el paté**

pork **la carne de cerdo, el cerdo**
rabbit **el conejo**
salami **el salami, el salchichón**
sausage **la salchicha**
sirloin **el solomillo**
steak **el filete**
stew **el guiso, el estofado**
veal **la (carne de) ternera**

Poultry & game

capon **el capón**
chicken **el pollo**
chicken breast **la pechuga de pollo**
duck **el pato**
goose **el ganso**
partridge **la perdiz**
pheasant **el faisán**
poultry **la carne de ave, la ave**
quail **el codorniz**
turkey **el pavo**
wild boar **el jabalí**
woodcock **la becada**

Traditional dishes

albóndigas spiced meatballs
almejas a la marinera clams in paprika sauce
calamares a la romana deep-fried squid
caldo gallego meat and vegetable broth
[chile con carne] stew of kidney beans, chilli and minced beef
chorizo spicy sausage made of pork, garlic and paprika
conejo al ajillo rabbit with garlic
empanada gallega tenderloin of pork, onions and chili peppers in a pie
empanadillas savoury pasties

stuffed with meat or fish
gambas a la plancha grilled prawns
menestra de pollo casserole of chicken and vegetables
paella valenciana saffron rice with chicken, shrimp, mussels, prawns, squid, peas, tomato, chili pepper and garlic
riñones al jerez kidneys braised in sherry
sopa de mariscos seafood soup
sopa de pescado fish soup
[taco] cornmeal pancake stuffed with meat, chilli-pepper sauce and mashed avocado

10c Vegetables, fruit & dessert

Vegetables

artichoke   la alcachofa
asparagus   el espárrago
aubergine/eggplant   la berenjena
avocado   el aguacate
baked-beans   las judías cocidas,
  [los frijoles cocidos]
beans   las judías, las habas
beetroot/beets   la remolacha
broccoli   el brécol, [el brócoli]
Brussels sprout   la col de bruselas
cabbage   la col, [el repollo]
carrot   la zanahoria
cauliflower   la coliflor
celeriac   el apio
celery   el apio
chick-pea   el garbanzo
corn/maize   el maíz
  corn on the cob   la mazorca
courgette/zucchini   el calabacín
cucumber   el pepino, [el
  cohombro]
eggplant   la berenjena
endive/chicory   la endivia
French bean   la judía enana, el
  frijol
garlic   el ajo
gherkin   el pepinillo
haricot bean   la alubia, la judía
herb   la hierba aromática
leek   el puerro
lentil   la lenteja
lettuce   la lechuga
marrow   el tuétano

mushroom   el champiñón
onion   la cebolla
parsley   el perejil
parsnip   la chirivía, la pastinaca
pea   el guisante, [la alverja]
pepper (red/green)   el pimiento
  (verde/rojo)
potato   la patata
pumpkin   la calabaza
radish   el rábano
rice   el arroz
salad   la ensalada
spinach   la espinaca
sweetcorn   el maíz dulce
tomato   el tomate
turnip   el nabo
vegetable   la verdura
  vegetable (adj)   vegetal
watercress   el berro

Fruit

apple   la manzana
apricot   el albaricoque
banana   el plátano
berry   la baya, el grano
bilberry   el arándano
blackberry   la mora, la zarzamora
blackcurrant   la grosella
brazil nut   la nuez del Brasil
bunch of grapes   el racimo de
  uvas
cherry   la cereza
chestnut   la castaña
coconut   el coco

Traditional dishes

arroz con leche   rice pudding
bizcocho   sponge cake
crema catalana   caramel
  pudding
guacamole   mashed avocado

pastel de queso   cheesecake
[papusa]   pancake with cheese
  or bacon
tortilla de patatas   potato
  omelette

currant   **la pasa de corinto**
date   **el dátil**
fig   **el higo**
fruit   **la fruta**
gooseberry   **la grosella espinosa**
grape   **la uva**
grapefuit   **el pomelo**
hazelnut   **la avellana**
kiwi-fruit   **el kiwi**
lemon   **el limón**
lime   **la lima**
melon   **el melón**
nut   **la nuez**
olive   **la aceituna**
orange   **la naranja**
passion fruit   **la fruta de la pasión,**
   [el maracuyá]
peach   **el melocotón**
peanut   **el cacahuete**
pear   **la pera**
peel   **la piel, la cáscara**
I peel   **pelo, quito la cáscara**
peeled   **pelado**
piece of fruit   **una fruta**
pineapple   **la piña**
pip   **la pepita**
plum   **la ciruela**
pomegranate   **la granada**
prune   **la ciruela seca**
raisin   **la pasa, [la uva pasa]**
raspberry   **la frambuesa**
redcurrant   **la grosella roja**
rhubarb   **el ruibarbo**
stone   **el hueso**
strawberry   **la fresa**
sultana   **la pasa**

tangerine   **la mandarina**
walnut   **la nuez**

Dessert
biscuit/cookie   **la galleta**
cake   **el pastel**
caramel   **el caramelo**
chocolate   **el chocolate**
chocolates   **los bombones**
cream   **la nata**
creme caramel   **el flan**
custard   **las natillas**
dessert   **el postre**
flan   **la tarta, [el flan]**
flour   **la harina**
fresh fruit   **la fruta fresca**
fruit of the day/season   **la fruta de**
   la estación
fruit salad   **la macedonia, [la**
   ensalada de frutas]
gateau   **el gateau**
ice cream   **el helado**
mousse   **la mousse**
pancake   **la hojuela, [el**
   panqueque]
pastry   **la pastita**
pie   **el pastel**
pudding   **el puding, el dulce, el**
   postre
sweet   **dulce**
tart   **la tarta dulce**
trifle   **la trufa**
vanilla   **la vainilla**
whipped cream   **la nata batida**
yoghurt   **el yogur**

I'd rather have boiled potatoes
than chips/fries.

**Prefiero las patatas [papas]
cocidas a las patatas [papas]
fritas.**

Two strawberry ice-creams. Have
you got any apple pie?

**Dos helados de fresa. ¿Tiene
tarta [flan] de manzana?**

10d Cooking & eating

Food preparation

I bake	**cuezo al horno, horneo**
baked	**al horno**
barbecue	**la barbacoa**
I beat	**bato**
beaten	**batido**
I boil	**hiervo**
boiled	**hervido**
bone	**el hueso, la espina**
boned	**deshuesado, sin espinas**
boned *(fish)*	**sin espinas**
I bone	**deshueso, quito las espinas**
I braise	**braseo**
braised	**braseado**
in breadcrumbs	**empanado**
breast	**la pechuga**
I carve	**trincho**
I chop	**corto en trozos, pico**
I clear the table	**quito la mesa**
I cook	**cocino**
cooking/cuisine	**la cocina**
I cut	**corto**
I dice	**corto en cubitos**
dough	**la masa, la pasta**
I dry up	**seco (los platos)**
egg	**el huevo**
flour	**la harina**
food preparation	**la preparación de alimentos**
fried	**frito**

I fry	**frío**
I grate	**rallo**
grated	**rallado**
gravy	**la salsa de carne**
I grill	**aso (a la parrilla)**
grilled	**asado (a la parrilla)**
ingredient	**el ingrediente**
large	**grande**
I lay/set the table	**pongo la mesa**
I marinate	**pongo a marinar**
marinated	**marinado**
medium	**en su punto, término medio**
milk	**la leche**
I mix	**mezclo**
mixed	**mezclado**
olive-oil	**el aceite de oliva**
pastry	**la pasta**
short(crust) pastry	**la pasta quebradiza**
I peel	**pelo**
peeled	**pelado**
I pour	**sirvo**
rare	**poco hecho**
recipe	**la receta**
roast	**el asado**
I roast	**aso al horno**
in sauce	**en salsa**
I sift	**tamizo, cierno**
I slice	**corto en rodajas**
sliced	**en rodajas**

Chop 2 kilos of tomatoes and 1 kilo of peeled onions. Put into saucepan with 500 ml of malt vinegar. Add 500g soft sugar and 2 teaspoons of salt.

Cook, stirring frequently for 40 mins until mixture thickens.

Pique 2 kilos de tomates y 1 kilo de cebollas peladas. Póngalos en una cacerola con 500 ml de vinagre de malta. Agregue azúcar refinada y dos cucharaditas de sal.
Cocínelo durante 40 minutos, revolviendo continuamente hasta que espese.

I spread **extiendo**
stewed **estofado, guisado**
sunflower oil **el aceite de girasol**
I toast **tuesto**
toasted **tostado**
I wash up **friego, lavo**
I weigh **peso**
well-done **muy hecho, bien cocinado**
I whip **bato**
whipped **batido**
I whisk **bato (con batidora)**
whisked **batido (con batidora)**

Eating

additive **el aditivo**
I am hungry **tengo hambre**
I am thirsty **tengo sed**
appetite **el apetito**
appetizing **apetitoso**
bad **malo**
I bite **muerdo**
bitter **amargo**
calorie **la caloría**
    low-calorie **bajo en calorías**
I chew **mastico**
cold **frío**
delicious **delicioso**
diet **el régimen, [la dieta]**
    I'm on a diet **sigo un régimen, [estoy a dieta]**
fatty/oily **graso**
fresh **fresco**

fresh(ly) *(adv)* **fresco**
healthy *(appetite)* **bueno**
    healthy *(food)* **sano**
I help myself **me sirvo**
hot **picante**
hunger **el hambre**
hungry **hambriento, con ganas de comer**
I like **me gusta**
mild **suave**
I offer **ofrezco**
I pass (salt) **paso**
piece **el trozo, el pedazo**
I pour **sirvo**
I provide **pongo, proporciono**
rancid *(cheese)* **rancio**
salty **salado**
I serve **sirvo**
sharp **ácido**
slice **la rebanada**
I smell **huelo**
soft **blando**
spicy **picante**
stale (bread) **duro**
still **no espumoso, sin gas**
strong **fuerte**
I swallow **trago**
tasty **sabroso**
thirst **la sed**
thirsty **sediento**
I try **pruebo**
vegan **vegetariano estricto**
vegetarian **vegetariano**

Pass the salt, please.	**Pase la sal, por favor.**
Just a small portion.	**Sólo una porción pequeña.**
Nothing more, thanks.	**Nada más, gracias.**

Sickness & health

11a Accident & emergencies

accident **el accidente**
ambulance **la ambulancia**
I attack **ataco**
break **la rotura, la ruptura, el rompimiento**
I break **rompo, me rompo**
I break my arm **me rompo el brazo**
breakage **la rotura, la ruptura, el rompimiento**
broken **roto**
I have broken my leg **me he roto la pierna**
bruise **la contusión, el cardenal, la magulladura, el moretón**
I bruise **contundo, magullo**
burn **la quemadura**
I burn **me quemo**
casualty **el herido, la víctima**
casualty department **la sección de accidentes**
I catch fire **me enciendo, prendo**

fuego
I collide (with) **choco (con), colisiono (con)**
collision **la colisión, el choque**
I crash **choco, colisiono**
I crash (plane) **estrello (avión)**
crash **el choque, la colisión**
I crush **aplasto**
I cut (myself) **(me) corto**
I have cut my finger **me he cortado el dedo**
dead **muerto**
death **la muerte**
I die **muero**
emergency **la emergencia, urgencia**
emergency exit **la salida de emergencia/urgencia**
emergency services **las urgencias, los servicios de emergencia**
it explodes **estalla, explota,**

There has been an accident! My friend is injured.
We need an ambulance quickly.

Call the fire brigade!

I think I have broken my arm. It hurts a lot.

¡ Ha habido un accidente! Mi amigo está herido.
Necesitamos una ambulancia, pronto!

¡Llama a los bomberos!

Creo que tengo el brazo roto. Me duele mucho.

explosiona
explosion **la explosión, el estallido**
I extinguish **apago, extingo**
I fall **caigo**
fatal **fatal, mortal**
fine **la multa**
fire **el fuego, el incendio**
fire brigade **el cuerpo de bomberos**
fire engine **el coche de bomberos**
fire extinguisher **el extintor**
fireman **el bombero**
first aid **los primeros auxilios**
graze **el roce, la abrasión, la rozadura**
I graze **raspo**
I have an accident **sufro un accidente**
hospital **el hospital**
impact **el impacto, el choque**
incident **el incidente**
I injure **hiero, hago daño a, lastimo, lesiono**
injury **la herida**
injured **herido**
insurance **el seguro, los seguros**
I insure **aseguro**

I kill **mato**
killed **matado, muerto**
life-belt **el cinturón salvavidas**
life-jacket **el chaleco salvavidas**
oxygen **el oxígeno**
para-medic **el paramédico**
I recover **recupero, me recobro**
recovery **la recuperación**
I rescue **rescato, salvo**
rescue **el rescate, el salvamento**
rescue services **los servicios de rescate**
I run over **atropello**
I rush **voy de prisa, me apresuro**
safe **salvo, seguro**
safe and sound **sano y salvo**
safety-belt **el cinturón de seguridad**
salvage **el salvamento, la recuperación**
I save **rescato, salvo**
seat-belt **el cinturón de seguridad**
terrorist attack **el ataque de terroristas**
third-party **la tercera persona**
witness **el testigo**

It was your fault, not mine.	**Ha sido culpa tuya, no mía.**
Are you a doctor?	**¿Es usted médico?**
Where's the nearest hospital?	**¿Dónde está el hospital más cercano?**

➤ MEDICAL TREATMENT 11c; HEALTH & HYGIENE 11d

11b Illness & disability

ache   **el dolor**
alive   **vivo**
I am ill/sick   **estoy enfermo**
I am sick/vomit   **vomito, devuelvo**
he amputates   **amputa**
amputee   **el amputado**
amputation   **la amputación**
arthritis   **la artritis**
asthma   **el asma** *(f)*
black eye   **el ojo amoratado**
I bleed   **desangro, sangro**
blind   **ciego**
blind man/woman   **el ciego, la ciega**
blood   **la sangre**
breath   **el aliento, la respiración**
I breathe   **respiro**
breathless   **falto de aliento, desalentado, jadeante**
catarrh   **el catarro**
I catch cold   **cojo frío, cojo un resfriado**
cold   **el resfriado, el catarro**
constipated   **estreñido**
constipation   **el estreñimiento**
convalescence   **la convalecencia**
I am convalescing   **convalezco**
cough   **la tos**

I cough   **toso**
cripple   **el lisiado, el mutilado**
I cry   **lloro**
dead   **muerto**
deaf   **sordo**
deafness   **la sordera**
death   **la muerte**
depressed   **deprimido**
depression   **la depresión, el abatimiento**
diarrhoea   **la diarrea**
I die   **muero**
diet   **el regimen, la dieta**
disabled   **minusválido**
disease   **la enfermedad, el mal**
dizziness   **el mareo, el vértigo**
dizzy   **mareado**
drug   **la droga**
drugged   **drogado**
drunk   **borracho**
dumb   **mudo**
earache   **el dolor de oídos**
I feel dizzy   **me siento mareado**
I feel ill/unwell   **me siento enfermo**
I feel (well)   **me siento (bien)**
fever   **la fiebre**
feverish   **febril**
flu   **la gripe**

I feel dizzy if I stand up.   **Al levantarme me siento mareado.**

I don't usually faint!   **No suelo desmayarme.**
I have been sick/vomited several times.   **He vomitado varias veces.**

I suffer from high blood-pressure.   **Padezco de hipertensión.**

My children have diarrhoea. I seem to be constipated.   **Mis niños tienen la diarrea. Yo debo estar estreñido.**

I get drunk   **me emborracho**
I got better   **me mejoré, me repuse, me restablecí**
I had an operation   **me han operado**
I have a cold   **tengo un resfriado**
I have a temperature   **tengo fiebre**
headache   **el dolor de cabeza**
health   **la salud**
healthy   **bien de salud**
heart attack   **el ataque cardíaco**
high blood pressure   **la hipertensión**
HIV-positive   **VIH positivo**
hurt   **el dolor**
I hurt   **me duele, tengo dolor de ...**
it hurts   **me duele**
ill   **enfermo**
illness   **la enfermedad**
jaundice   **la ictericia**
I live   **vivo**
I look (ill)   **parezco enfermo**
mental illness   **la enfermedad mental**
mentally handicapped   **minusválido mental**
mentally sick   **enfermo de la mente**
migraine   **la jaqueca**
mute   **el mudo**

mute *(adj)*   **mudo**
pain   **el dolor**
painful   **doloroso**
pale   **pálido**
paralysis   **la parálisis**
paralyzed   **paralizado**
physically handicapped   **mutilado, minusválido**
recovery   **el restablecimiento**
rheumatism   **el reumatismo**
sick   **enfermo**
I sneeze   **estornudo**
sore throat   **el dolor de garganta**
sting   **la picadura, el escozor, el picazón**
it stings   **me pica, me rasca**
stomach   **el estómago**
stomach ache   **el dolor de estómago**
stomach upset   **el trastorno estomacal**
I take drugs   **tomo drogas, me drogo**
temperature   **la fiebre**
tonsillitis   **la amigdalitis**
toothache   **el dolor de muelas**
I vomit   **vomito, devuelvo**
what's wrong?   **¿qué (te) pasa?**
I wound   **hiero**
wounded   **herido**

I don't know what is wrong with her.
No sé qué tendrá.

She seems to have a temperature.
Parece tener fiebre.

I have a sore throat and I have a migraine coming on.
Tengo dolor de la garganta y me llega [me está empezando] una jaqueca.

➤ PARTS OF THE BODY App.5b; ACCIDENTS & EMERGENCIES 11a

11c Medical treatment

anaesthetic/anesthetic **el anestésico**
    I am under anaesthetic/
    anesthetic **estoy anestesiado**
appointment **la cita**
bandage **la venda**
blood **la sangre**
blood test **el análisis sanguíneo/de la sangre**
blood pressure **la presión sanguínea**
capsule **la cápsula**
chemist/pharmacist **la farmacia**
chemotherapy **la quimoterapia**
cure **la cura**
danger to life **el peligro mortal**
dangerous **peligroso**
death **la muerte**
I diet **estoy a régimen/[dieta]**
doctor (Dr) **el médico**
dressing **el vendaje**
drop **la gota**
drug **la droga**
E111-form **el formulario/la ficha de E111**

I examine **examino**
examination **el examen**
I fill **(re)lleno**
glasses **las gafas**
I have **tengo**
heating **la calefacción**
hospital **el hospital**
I improve **me restablezco, me repongo**
injection **la inyección**
insurance certificate **el certificado de seguro**
I look after **cuido de**
medical **medical**
medicine **la medicina**
midwife **la comadre, la comadrona, la partera**
nurse **la enfermera**
I nurse **cuido, atiendo**
I operate **opero**
operation **la operación, la intervención quirúrgica**
pastille **la pastilla**
patient **el paciente, el enfermo**
physiotherapy **la fisioterapia**

Call a doctor!

¡Llama a un médico!

Is he a good doctor? Can he diagnose the symptoms and prescribe a cure?

¿Es buen médico? ¿Puede diagnosticar las síntomas y recomendar una cura?

He does not like injections. He has never had an X-ray.

No le gustan las inyecciones. Nunca le han radiografiado.

Will I need an operation? I have my medical insurance.

¿Necesitaré una operación? Tengo mi seguro de enfermedad.

physiotherapist **el fisioterapeuta**
pill **la píldora**
plaster (of Paris) **el yeso mate**
I prescribe **receto**
prescription **la receta**
radio therapy **la radioterapia**
receptionist **el/la recepcionista**
service **el servicio**
I set **encaso**
spa resort **el balneario, la estación balnearia, la estación termal**
specialist **el/la especialista**
stitch **el punto de sutura**
stitches **los puntos de sutura**
sticking plaster **el esparadrapo**
surgery **la cirugía**
surgery hours **las horas de consulta**
syringe **la jeringa, la jeringuilla**
tablet **la tableta, el comprimido, la pastilla**
therapeutic **terapéutico**
therapy **la terapia, la terapéutica**
therapist **el/la terapeuta**
thermometer **el termómetro**
I treat **trato, curo, atiendo**
treatment **el tratamiento, la cura**

ward **la sala, la crujía**
wound **la herida**
x-ray **el rayo x**
I x-ray **radiografío**

Dentist & optician

abscess **el flemón**
contact lens **el contacto**
dentist **el dentista**
denture **la dentadura**
I extract **saco**
eyesight **la vista**
filling **el empaste**
frame **la montura**
lens **el lente**
long-sighted **présbite**
optician **el óptico**
short-sighted **miope**
spectacles/glasses **las gafas**
spectacles case **el estuche para gafas**
sunglasses **las gafas de sol**
tinted **ahumado**
I test/check **controlo**
I have toothache **tengo dolor de muelas**

I have lost my tablets. I have to take them four times a day.

He perdido mis comprimidos [tabletas/pastillas]. Debo tomarlos cuatro veces al día.

Can I have a prescription?

¿Me puede dar una receta?

He had an operation recently. He seems to be recovering.

Le operaron recientemente. Parece que se está restableciendo.

We are so relieved - all the tests proved negative.

Estamos aliviados - todos los análisis salieron negativos.

➤ HOSPITAL DEPARTMENTS App.11c

11d Health & hygiene

Physical state

aching **el dolor**
  aching *(adj)* **adolorido**
asleep **dormido**
awake **despierto**
blister **la ampolla**
boil **el divieso, el furúnculo**
bruise **la contusión, el cardenal,**
  la magulladura, el magullón,
  el moretón
comfort **la comodidad**
comfortable **cómodo, confortable**
discomfort **el malestar**
dizziness **el mareo, el vértigo**
dizzy **mareado**
drowsiness **la somnolencia**
drowsy **soñoliento**
I exercise **ejercito**
exercise bike **la bicicleta estática**
faint **mareado**
I faint **me desmayo, pierdo el**
  conocimiento
I feel **me siento**
fit **en buena forma, en buen**
  estado físico, sano, bien de
  salud
fitness **la buena salud, el (buen)**
  estado físico
graze **el roce, la abrasión, la**
  raspadura
I am hot/cold **tengo calor/frío**
hunger **el hambre** *(f)*
hungry **hambriento**
I am hungry **tengo hambre**
ill **enfermo**

I lie down **me acuesto**
I look **parezco**
queasy **mareado, bascoso**
I relax **me relajo**
I rest/have a rest **descanso**
seasick **mareado**
sick **enfermo**
I sleep **duermo**
sleepy **soñoliento**
stamina **la resistencia, el aguante**
strange **extraño, curioso, raro**
thirst **la sed**
thirsty **sediento**
I am thirsty **tengo sed**
tired **cansado**
I am tired **tengo sueño, estoy**
  cansado
tiredness **el cansancio, la fatiga,**
  el sueño
uncomfortable **incómodo,**
  molesto
under the weather **indispuesto**
unfit **enfermo, indispuesto, de**
  mala salud
unwell **enfermo, indispuesto**
I wake up **me despierto**
well **bien de salud**
well-being **el bienestar**

Beauty & hygiene

bath **el baño**
beauty **la belleza**
beauty contest **el concurso de**
  belleza
beauty salon/parlor **el salón de**

I need a shower.

I'd like a haircut, please. Don't cut
it too short.

Necesito ducharme.

**Quiero un corte de pelo, por
favor. No me lo corte mucho.**

belleza
beauty queen **la reina de la belleza**
beauty treatment **el tratamiento de belleza**
body odour/odor **el olor a sudor**
I burp/belch **eructo**
I brush **cepillo**
brush **el cepillo**
I clean **limpio**
clean **limpio**
I clean my teeth **me limpio los dientes**
comb **el peine**
I comb my hair **me peino**
condom **el condón, el preservativo**
contraceptive **el anticonceptivo**
contraception **la contracepción, las medidas anticonceptivas**
I cut **corto, me corto ...**
dandruff **la caspa**
I defecate **defeco**
dirty **sucio**
diet *(usual food)* **la dieta**
I am on a diet **sigo un régimen**
electric razor **la afeitadora (eléctrica)**
face-pack **el tratamiento facial**
flannel **la manopla**
fleas **las pulgas**
hairbrush **el cepillo para el pelo**
haircut **el corte de pelo**
I get my hair cut **me hago cortar el pelo**
hairdo **el peinado**
healthy *(person)* **sano, con buena salud**

healthy *(diet, place)* **saludable**
laundry *(establishment)* **el lavadero, la lavandería**
laundry *(linen)* **la ropa sucia, la ropa por lavar**
louse/nit **el piojo**
I'm losing my hair **pierdo el pelo, me estoy quedando calvo**
manicure **la manicura, [el manicure]**
I menstruate **menstruo**
menstruation **la menstruación**
nailbrush **el cepillo para las uñas**
period **el período, la regla**
period pains **los dolores de la regla**
razor **la afeitadora, la rasuradora, la maquinilla de afeitar**
sanitary **sanitario, higiénico**
sanitary towel **el paño higiénico, la compresa (higiénica), [la toalla higiénica]**
scissors **las tijeras**
I shave **me afeito**
shower **la ducha**
smell *(bad)* **el olor**
I smell *(badly)* **huelo**
soap **el jabón**
I sweat **sudo**
sweat **el sudor**
I take a bath **me baño**
I take a shower **me ducho**
tampon **el tampón**
toothbrush **el cepillo de dientes**
toothpaste **la crema de dientes, la pasta dentífrica**
towel **la toalla**
I wash **me lavo**

A little more off the back and sides, please. | **Un poco más por detrás y en los lados.**

Please trim my moustache. | **¿Quiere usted cortarme el bigote?**

Social issues

12a Society

abnormal **anormal**
alternative **la alternativa**
amenity **la amenidad**
anonymous **anónimo**
attitude **la actitud**
available **disponible**
basic **básico**
basis **la base**
burden **la carga, el peso**
campaign **la campaña**
care **el cuidado**
cause **la causa**
change **el cambio**
circumstance **la circunstancia**
community **la comunidad**
compulsory **obligatorio**
contribution **la contribución**
cost **el precio, el coste, el costo**
I counsel **aconsejo, asesoro**
counselling **el asesoramiento, la asistencia**
criterion **el criterio**
debt **la deuda**
I am in debt **tengo deudas**
dependence **la dependencia**
dependent **dependiente**
depressed **deprimido, abatido**
depression **la depresión, la crisis**
deprived **privado de**
difficulty **la dificultad**

effect **el efecto**
effective **efectivo, eficiente**
fact **el hecho**
finance **las finanzas**
financial **financiero**
frustrated **frustrado**
frustration **la frustración**
guidance **la dirección, la orientación**
increase **el aumento**
inner city **el barrio céntrico de la ciudad**
institution **la institución**
loneliness **la soledad**
lonely **solitario**
long-term **a largo plazo**
measure **medida**
negative **negativo**
normal **normal, común**
policy **la política, los principios, los criterios**
positive **positivo**
power **el poder**
prestige **el prestigio**
problem **el problema, la cuestión**
protest movement **el movimiento de protesta**
I provide (with) **proporciono, suministro**
provision **la provisión, el**

There are immense social problems in the inner city. | **Existen enormes problemas sociales en los barrios céntricos de las ciudades.**

The unemployed often feel frustrated and lonely, as a result of unemployment. | **Los desempleados suelen sentirse frustrados y solitarios como consecuencia del paro.**

suministro, la estipulación, la disposición
psychological **psicológico**
quality of life **la calidad de vida**
question/issue **la cuestión, el asunto**
rate **la tasa**
responsibility **la responsabilidad**
responsible (ir-) **(ir)responsable**
result **el resultado**
role **el papel**
rural **rural**
scarcity **la escasez**
scheme **el esquema**
I am on the scrap heap **no encuentro trabajo**
secure (in-) **(in)seguro**
security (in-) **la (in)seguridad**
self-esteem **la autoestima**
short-term **a corto plazo**
situation **la situación**
social **social**
society **la sociedad**
stable (un-) **(in)estable**
stability (in-) **la (in)estabilidad**
statistics **las estadísticas**
status **el estatus, la posición**
stigma **el estigma, la marca**
stress **el estrés, la fatiga**
stressful **estresante**
structure **la estructura, la configuración**
superfluous **superfluo**
support **el soporte, el apoyo, el sostén, la ayuda**
urban **urbano**
value **el valor**

Some useful verbs

I adapt/conform **me ajusto, me acomodo**
it affects **afecta**
I afford **me puedo permitir**
I alienate **enajeno, traspaso**
I break down **fracaso**
I campaign **hago campaña**
I care for **me preocupo por**
I cause **causo**
it changes **cambia**
I contribute **contribuyo**
I cope **me arreglo, me las ingenio**
I depend on **dependo de**
I deprive **privo**
I discourage **desaliento**
I dominate **domino**
I encourage **aliento, animo**
I help **ayudo**
I increase **aumento**
I lack **carezco de**
I look after **cuido de**
I need **necesito**
I neglect **descuido, abandono**
I owe **debo**
I protest **protesto**
I provide for **proporciono, suministro**
I put up with **(me) aguanto**
I rely on **confío en, cuento con**
I respect **respeto**
I share **comparto**
I solve **resuelvo**
I suffer from (disease) **tengo**
I support **mantengo**
I tackle **hago frente a**
I value **valoro**

Financial difficulties lead to loss of status and family problems.

The quality of life suffers because of it.

Las dificultades económicas llevan a una pérdida de estatus y problemas familiares.

Como consecuencia, se compromete la calidad de la vida.

12b Poverty & social services

Social services

aid **la ayuda**
agency **la agencia, la oficina**
authority **las autoridades**
benefit **el beneficio**
I benefit **me beneficio**
charity **la caridad, la organización caritativa**
claim **la solicitud**
I claim **solicito**
claimant **el solicitante**
disability **la invalidez, la incapacidad**
disabled **el inválido, el minusválido**
I am eligible for **tengo derecho a, cumplo los requisitos para**
frail **débil, delicado**
frailty **la debilidad**
grant **la concesión, la beca**
handicap **la minusvalía, el obstáculo, la incapacidad**
handicapped **el minusválido, el incapacitado**
ill-health **la mala salud**
income support **la pensión de subsistencia**
loan **el préstamo**

maintenance **el mantenimiento**
official **oficial**
reception centre/center **el centro de recepciones**
Red Cross **la Cruz Roja**
refuge **el refugio**
refugee **el refugiado**
I register **me inscribo**
registration **la inscripción**
Salvation Army **el Ejército de Salvación**
service **el servicio**
social security **la seguridad social**
social services **los servicios sociales**
social worker **el asistente social**
support **la ayuda**
I support **ayudo**
welfare **el bienestar social**

Wealth & poverty

affluence **la prosperidad**
I beg **mendigo, pido**
beggar **el mendigo**
I am broke **no tengo un céntimo**
debt **la deuda**
in debt **tengo deudas**
deprivation **la privación, la**

– What social services are available to those in need?

– There is a reception centre/center for the homeless. Many charities are active in this way.
The physically handicapped can apply for help too.
They are particularly vulnerable to unemployment.

– ¿Cuáles servicios sociales están a la disposición de los necesitados?
– Hay un centro de recepción para las personas sin hogar. Muchas sociedades benéficas son activas del mismo modo.
Los minusválidos también pueden solicitar ayuda.
Ellos son muy vulnerables en lo que se refiere al desempleo.

pérdida
deprived **desventajado, desvalido**
destitute **el indigente, necesitado**
living standards **las condiciones de vida**
millionaire **el millonario**
need **la necesidad**
nutrition **la nutrición**
poor **pobre**
poverty **la pobreza, la miseria**
subsistence **la subsistencia**
tramp/vagrant **el vagabundo**
vulnerability **la vulnerabilidad**
vulnerable **vulnerable**
wealth **la riqueza**
I am well off **soy acomodado**

Unemployment

I cut back *(jobs)* **recorto, reduzco**
I dismiss **despido**
dismissal **el despido**
dole **el subsidio de desempleo**
I give notice **aviso**
job **el empleo, el trabajo**
job centre/employment center **la oficina de empleo**
job creation scheme **el programa de creación de empleo**
long-term unemployed **el**

deempleado de larga duración
I have lost my job **he perdido mi empleo**
part-time **la media jornada**
redundancy **el despido**
redundant **despedido**
retraining **la recapacitación, el entrenamiento adicional**
I refuse a job **rechazo un empleo**
I resign **dimito, renuncio**
short-time working **la jornada reducida**
skill **la habilidad, la aptitud, la técnica, el oficio**
staffing **empleo de personal**
training scheme/program **la programa de formación**
unemployable **inútil para el trabajo**
unemployed **desempleado, parado**
unemployment **el paro, el desempleo**
unemployment benefit **el subsidio de paro/desempleo**
unemployment rate **la tasa de desempleo**
unskilled worker **trabajador no especializado**
vacancy **la vacante**

– How high is the level of unemployment?
– In some areas it is about 15%.

– Can people retrain or work part-time?

– Yes, sometimes, and many retire early.
Not everyone gets the dole, as many have not worked for a long time.

– ¿Cuál es la tasa del desempleo?
– En algunas zonas llega a unos 15%.

– La gente, puede recapacitarse o trabajar en horario de jornada reducida?

– Sí, a veces, y muchos se toman la jubilación anticipada.
No todos reciben el subsidio del paro, pues muchos llevan mucho tiempo sin trabajar.

12c Housing & homelessness

accommodation **la vivienda**

I build **construyo**

building **la construcción, el edificio**

    building land **los terrenos edificables/urbanizables**

    building plot **el solar para la construcción, [el lote]**

    building site **la obra**

camp **el campamento**

comfortable/homely **confortable, cómodo**

commune **la comuna**

dilapidated **desmoronado, ruinoso**

I demolish **demuelo**

demolition **la demolición**

it deteriorates **se deteriora, deteriora**

digs/unfurnished rooms **las habitaciones sin muebles**

drab **monótono, triste**

estate/real estate agent **el agente de propiedad/de finca raíz**

I evict **desalojo, desahucio**

it falls down **está en ruinas**

flat/apartment **el piso, el apartamento**

    block of flats/apartment house **el bloque de pisos/apartamentos**

furnished **amueblado**

homeless **sin hogar**

homelessness **la carencia de hogar**

hostel **el hostel**

house **la casa**

    detached house **el chalet**

    council house **la casa protegida, la casa del ayuntamiento, [la vivienda estatal]**

    semi-detached house **la casa adosada**

housing **la vivienda**

    housing association **la sociedad constructora**

    housing shortage **la escasez de viviendas**

inner city **el barrio céntrico de la ciudad**

– Why do so many houses in Spain stand empty?
The houses deteriorate fast and squatters move in.

– ¿Por qué quedan vacías tantas casas en España?
Las casas se deterioran rápidamente, y luego las ocupan los squátters.

Aren't the town planners intending to demolish the houses?

Y los urbanistas, ¿no tienen la intención de demoler estas casas?

– Yes, but at the same time so many are homeless. They sleep rough or squat.

– Sí, pero al mismo tiempo hay tantos sin hogar. Duermen al descubierto o ocupan las casas ilegalmente.

– Is the council/municipality still building council/public housing?

– Y el ayuntamiento [la alcaldía] ¿sigue construyendo viviendas protegidas?

landlord   **el dueño, el propietario (de la casa)**
I let/rent   **alquilo, arriendo**
living conditions   **las condiciones de vida**
I maintain   **mantengo**
I modernize   **modernizo**
mortgage   **la hipoteca, el préstamo hipotecario**
mortgage rate   **el tipo de interés hipotecario**
I move house   **me mudo de casa**
I occupy   **ocupo**
overcrowded   **lleno de gente, atestado**
overcrowding   **la superpoblación, la masificación**
own   **propio**
owner-occupied   **ocupado por el dueño**
I pull down   **demuelo, derribo**
I redevelop   **reorganizo, reconstruyo**
I renovate   **renuevo**
I rent   **alquilo, arriendo**
rent   **la renta, el alquiler**
I repair   **reparo**

repairs   **las reparaciones**
shanty town   **el barrio de chabolas, [el arrabal]**
shelter   **el refugio**
slum   **la barriada, el barrio pobre**
I sleep rough   **duermo en la calle, estoy en la calle**
social housing/council housing/public housing   **la vivienda protegida**
slum clearance   **la demolición de barrios pobres**
speculator   **el especulador**
squalid   **miserable, escuálido**
I squat   **ocupo sin derecho, usurpo la propiedad**
squatter   **el ocupante sin derecho, el intruso, el usurpador**
suburb   **el suburbio**
it stands empty   **está vacío**
tenant   **inquilino**
town planning   **el planeamiento urbano**
urban   **urbano**
urban development   **el desarrollo urbano**
unfurnished   **desamueblado**
waste land   **la tierra baldía**

– Yes, but not enough. Living conditions in the blocks of flats/apartment blocks are extremely poor. They are overcrowded and the landlords no longer repair them.

Despite campaigns to help the homeless and unemployed, the situation remains serious.

It is impossible to find a furnished flat/apartment to rent. The area is fast becoming a slum.

– **Sí, pero no bastan. Las condiciones de vida en los bloques de viviendas protegidas son malísimas. Están masificadas, y los propietarios ya no las reparan.**

A pesar de las campañas para ayudar a los sin hogar y a los desempleados, la situación sigue siendo grave.

Es imposible encontrar un piso amueblado para alquilar. Este barrio se está convirtiendo rápidamente en un barrio bajo.

12d Addiction & violence

abuse **el abuso**
I abuse **abuso**
act of violence **el acto de violencia**
addict *(adj/n)* **adicto**
addiction **la adicción**
addictive **adictivo**
aggression **la agresión**
aggressive **agresivo**
alcohol **el alcohol**
alcoholic **el alcohólico**
alcoholism **el alcoholismo**
anger **la rabia, el enfado**
angry **enfadado**
I attack **ataco**
attack **el ataque**
I beat up **doy una paliza**
I bully **intimido**
bully **la intimidación**
child abuse **el maltrato de los hijos**
consumption **el consumo**
dangerous **peligroso**
I drink **bebo**
I get drunk **me emborracho**
drunk **borracho**
drunken driving **la conducción bajo los efectos del alcohol**
I dry out **me desalcoholizo**

effect **el efecto**
fatal **fatal, mortal**
fear **el temor, el miedo**
I fear **temo, tengo miedo de**
force **la fuerza**
gang **la banda**
harass **hostigar, perseguir**
hooligan **el gamberro, el vándalo**
hostile **hostil**
hostility **la hostilidad**
insult **el insulto**
I insult **insulto**
intoxication **la intoxicación**
legal (il-) **(i)legal**
I legalize **legalizo**
I mug **asalto, aporreo**
mugger **el asaltante**
nervous **nervioso**
nervousness **los nervios, el estado nervioso**
pimp **el chulo, el proxeneta**
porno **pornográfico**
pornography **la pornografía**
prostitution **la prostitución**
punk **el punki**
rape **la violación**
he rapes **viola**
rapist **el violador**

Violence and vandalism are common. Older people and women are sometimes afraid to go out alone.

Many young people have a drug problem. They start by sniffing solvents, or by taking soft drugs. Cannabis is the most common, and gives a feeling of intoxication. Then they go onto hard drugs.

La violencia y el vandalismo son muy frecuentes. Los ancianos y las mujeres a veces tienen miedo de salir solos.

Muchos jóvenes tienen problemas con la toxicomanía. Empiezan inhalando disolventes o tomando drogas blandas. El cánabis es el más común, y da la sensación de intoxicación. Luego pasan a las drogas duras.

rehabilitation   **la rehabilitación**
I revert   **revierto, reincido**
rocker   **el rocker**
I seduce   **seduzco, convenzo**
sexual harassment   **el hostigamiento sexual**
skinhead   **el cabeza rapada**
I smoke   **fumo**
stimulant   **el estimulante**
stimulation   **la estimulación**
I terrorize   **aterrorizo**
I threaten   **amenazo**
thug   **el gamberro, el desalmado**
vandal   **el gamberro, el vándalo**
vandalism   **el gamberrismo, el vandalismo**
victim   **la víctima**
violent   **violento**

Drugs

addicted to drugs   **drogadicto**
AIDS   **SIDA**
cannabis   **el cánabis, la marihuana**
cocaine   **la cocaína**
crack   **el crack**
I deal   **trafico**
drug   **la droga**
drug scene   **la escena de drogas, el barrio de drogas**

drug traffic   **el tráfico de drogas, el narcotráfico**
I get infected   **me infecto**
glue   **el pegamento, el pegante**
hard drugs   **las drogas duras**
hash   **el hachís**
I have a fix   **estoy enganchado, estoy drogado**
heroin   **la heroína**
HIV-positive   **VIH positivo**
I inject   **inyecto**
junkie   **el yonqui, el drogadicto**
I kick (the habit)   **me desintoxico**
LSD   **LSD**
narcotic   **el narcótico**
pusher   **el camello, el traficante de drogas**
I sniff   **esnifo, inhalo**
soft drugs   **las drogas blandas**
solvent   **el disolvente**
stimulant   **el estimulante**
syringe   **la jeringuilla**
I take drugs/a fix   **tomo drogas, estoy enganchado**
tranquillizer   **el tranquilizante**
withdrawal   **la retirada, el desenganchamiento**

Junkies inject or smoke drugs.

Los toxicómanos se inyectan con las drogas o los fuman.

All drugs are dangerous, but injecting them brings risks of AIDS.
.

Todas las drogas son peligrosas, pero inyectarlas trae el peligro del SIDA.

The drug scene is worrying as so many people become dealers or turn to crime.

El mundo de las drogas es muy preocupante, pues muchas personas se hacen camellos [traficantes] o recurren a la criminalidad.

Withdrawal symptoms are very unpleasant.

El síndrome de la abstinencia es muy desagradable.

12e Prejudice: race & sexuality

asylum seeker **el solicitante de asilo político**
I call names **insulto**
citizenship **la ciudadanía**
country of origin **el país de origen**
cultural **cultural**
culture **la cultura**
I discriminate **discrimino**
discrimination **la discriminación**
dual nationality **la doble nacionalidad**
emigrant **el emigrante**
emigration **la emigración**
equal (un-) **(des)igual**
equal opportunities **las oportunidades iguales**
equal pay **la paga igualitaria**
equal rights **los derechos igualitarios**
equality (in-) **la (des)igualdad**
ethnic **étnico**
far right **la extrema derecha**
fascism **el fascismo**
fascist **el fascista**
foreign **el extranjero**
foreign worker **el trabajador extranjero**

freedom **la libertad**
    freedom of speech **la libertad de expresión**
ghetto **el gueto**
human rights **los derechos humanos**
I immigrate **inmigro**
immigrant **el inmigrante**
immigration **la inmigración**
I integrate **me integro**
integration **la integración**
intolerance **la intolerancia**
intolerant **intolerante**
majority **la mayoría**
minority **la minoría**
mother tongue **la lengua madre**
I persecute **persigo**
persecution **la persecución**
politically correct **políticamente correcto**
prejudice **el prejuicio**
prejudiced **lleno de prejuicios**
rabid **fanático**
race riot **la manifestación racial**
racism **el racismo**
racist **el racista**
    racist *(adj)* **racista**

– Is racism a serious problem?

– Yes, black and dark-skinned people suffer particularly from discrimination.
– What about the ethnic minority population resident here?
– Unfortunately they tend to get the worst jobs and to be paid less. They are more likely to be unemployed and can only afford cheap accommodation.

– **¿Es un problema serio el racismo?**
– **Sí, los negros y la gente de piel morena sobre todo sufren la discriminación.**
– **¿Y qué pasa con la minoría étnica que vive aquí?**
– **Desafortunadamente suelen obtener los peores empleos, y les pagan menos. Tienen más probabilidad de quedar desempleados, y sólo llegan a tener viviendas muy malas.**

refugee **el refugiado**
I repatriate **repatrio**
residence permit **el permiso de residencia**
right **el derecho**
 right to asylum **el derecho de asilo**
 right to residence **el derecho de residencia**
stereotypical **estereotípico**
tolerance **la tolerancia**
tolerant **tolerante**
I tolerate **tolero**
work permit **el permiso de trabajo**

Race

anti-Semitic **antisemítico**
anti-Semitism **el antisemitismo**
Asian **asiático**
black **el negro**
Caribbean **el caribe**
 Caribbean *(adj)* **del Caribe**
coloured/colored **de color**
dark-skinned **de piel oscura**
Jew **el judío, el hebreo**
Jewish **judío**
Neo-Nazism **neo fascismo**
white **el blanco**

Sexuality

female **la mujer, la hembra**
feminine **femenino**
feminism **el feminismo**
feminist **la feminista**
gay **el marica, el homosexual**
gay club **el club para gays**
gay movement **el movimiento homosexual**
heterosexual **el heterosexual**
 heterosexual *(adj)* **heterosexual**
homosexual **el homosexual**
 homosexual *(adj)* **homosexual**
homosexuality **la homosexualidad**
lesbian **la lesbiana**
 lesbian *(adj)* **lesbiana**
male **varón**
sexual **sexual**
sexuality **la sexualidad**
women's lib **la liberación de la mujer**
women's libber **la activista por la liberación de la mujer**
women's rights **los derechos de la mujer**

The law still discriminates against male homosexuals, although society is getting more tolerant.

La ley sigue discriminando a los homosexuales masculinos, aunque la sociedad se está haciendo más tolerante.

– Is there still anti-Semitism?
– Unfortunately, although the position has improved overall, there is still renewed prejudice against the Jews.

– ¿Existe aún el antisemitismo?
– Por desgracia, aunque la posición ha mejorado, sigue habiendo prejuicio en contra de los judíos.

The feminist movement is still demanding equal rights for women.

El movimiento feminista sigue exigiendo derechos iguales para las mujeres.

Religion

13a Ideas & doctrines

agnostic **el agnóstico**
anglican **el anglicano**
apostle **el apóstol**
atheism **el ateismo**
atheist **el ateo**
atheistic **ateístico**
authority **la autoridad**
belief **la creencia**
I believe (in) **creo (en)**
believer **el creyente**
Bible **la Biblia**
biblical **bíblico**
blessed **bendito**
Buddha **Buda**
Buddhism **el Budismo**
Buddhist **el budista**
calvinist **el calvinista**
he canonises **canoniza**
cantor **el cantor**
catholic **el católico**
charismatic **carismático**
charity **la caridad**
Christ **Cristo**
Christian **el cristiano**
Christianity **la cristianidad, el cristianismo**
church **la iglesia**
commentary **el comentario**
conscience **la conciencia**
conversion **la conversión**

covenant **la alianza, el pacto**
disciple **el discípulo**
divine **lo divino**
doctrine **la doctrina**
duty **el deber, la obligación**
ecumenism **el ecumenismo**
ethical **ético**
evil **el mal**
faith **la fe**
faithful **fiel**
I forgive **perdono**
forgiveness **el perdón**
free will **la libre voluntad**
fundamentalism **el fundamentalismo**
fundamentalist **el fundamentalista**
God **el Dios**
god **el dios**
goddess **la diosa**
Gospel **el evangelio**
grace **la gracia**
heaven **el cielo, el paraiso**
Hebrew **el hebreo**
hell **el infierno**
heretical **herético**
Hindu **el hindú**
Hinduism **el hinduismo**
holiness **la santidad**
holy **santo, sagrado**
Holy Spirit **el espíritu santo**

The five pillars of Islam are belief in the One True God and his Prophet, prayer, fasting, giving alms and pilgrimage to Mecca.

Los cinco pilares de la fe musulmana son la creencia en el Unico Dios Verdadero y en su Profeta, la oración, el ayuno, la limosna y el pelerinaje a Meca.

hope **la esperanza**
human **humano**
human being **el ser humano**
humanism **el humanismo**
humanity **la humanidad**
infallibility **la infalibilidad**
infallible **infalible**
Islam **el islam**
Islamic **islámico**
Jesus **Jesús**
Jew **el judío**
Jewish **el judío**
Judaic **judaico**
Judaism **judaismo**
Lord **El Señor**
merciful **misericordioso**
mercy **la misericordia**
Messiah **El Mesías**
Mohammed **Mahoma**
moral **moral**
morality **la moralidad**
Muslim **musulmán**
mystical **místico**
mysticism **la mística, el misticismo**
myth **el mito**
New Testament **El Nuevo Testamento**
nirvana **la nirvana**
Old Testament **El Viejo Testamento**
orthodox **el ortodoxo**
pagan **el pagano, el infiel**
parish **la parroquia**
Pentateuch **el Pentateuco**
prophet **el profeta**
protestant **el protestante**

protestantism **el protestantismo**
Quaker **el cuáquero**
Q'uran/Koran **El Corán**
redemption **la redención, el perdón**
religion **la religión**
sacred **sagrado**
saint **el santo**
Saint Peter **San Pedro**
he sanctifies **santifica**
Satan **Satanás**
he saves **salva**
scripture **las escrituras** *(pl)*
service **el servicio religioso, la misa**
Sikh **sij**
Sikhism **sijismo**
sin **el pecado**
sinful **pecaminoso**
sinner **el pecador**
soul **el alma**
spirit **el espíritu**
spiritual **espiritual**
spirituality **la espiritualidad**
Talmud **el Talmud**
Taoism **el taoísmo**
theological **teológico**
theology **la teología**
traditional **tradicional**
transcendental **trascendental**
Trinity **la trinidad**
true **verdadero**
truth **la verdad**
vision **la visión**
vocation **la vocación**

There is considerable disagreement about the ordination of women to the priesthood.

Hay un desacuerdo apreciable con respecto a la ordenación de las mujeres al sacerdocio.

John Wesley said, "The world is my parish."

John Wesley dijo, "El mundo es mi parroquia."

13b Faith & practice

archbishop **el arzobispo**
baptism **el bautismo, el bautizo**
bar-mitzvah **el bar-mitzah**
I bear witness to **testifico, doy testimonio**
bishop **el obispo**
bishopric/see **el obispado**
burial **el entierro**
cathedral **la catedral**
chapel **la capilla**
christening **el bautizo, el bautismo**
clergy **el clero**
clergyman **el clérigo**
communion **la comunión**
  holy communion **la santa comunión**
community **la comunidad**
I confess *(faith)* **soy**
I confess *(sins)* **confieso**
confession **la confesión**

confirmation **la confirmación**
congregation **la congregación**
  congregation *(of cardinals)* **la curia**
convent **el convento**
I convert *(others)* **convierto**
I convert *(self)* **me convierto**
Eucharist **La Eucaristía**
evangelical **evangélico**
evangelist **el evangelista**
I give alms **doy limosna**
I give thanks **doy gracias**
Imam **el Imam, el Imán**
intercession **la intercesión, la mediación**
laity **el laicado**
lay **seglar, profano**
layperson **el seglar, el laico**
the Lord's Supper **La Santa Cena**
Mass **La Misa**
I meditate **medito**

Bishops in the Church of England are not afraid to speak about social problems.

Los obispos de la Iglesia Anglicana no tienen miedo de hablar de los problemas sociales.

The sacrament of Holy Communion will be celebrated on Sunday at 9 o'clock.

El Sacramento de la Sagrada Comunión se celebrará el domingo a las nueve.

The Parish Council meets regularly.

El Consejo Paroquial se reúne con regularidad.

Every Muslim is called to prayer five times a day.

A todos los musulmanes se les llama a rezar cinco veces al día.

During the Holy month of Ramadan, Muslims fast from dawn to dusk. The month ends with the celebrations of the festival of Eid.

Durante el Mes Sagrado de Ramadán, los musulmanes ayunan desde el amanecer hasta el anochecer. El mes termina con las festividades de la fiesta de Eid.

meditation **la meditación**
minister **el ministro de la iglesia**
I minister to the parish **soy el párroco, administro la parroquia**
ministry **el ministerio eclesiástico**
mission **la misión**
missionary **el misionario, el misionero**
monastery **el monasterio**
monk **el monje**
mosque **la mezquita**
mullah **mullah**
nun **la monja**
parish **la parroquia**
parishioner **el feligrés**
pastor **el pastor, el sacerdote**
pastoral **pastoral**
pilgrimage **el peregrinaje**
Pope **El Papa**
I praise **rezo, oro**
I pray (for) **rezo (por), pido (por)**
prayer **la oración**

priest **el sacerdote, el cura**
rabbi **el rabino**
reformation **la reformación, la reforma**
I repent **me arrepiento**
repentance **el arrepentimiento**
repentant **el arrepentido**
I revere **venero, reverencio**
reverence **la veneración, la reverencia**
reverent **reverente**
rite **el rito**
ritual **el ritual**
sacrament **el sacramento**
synagogue **la sinagoga**
synod **el sínodo**
temple **el templo**
vow **el voto**
wedding **la boda**
witness **el testigo**
I witness **testifico**
worship **la adoración**
I worship **adoro**

Those who are called to ministry must demonstrate their vocation before being accepted in theological colleges.

Los que tienen vocación por el sacerdocio tienen que manifestar su vocación antes de ser aceptados en los seminarios.

The Baptist tradition is very strong in the American South.

La tradición de la Iglesia Bautista es muy fuerte en el Sur de los Estados Unidos.

A few Muslim schoolgirls in France have come into conflict with the authorities because they chose to wear the veil at school.

Algunas colegialas musulmanas han entrado en conflicto con las autoridades por decidir llevar el velo en el colegio.

Religious fundamentalism can lead to fanaticism and intolerance in any religion.

En cualquier religión, el fundamentalismo religioso puede llevar al fanatismo y a la intolerancia.

Business & economics

14a The economics of business

I administer **administro**
I agree (to do) **acepto (hacer)**
agreement **el acuerdo**
bureaucracy **la burocracia**
business **los negocios**
  a business **un negocio, un acuerdo negocial**
capacity (*industrial*) **la capacidad**
commerce **el comercio**
commercial **comercial**
company **la empresa, la compañía, la sociedad**
deal **el trato**
I deliver **suministro, envío**
demand **la demanda**
the product is in demand **el producto está en demanda, el producto tiene demanda**
development **el desarrollo**
I earn (a living) **(me) gano (la vida)**
I employ **empleo**
employment **el empleo**
executive **el ejecutivo**
I export **exporto**
exports **las exportaciones**
fall **la caída**
goods **los bienes**
it grows **crece**
I import **importo**

I increase **incremento, aumento**
increase **el incremento, el aumento**
industrial output **la producción industrial**
industry **la industria**
I invest **invierto**
investment **la inversión**
lay-offs **los despidos**
living standards **el nivel de vida**
I manage **dirijo, gestiono, administro**
management **la dirección, la gestión, la administración**
multinational **la multinacional**
I negotiate **negocio**
negotiations **las negociaciones**
  one-to-one **cara a cara**
priority **la prioridad**
I produce **produzco**
producer **el productor**
production line **la línea de producción**
productivity **la productividad**
quality **la calidad**
I raise (*prices*) **subo, incremento**
reliability **la fiabilidad**
rise/raise **el aumento**
  wages rise **el aumento salarial**
services **los servicios**

Strikers blocked the port of Bilbao and all main roads to Barajas Airport.	**Los huelguistas obstruyeron el puerto de Bilbao y todas las carreteras que llevan al Aeropuerto de Barajas.**
Unemployment is rising to 12%.	**El desempleo alcanza el 12%.**

I set (priorities) **establezco**
sick-leave **la baja/licencia por enfermedad**
I sign (contracts) **firmo**
skilled labour/labor **el trabajo especializado**
workers' unrest **el descontento laboral**
social welfare **el bienestar social**
I strengthen **refuerzo**
supplier **el proveedor**
supply **el suministro**
tax **el impuesto**
I tax **cobro un impuesto**
unemployment **el desempleo**
unemployment benefit **el subsidio de desempleo**
unskilled labour/labor **el trabajo no especializado**
work ethic **la ética laboral, la ética del trabajo**
workforce **los trabajadores**
working week **la semana laboral**

Industrial/Labor dispute

I am on strike **estoy en huelga**
I blackleg **trabajo durante una huelga, soy esquirol**
I boycott **boicoteo**
I cross the picket line **cruzo la línea de piquetes**
demonstration **la manifestación**
dispute **la disputa**
I go slow/slow down **desciendo el ritmo de trabajo**
industrial/labor dispute **la disputa laboral, el conflicto laboral**

industrial relations **las relaciones industriales**
I lock-out **dejo en la calle, cierro la puerta**
lock-out **quedarse en la calle**
minimum wage **el salario mínimo**
I picket **hago de piquete**
picket **el piquete**
productivity bonus **el bono de productividad, la prima de productividad**
I resume work **reanudo, vuelvo al trabajo**
settlement **el ajuste**
stoppage **la suspensión, la huelga**
strike **la huelga**
unofficial strike **la huelga no autorizada**
I strike **hago huelga**
strike ballot **la votación de la huelga**
strikebreaker **el esquirol**
striker **el huelguista**
trade union **el sindicato**
trade unionist **el sindicalista**
unfair dismissal **el despido injustificado**
I unionize **me sindico, me sindicalizo**
unionized labour/labor **los trabajadores sindicados**
unrest **el descontento**
wage demand **la demanda salarial**
work to rule **la huelga de celo, el paro técnico**

The unions called for a reduction in the average weekly hours of work.

Los sindicatos exigieron una reducción en el promedio de horas semanales de trabajo.

The President has agreed to meet union leaders for talks.

El Presidente ha consentido en entrevistarse con los líderes de los sindicatos.

14b At work

agenda   **el orden del día**
   on the agenda   **en el orden del día**
I am away on business   **estoy en viaje de negocios**
business trip   **el viaje de negocios**
canteen   **la cantina, el bar**
career   **la carrera, la trayectoria profesional**
I chair a meeting   **presido a una reunión**
I delegate   **delego**
disciplinary proceedings   **el procedimiento disciplinario**
free   **gratis**
grant   **la beca, la ayuda**
I grant (someone)   **beco, concedo una ayuda**
holiday/vacation   **las vacaciones**
job   **el trabajo, el empleo**
manager   **el gerente**
management functions   **las funciones directivas**
I market   **comercio (al por mayor)**
meeting   **la reunión**
misconduct   **la mala conducta**
occupation   **la ocupación, la profesión**
I'm off work   **no trabajo, estoy de baja**
post   **el puesto de trabajo**
profession   **la profesión**
professional   **el profesional**
publicity   **la publicidad**
I qualify   **me cualifico**
I report to ...   **mi superior inmediato es ...**
I am responsible for   **soy responsable de**
research   **la investigación**
I sell   **vendo**
semi-skilled   **semiespecializado**
I teach   **enseño**
I toil   **trabajo duro**

trade   **el comercio**
training   **el aprendizaje, el entrenamiento**
training course   **el curso de aprendizaje, el curso de entrenamiento/capacitación**
I transfer   **me traslado**
vocation   **la vocación**
wage-earner   **el asalariado**
warning (verbal)   **la amonestación verbal**
   written warning   **la amonestación por escrito**
I work   **trabajo**
work   **el trabajo**
worker   **el trabajador**
workforce   **los trabajadores, la fuerza laboral**

In the office

business lunch   **la comida de negocios**
business meeting   **la reunión de negocios**
computer   **el ordenador, [el computador]**
conference call   **la convocatoria de la conferencia**
conference room   **la sala de conferencias**
correcting fluid   **el líquido corrector**
desk   **la mesa, el mostrador**
I dictate   **dicto**
dictating machine   **el dictáfono**
electronic mail   **el correo electrónico**
extension   **la extensión**
fax   **el fax**
fax machine   **la máquina de fax**
I fax   **mando un fax**
file   **el archivo**
I file   **archivo**
filing cabinet   **el archivador**

intercom   **el interfono**
open-plan   **la oficina de plan abierto**
photocopier   **la fotocopiadora**
photocopy   **la fotocopia**
I photocopy   **fotocopio**
pigeonhole   **el casillero**
reception   **la recepción**
receptionist   **el recepcionista**
shorthand   **la taquigrafía**
swivel chair   **la silla giratoria**
telephone   **el teléfono**
typing pool   **la sala de mecanógrafos**
wastebasket   **la papelera**
word processor   **el procesador de textos**
work station   **el puesto de trabajo, la estación de trabajo**

In the factory & on site

automation   **la automatización**
blue-collar worker   **los trabajadores, los obreros**
I build   **construgo**
bulldozer   **la aplanadora**
car/automobile industry   **la industria automotriz/del automóvil**
component   **el componente, la pieza**
concrete   **el hormigón**
construction industry   **la industria de la construcción**
crane   **la grúa**
fork-lift truck   **la carreta elevadora**
I forge   **forjo**
industry   **la industria**
   heavy industry   **la industria pesada**
   light industry   **la industria ligera**
I manufacture   **fabrico**
manufacturing   **la fabricación**
mass production   **la producción en masa**
mining   **la minería**
power industry   **la industria eléctrica**
precision tool   **el instrumento de precisión**
prefabricated   **prefabricado**
process   **el proceso**
I process   **proceso**
product   **el producto**
on the production line   **en línea de producción**
raw materials   **las materias primas**
robot   **el robot**
scaffolding   **el andamio**
shipbuilding   **la construcción naval**
steamroller   **la apisonadora**
steel smelting   **la fundición del acero**
textile industry   **la industria textil**

Employment patterns are shifting from traditional models of regular permanent jobs for one employer to a wide range of professional services delivered as a freelance to various employers.

La estructura del empleo está cambiando: en lugar del modelo tradicional de puestos regulares y permanentes con un solo patrón, está cambiando a una amplia gama de servicios profesionales prestados a varios patrones por trabajadores independientes.

➤ STATIONERY App.27b; COMPUTERS 15D

14c Pay & conditions

apprentice **el aprendiz**
bonus **la prima**
I clock in/out **ficho la entrada/salida, marco tarjeta**
commission **la comisión**
on commission **a comisión**
company car **el coche de la empresa**
contract **el contrato**
I am employed **tengo trabajo**
expenses **los gastos**
expense account **la cuenta de gastos**
flexi-time/flextime **la jornada flexible**
freelance **autónomo**
I work freelance **soy autónomo**
full-time **la jornada completa/a tiempo completo**
income **los ingresos** *(pl)*
overtime **las horas extraordinarias** *(pl)*
overworked **el recargado de trabajo**
part-time **la jornada a tiempo parcial, medio tiempo**
payday **el día de paga**
payslip **la hoja de sueldo**
payrise/pay raise **el incremento salarial, la subida de sueldo**
payroll **la nómina**
pension **la pensión**
perk **el gaje, los beneficios** *(pl)* **adicionales**
permanent **permanente, fijo**
I retire **me retiro, me jubilo**
retirement **el retiro**
salary **el salario, el sueldo**
self-employed **autónomo**
sexual harassment **el hostigamiento sexual**
shift **el turno**
day shift **el turno de día, el turno diurno**
night shift **el turno de noche, el turno nocturno**
temporary **temporal**
trial period **el período de prueba**
working-hours **las horas laborales**
wages **el salario, el sueldo**

The conditions in this office are not good enough for your staff, Mr Abril.

The place is cold, badly lit, and poorly ventilated. And you have far too many electrical appliances plugged into one socket. Unless you make considerable changes within three months, I shall be forced to close the office down. I shall come back next week to discuss your plans. Goodbye!

Las condiciones de trabajo en esta oficina no son bastante buenas para su personal, Señor Abril.

El lugar es frío, es mal iluminado, y mal ventilado. Y tienen ustedes un gran exceso de aparatos eléctricos conectados a un sólo enchufe. Si ustedes no introducen todos los cambios necesarios en un plazo de tres meses, me veré obligado a cerrar la oficina. Volveré la semana que viene para discutir con usted su plan de acción. ¡Adiós!

Job application

I advertise for a secretary   **anuncio un puesto de secretaria**

advertisement   **el anuncio de trabajo**

I have been made redundant   **he sido despedido**

I apply for a job   **solicito un trabajo**

classified ad(vertisement)   **los anuncios por palabras, [los avisos clasificados]**

curriculum vitae/resumé   **la hoja de vida**

discrimination   **la discriminación**

   racial discrimination   **la discriminación racial**

   sexual discrimination   **la discriminación sexual**

employment agency   **la agencia de trabajo**

interesting   **interesante**

interview   **la entrevista**

I interview   **entrevisto**

job application   **la solicitud de trabajo**

job centre/center *(government)*   **la oficina de empleo**

job description   **la descripción del trabajo**

I find a job   **encuentro un trabajo**

I look for   **busco**

I promote (someone)   **asciendo (a alguien)**

I am promoted   **soy ascendido**

opening *(vacancy)*   **la creación (de un puesto)**

promotion   **la promoción**

qualification   **la titulación**

qualified   **titulado, cualificado**

situations vacant   **los puestos vacantes**

I start work (for)   **empiezo a trabajar (para)**

I take on *(employee)*   **empleo**

vacancy   **una vacante**

work experience   **la experiencia laboral**

– Hello. Could I speak to the personnel manager, please.

– Speaking. What can I do for you?

– I saw your advert in the paper for a sales executive. Could you send me the job description and application forms? How many referees are you asking for?

– Two, including your present or last employer.

– Oiga. Quisiera hablar con el **jefe de la administración del personal.**

– Soy yo. ¿En qué puedo servirle?

– Vi su anuncio en el diario en el que se pedía un ejecutivo de ventas. ¿Podría usted mandarme la descripción del trabajo y las hojas de solicitud? ¿Cuántas referencias piden ustedes?

– Dos, incluyendo a su jefe actual o el último empleador que ha tenido.

14d Finance & industry

account **la cuenta**
advance **el anticipo**
  in advance **(por) adelantado**
I advertise **anuncio**
advertisement **el anuncio**
advertising **la publicidad**
advertising agency **la agencia de publicidad**
advice note **el aviso**
audit **la auditoría**
bill **la factura**
board **la junta**
bond **el bono**
branch *(of company)* **la sucursal**
budget **el presupuesto**
capital **el capital**
capital expenditure **los gastos de inversión**
chamber of commerce **la cámara de comercio**
collateral **la garantia**
company **la empresa, la compañia, la sociedad**
I consume *(resources)* **consumo**
consumer goods **los bienes de consumo**
consumer spending **los gastos de consumo**
cost of living **el coste de la vida**
costing **la estimación, la cotización**

costs **los costes**
credit **el crédito, el activo**
debit **el debe, el pasivo**
deflation **la deflación**
economic **económico**
economy **la economía**
funds **los fondos**
government spending **el gasto público**
income **el ingreso, los ingresos**
income tax **el impuesto sobre la renta**
instalment **el plazo**
interest rate **el tipo de interés**
I invest in **invierto en**
investment **la inversión**
invoice **la factura**
labour/labor costs **los costos laborales**
liability **la responsabilidad**
manufacturing industry **la industria de fabricación**
market **el mercado**
market economy **la economía de mercado**
marketing **la comercialización, el márketing**
merchandise **la mercancía**
national debt **la deuda nacional**
I nationalize **nacionalizo**
output **la producción, el**

Morales SA announced its takeover bid for the Dani supermarket chain.

The company informed shareholders that this year's operating profits will not match the level seen last year.

Morales S.A. anunció su oferta pública de adquisición de la cadena de supermercados Dani.

La compañia informó a sus accionistas que los beneficios netos este año no alcanzarán el valor de los del año pasado.

rendimiento

pay **el pago**

price **el precio**

private sector **el sector privado**

I privatiz/e **privatizo**

product **el producto**

production **la producción**

public sector **el sector público**

quota **la cuota**

real estate/realty **la propiedad inmobiliaria**

retail sales **las ventas al por menor**

retail trade **la venta al por menor**

salaries **los salarios**

sales tax **el impuesto sobre las ventas**

service sector **el sector de servicios**

share **la acción**

shares going up/down **la subida/ bajada de las acciones**

share index **el índice de la bolsa**

statistics **las estadísticas**

Stock Exchange **la bolsa de valores**

I subsidize **subvenciono**

subsidy **el subsidio**

supply and demand **la oferta y la demanda**

supply costs **los costos de suministro**

I tax **cobro un impuesto**

tax **el impuesto**

tax increase **el incremento/la subida de los impuestos**

taxation **la imposición**

taxation level **el nivel de imposición**

turnover **la facturación**

VAT/sales tax **el IVA (impuesto sobre el valor añadido)**

viable **viable**

wages **el salario**

Financial personnel

accountant **el contable**

actuary **el actuario**

auditor **el auditor**

banker **el banquero**

   investment banker **el banquero (del banco) de inversiones**

   merchant banker **el banquero (del banco) comercial**

bank manager **el director del banco**

broker **el agente de negocios**

   insurance broker **el agente de seguros**

consumer **el consumidor**

investor **el inversionista**

speculator **el especulador**

stockbroker **el agente de bolsa**

trader *(Wall St.)* **el comerciante**

Spantax Air expressed cautious optimism and suggested that the worst recession in the history of the aviation industry is coming to an end.

La compañía aérea Spantax hizo una declaración de optimismo prudente, e indicó que está terminando la peor recesión de la historia de la industria de la aviación.

News of the budget deficit caused panic in the Stock Exchange today.

La Bolsa fue presa del pánico hoy al recibir las noticias del déficit presupuestario.

14e Banking & the economy

Banking & personal finance

account **el contable**
automatic teller/cashpoint **el cajero automático**
bank **el banco**
bank loan **el préstamo bancario**
I bank (money) **pongo dinero en el banco**
bankrupt **la bancarrota**
building society/savings and loan association **la sociedad de crédito inmobiliario**
cash **dinero efectivo, metálico**
I cash a cheque/check **cobro un cheque, hago efectivo un cheque**
cashcard **la tarjeta de dinero, la tarjeta para el cajero automático**
cashdesk **la caja**
I change **cambio**
cheque/check **el cheque**
credit card **la tarjeta de crédito**
currency **la moneda, la divisa**
deposit *(in a bank)* **el deposito, el ingreso**

deposit *(returnable)* **el depósito retornable**
down payment/deposit **el desembolso inicial, la entrada**
eurocheque **el eurocheque**
exchange rate **el tipo de cambio**
hire purchase/installment plan **la venta a plazos**
I'm in credit by **tengo un crédito de, tengo un saldo positivo de**
in deficit **en déficit**
in the red **descubierto, en números rojos**
I lend **presto**
loan **el préstamo**
mortgage **la hipoteca, el crédito hipotecario**
I mortgage **hipoteco, obtengo un crédito hipotecario**
I open *(account)* **abro**
overdraft **el descubierto, el sobregiro**
repayment **el reembolso**
I save **ahorro**
savings **los ahorros**

– I'd like to open an account here.
– Certainly, sir. What sort of account do you need?
– Just a normal current account.

– Could you fill in this form with all your details?

– Certainly. What overdraft facilities are available for students.

– I need to check that for you.

– **Quisiera abrir una cuenta aquí.**
– **Por cierto ,señor. ¿Qué tipo de cuenta necesita usted?**
– **Una cuenta corriente, nada más.**

– **Haga el favor de rellenar este formulario con todos sus detalles personales.**

– **De acuerdo. ¿Qué posibilidades de crédito al abierto tienen ustedes a disposición de estudiantes [con estudios]?**

– **Tendré que verificarlo.**

travellers' cheque/traveler's check
los cheques de viaje
I withdraw **retiro**

Growth

amalgamation **la fusión**
appreciation **el incremento de valor**
assets **el activo, los bienes, el capital**
assurance **la garantía**
auction **la subasta**
boom **el boom, el auge**
competition **la competencia, la concurrencia**
economic miracle **el milagro económico**
efficiency **la eficacia**
material growth **el incremento de bienes**
merger **la fusión, el fusionamiento**
profit **el beneficio**
profitable **rentable, lucrativo**
progress **el progreso**
prosperity **la prosperidad**
prosperous **próspero, floreciente**

recovery **la recuperación**
takeover **la adquisición, la toma de control**
takeover bid **la oferta pública de adquisición de acciones**

Decline

bankrupt **la bancarrota**
credit squeeze **la restricción**
debt **la deuda**
it is declining **está en baja**
deficit **el déficit**
depreciation **la depreciación**
I dump **hago dúmping**
inflation **la inflacción**
inflation rate **el índice de inflación**
loss **la pérdida**
no-growth economy **la economía sin crecimiento**
slow-down **la ralentización de la economía**
slump **la recesión**
spending cuts **los recortes presupuestarios**
stagnant **estancado**
stagnation **el estancamiento de la economía**

– Did you hear about Borges & Sons?
– No - what about them?
– Unfortunately, they went bankrupt. They borrowed too heavily in order to introduce a new line which just didn't sell.

– And what was it?
– A range of battery powered toys which clearly couldn't compete with the videogames market.

– **¿Has oído las noticias acerca de Borges e Hijos?**
– **No. ¿Qué les pasa?**
– **Desafortunandamente, han quebrado. Tomaron demasiado dinero prestado para poder introducir un nuevo producto, que luego no se vendió.**
– **¿Y qué fue?**
– **Fue una gama de juguetes a pila que, está claro, no pudo hacer competencia contra el mercado de los videojuegos.**

Communicating with others

15a Social discourse

Meeting

I accept **acepto**
appointment **la cita**
at home **en casa**
ball **el baile**
banquet **el banquete**
I bump into *(someone)* **topo con**
I'm busy **estoy ocupado**
I celebrate **celebro**
celebration **la celebración**
club **el club**
I come and see **vengo a ver**
dance **el baile**
I dance **bailo**
date *(appointment)* **la cita, el compromiso**
diary/datebook **la agenda**
I drop in on *(someone)* **paso a ver**
I expect **espero**
I'm expecting ... for dinner **espero a ... para cenar**
I'm free **estoy libre**
I fetch someone **busco a alguien**
I greet **saludo**
guest **el invitado, el convidado, el huésped**
handshake **el apretón de manos**
I have fun **me divierto**
invitation **la invitación**
I invite **invito**
I join **me uno a, me reúno (con), me junto con**
 I join *(a society)* **me hago socio de, ingreso en**
I keep *(a date)* **cumplo**
meeting **la reunión**
I meet **encuentro, me reúno con**
member **el miembro**
party **el partido**
 I throw a party **doy una fiesta**

reception **la recepción**
I see **veo**
I shake hands with **estrecho manos con**
social life **la vida social**
I socialize **socializo**
I take part **tomo parte**
I talk **hablo**
visit **la visita**
I visit **visito**

Greetings & congratulations

bow/curtsey (to someone) **la reverencia**
Cheers! **¡Salud!**
Come in! **¡Pase/Entre (usted)!**
I congratulate **felicito**
Congratulations! **¡Felicitaciones!, ¡Enhorabuena!, ¡Felicidades!**
Good afternoon/evening **Buenas tardes/noches**
Good morning **Buenos días**
Good night **Buenas noches**
I greet **recibo, saludo**
Hallo/hello **Hola**
Happy Christmas **Feliz Navidad**
Happy Easter **Feliz Pascua**
Happy New Year **Feliz Año Nuevo**
Here's to ... **¡Vaya por ....!, ¡Bebemos a la salud de ...¡**
toast **el brindis**
I toast **brindo por**
Well done! **¡Bravo!, ¡Muy bien!**

Introduction

Bill, meet Jan. **Bill, te presento a Jane**
Doctor ... **Doctor ...**
How do you do? **¿Cómo está usted?**

I introduce   **le presento a**
I introduce myself   **me presento**
introduction   **la presentación**
I'd like you to meet …   **Quiero presentarle a …**
Madam   **Señora**
May I introduce …?   **Quiero presentarle a …**
Miss   **Señorita**
Mr.   **Señor**
Mrs.   **Señora**
Pleased to meet you   **¡Mucho gusto!, Encantado**
Professor …   **Profesor …**
sir   **señor**
This is …   **Este es …**
I welcome   **doy la bienvenida, acojo, recibo**

Pleasantries

I address (someone)   **me dirijo a**
I address as "tú"   **tuteo, trato de tú**
I address as "usted"   **trato de usted**
Best regards from …   **un saludo de**
Bless you!/Gesundheit!   **¡Jesús!**
I'm fine, thank you   **Estoy (muy) bien, gracias**
health   **la salud**
I hope you get well soon   **(Espero) que te mejores pronto**
How are you (keeping)?   **¿Cómo está usted?**
How are you feeling?   **¿Cómo te sientes?**
Much better, thank you   **Mucho mejor, gracias**
the same to you (polite)   **(Y) a usted, igualmente**
so-so   **regular, ni bien ni mal**
Your (very good) health!   **¡Salud!**

Thanking

Many thanks   **Muchas gracias**
Nice/good of you to …   **Es usted muy amable …**
Not at all!/It's a pleasure   **¡De**

nada!, ¡No hay de qué!**
I thank   **agradezco**
Thanks!   **¡Gracias!**
Thank you so much   **Muchísimas gracias**
No, thank you!   **¡No, gracias!**
I'm (very) grateful to you for …   **Le estoy muy agredecido por …**

Apologizing

I apologise   **me disculpo, pido perdón**
I do apologize   **le ruego me disculpe**
I beg your pardon   **le ruego me perdone**
I excuse   **perdono**
Excuse me   **Discúlpeme**
Excuse me, please   **¡Perdón!, ¡Por favor!, ¡Con (su) permiso!**
Forget it!   **¡Olvídelo!, ¡No se preocupe!, ¡No importa!**
I forgive   **perdono, disculpo**
it doesn't matter (at all/a bit)   **no importa (nada), es igual**
Oh dear!   **¡Ay!, ¡Dios mío!**
I refuse   **rehuso, rechazo**
I'm (so very) sorry that …   **Siento (muchísimo) que …**
What a shame/pity (that …)!   **¡Qué lástima (que …)!**

Farewells

All the best!   **¡Que tenga suerte!**
(Good-)bye!   **¡Adiós!**
Cheerio!   **¡Hasta luego!**
Good luck!   **¡Que tenga suerte!**
I say goodbye   **me despido**
Have a good time!   **¡Que usted se divierta!, ¡Que lo pase bien!**
Have a safe journey home!   **¡Buen viaje!**
See you later!   **¡Hasta luego!**
I will see you later/ tomorrow   **Nos veremos más tarde/mañana**
Sweet dreams!   **¡Duerma usted bien!**

15b Comments & exclamations

Approval & disapproval

I quite agree! **¡estoy totalmente de acuerdo!**
agreement **el acuerdo**
approval **la aprobación**
I approve **apruebo**
Is this all right? **¿Vale?, ¿Está bien?**
Fine! **¡Estupendo!, ¡Magnífico!**
I'm glad/pleased (that …) **Me alegro (de que …)**
Good! **¡Bueno!, ¡Muy bien!**
How nice **¡Qué bien!**
You should(n't) have … **(No) debería haber …**
Quiet! **¡Silencio!, ¡A callar!, ¡Cállate!, ¡Cállese!**
sh! **¡chitón!, ¡chist!**
tut-tut *(clicks)* **¡Vamos!, ¡Eso no!, ¡Qué horror!, ¡Pche!**
That's enough. **Basta (ya).**
That's just what I need. **Es precisamente lo que necesito.**

Permission & obligation

That's (quite) all right **(Eso) está (muy) bien**
allowed **permitido**
I allow **permito, dejo**
I am allowed to … **se me permite …**
It is not allowed/permitted **No se permite**
Can I ..? **¿Puedo …, ¿Se puede …?**
I can (not) **(no) puedo**
You cannot (can't) **No puede(s)**
I have to **tengo que, debo**
May I …? **¿Puedo …?**
I may (not) **(no) puedo**
I must (not) **(no) debo**
No **No**
Not now/here/tonight **Ahora/aquí/esta noche no**

I ought to … **debería …**
you ought to … **deberías …**
permission **el permiso**
permitted **permitido**
Please do! **Hágalo, por favor**
I'm (not) supposed to … **(no) debo …**
Have you got time to …? **¿Tiene usted tiempo de …?**
I should **debería**
You should(n't) … **(No) deberías …**

Surprise

Can that be …? **¿Es posible (eso)?**
That cannot (can't) be **No puede ser**
Fancy (that)! **¡Vaya!, ¡Fíjate!**
Good God! **¡Dios mío!**
Goodness! **¡Dios mío!**
Just as I expected **Ya me lo figuraba.**
Is it possible that …? **¿Es posible que …?**
Oh really! **¡Eh!, ¡Ca!, ¡Qué cosas pasan!**
surprise **la sorpresa**
I surprise **sorprendo**
surprising **sorprendente**
Does that surprise you? **¿Le sorprende eso?**
So what? **¿(Pues) y qué?**
Well? **¿Y entonces?**
Wow! **¡Caramba!, ¡Caray!**

Hesitating

er … **pues, es decir, esto …**
hesitation **la indecisión**
I hesitate **vacilo**
How shall I put it? **¿Cómo lo diría yo?**
Just a minute/moment! **Un momento, Un momentito**

Now let me think   **Déjame pensar,**
   Veamos, Vamos a ver
or rather ...   **o bien ...**
that is to say ...   **es decir ...**
That's not what I meant to say   **No**
   es lo que quería decir
thingummyjig   **la cosa, el chisme**
What's his/her name?   **¿Cómo se**
   llama (él/ella)?

Listening & agreeing/disagreeing

I agree/don't agree (that)...   **(no)**
   estoy de acuerdo que
Don't you agree (that) ?   **¿No crees**
   que ..?
I believe so/not   **Creo que sí/no**
Certainly!   **¡Desde luego!, ¡Por**
   supuesto!, ¡Por cierto!
Certainly not!   **¡De ninguna**
   manera!, ¡Ni hablar!
correct   **correcto, exacto, justo**
I don't think so   **Creo que no**
Exactly!   **¡Exactamente!**
I find (that)   **encuentro (que)**
Indeed!   **¡Por cierto!, ¡En efecto!,**
   ¡Claro que sí!, ¡Ya lo creo!
Just so!   **¡Exactamente!, ¡Eso es!,**
   ¡Perfectamente!, ¡Precisamente!
never   **nunca, jamás**
No!   **¡No!**
of course!   **¡claro!, ¡por supuesto!,**
   ¡naturalmente!
of course not!   **¡claro que no!**
Oh!   **¿De veras?**
Really?   **¿Verdad?, ¿De veras?**
right   **¡eso es!, ¡conforme!,**
   ¡justo!, ¡bueno!
rubbish!   **qué va! ¡tonterías!, ¡ni**
   pensar!
That's not so   **No es así**
that's (not) right/true.   **(no) es**
   correcto, (no) es verdad
that's right/correct   **es eso, eso es,**
   es correcto
I think so   **Creo que sí**
true   **verdad, verdadero**

uh-huh!   **¡a-ha!**
you're wrong   **está usted**
   equivocado
that's wrong!   **es equivocado, es**
   falso, no es correcto
yes!   **¡Sí!**

Clarification & meaning

a kind/sort of ...   **una especie de**
   ..., algo así como ...
Can you speak more slowly, please?
   Hable (usted) más despacio,
   por favor
Could you repeat that, please?
   Repite, por favor
Could you spell that, please?
   ¿Quiere usted deletrear eso,
   por favor?
Do you mean ...?   **¿Quiere usted**
   decir?
Did you say ... ?   **¿Dijo usted**
   que ...?
I explain   **explico**
How do you spell that, please?
   ¿Cómo se escribe eso, por
   favor?
I mean   **quiero decir**
I say   **digo**
Is that clear?   **¿Comprendido?,**
   ¿Entendido?, ¿Está claro?
it is spelt/you spell it ...   **se**
   escribe ...
That's just what I had in mind   **Es**
   exactamente lo que
   pensaba/buscaba
That's not what I had in mind   **No**
   es lo que yo había pensado
What did you say?   **¿Qué dijo**
   usted?
What do you mean by ... ?   **¿Qué**
   quiere(s) decir con ...?
What I said was ...   **Lo que dije**
   fue que ...
What is it in Spanish?   **¿Cómo es**
   en español?
you know   **usted sabe**

15c Post/Mail & telephone

Post/mail

abroad **el extranjero**
addressee **el destinatario, el consignatario**
airmail **el correo aéreo**
airmail letter **la carta por correo aéreo, el aerograma**
airmail paper **el papel para avión**
answer **la contestación, la respuesta**
collection **la recogida**
I correspond with **me escribo con**
correspondent **el corresponsal**
counter **el mostrador**
customs declaration **la declaración aduanera**
envelope **el sobre, la envoltura**
express delivery **la entrega urgente**
I finish (letter) **termino (la carta)**
first-class **el correo de primera clase**
freepost **Correo libre de franqueo**
I get/receive **recibo**
I hand in **entrego**
letter **la carta**
letter-box/mail box **el buzón**
letter/mail rate **la tarifa de cartas**
news **las noticias, las nuevas**
I note down **tomo apuntes**

note-paper **el papel para cartas, el papel para escribir**
package **el paquete, el bulto**
parcel **el paquete**
parcel-rate **la tarifa de paquetes**
pen-friend/pen pal **el amigo por correspondencia**
post/mail **Correo**
I post **echo a correos, llevo a correos, echo al post buzón**
postoffice **correos, la oficina de correos**
postage **los gastos de correo**
postal order **el giro postal**
postcard **la (tarjeta) postal**
postcode/zip code **el código postal**
poste-restante **la lista de correos**
postman/mailman **el cartero**
recorded/registered mail **el correo certificado**
reply **la contestación, la respuesta**
sealed **sellado**
I send **mando, envío**
I send (greetings) **mando (un saludo/recuerdos)**
sender **el remitente**
stamp **el sello**
I write **escribo**

When does the post/mail arrive?
I haven't heard from her for ages.

Dear Sir,
I am writing on behalf of my father, concerning. ...
I look forward to hearing from you ,

Yours sincerely, ...

¿A qué hora llega el cartero?
Hace mucho tiempo que no tengo noticias suyas.

Muy señor mío:
Le escribo de parte de mi padre, acerca de ...
Quedo a la espera de sus noticias,

Le saluda atentamente, ...

Telephone &
telecommunications

booth **la cabina**
button **el botón**
call-box/phone box **la cabina**
  telefónica
conversation **la conversación**
dial **el disco**
electronic mail **el correo**
  electrónico
engaged/busy *(phone)* **(está**
  comunicando/ ocupado
ex-directory/unlisted **no figura en**
  la guía
extension **la extensión, el**
  supletorio, el interno
extension number **el número de la**
  extensión
fax **el (tele)fax**
fax modem **el módem de fax**
local call **la llamada/conferencia**
  local
long-distance call **la conferencia**
  interurbana
nought/zero **cero**
operator **el/la telefonista**
out of order **no funciona**
receiver **el auricular**
reverse charge call **la llamada por**
  cobro revertido
slot **la ranura**
subscriber **el abonado**

telecommunications links **los**
  enlaces de telecomunicación
telecommunications **las**
  telecomunicaciones
telegram(me) **el telegrama**
telegraph **el telégrafo**
telephone **el teléfono**
telephone directory **la guía**
  telefónica
telephone kiosk **la cabina**
  telefónica
telephone/phone **el teléfono**
I transmit **transmito**
word **la palabra**
wrong number **el número**
  equivocado

Telephoning

I call **llamo**
I connect with **comunico con**
I dial **marco**
I fax **mando por fax, faxeo**
I hang up **cuelgo**
I hold **estoy en espera**
I pick up **descuelgo**
I press **pulso, aprieto**
I put … through (to) **me pongo**
  con …, (me) comunico con …
I speak to **hablo con**
I telephone/phone **llamo por/al**
  teléfono, telefoneo

Do you have change for the telephone?	¿Tiene usted moneda para el teléfono?
Can I dial/call direct?	¿Puedo marcar el número en directo?
Hallo/Hello! *(calling)*	¡Oíga(me), por favor!
Hallo/Hello! *(answering)*	¡Díga(me)!
Are you still there?	¿Aún está allí?
Can you hear me?	¿Me oye usted?
Could you fax it to me?	¿Me lo puede mandar por fax, por favor?

15d Computers

Computer applications

adventure game   **el videojuego de aventuras**
application   **la aplicación**
artificial intelligence   **la inteligencia artificial**
bar code   **el código de barras**
bar code reader   **el aparato lector de códigos de barras, la máquina lectora de códigos de barras**
calculator   **la calculadora, la minicalculadora**
computer control   **el control por ordenador**
computer science/studies   **la informática, las ciencias de la computación**
computerized   **computerizado, informatizado**
desk-top publishing/DTP   **la autoedición**
grammar checker   **el corrector de gramática, el consultor de gramática**
information   **la información**
information technology   **la informática**
office automation   **la ofimática, la buromática**
optical reader   **el lector óptico (de textos)**
simulation   **la simulación**
simulator   **el simulador**
spell-check   **el corrector ortográfico, el consultor de ortografía**
synthesizer   **el sintetizador**
text   **el texto**
thesaurus   **el diccionario de sinónimos, la antología**
word processor   **el procesador de palabras, el procesador de textos**
word-processing   **el proceso de textos, el tratamiento de textos**

Word processing & operating

I abort   **interrumpo (el programa), detengo prematuramente**
I access   **entro**
I append   **anexiono (al final)**
I back-up   **hago una copia de apoyo**
I block (text)   **agrupo**
I boot up   **arranco, cebo, inicializo**
I browse   **hojeo**
I cancel   **anulo**

Is it possible to replace the central processing unit? | ¿Es posible reemplazar la unidad procesadora central?
These computers are on a local area network. | Estos ordenadores están conectados a una red de área local.
The Macintosh and IBM systems are not yet compatible. | Los sistemas Macintosh y IBM aún no son compatibles.
How do you turn down the brightness? | ¿Cómo se baja el brillo?
Can you repair this keyboard? | ¿Puede usted reparar este teclado?

I click on **pulso el ratón**	I move **muevo**
I communicate **comunico**	I open (a file) **abro (un fichero),**
I copy **copio**	**entro a un fichero**
I count **cuento**	I print **imprimo, grabo**
I create **creo, abro (un archivo)**	I print out **imprimo**
I cut and paste **corto e inserto**	I (word) process **trato/manejo el**
I debug **depuro, quito el duende**	**texto**
de ...	I program(me) **programo**
I delete **cancelo, borro**	I read **leo, estudio**
I download **descargo**	I receive **recibo**
I embolden **pongo los caracteres**	I record **registro**
en negrita	I remove **quito**
I emulate **emulo**	I replace **reemplazo, sustituyo**
I enter **introduzco, entro a**	I retrieve **recupero, llamo**
I erase **borro**	I run **ejecuto**
I exit **salgo (del sistema)**	I save **salvo, grabo guardo**
I export **exporto**	I search **busco**
I file **ficho**	I send a copy to **envío una copia**
I format **formateo**	**a**
I handle (text) **trato (el texto)**	I send **envío, mando, emito**
I import **importo**	I shift **quito**
I install **instalo**	I simulate **simulo**
I keyboard **tecleo**	I sort **ordeno**
I list **listo**	I store **almaceno**
I log **apunto, anoto, registro**	I switch off **quito, apago,**
I log off/out **salgo del sistema,**	**desconecto**
finalizo la sesión, termino de	I switch on **enciendo, pongo,**
operar	**enciendo, conecto**
I log on/in **entro al sistema,**	I tabulate **tabulo**
accedo, inicio la sesión	I underline **subrayo**
I merge **fusiono**	I update **actualizo**

Don't show me your password!	**¡No me muestre su contraseña de acceso!**
I don't like the software package with this PC.	**No me gusta el paquete de programas que se ofrece con este ordenador personal**
Is this spreadsheet easy to use?	**¿Esta hoja electrónica, es fácil de utilizar?**
You can always consult the pull-down menu.	**Siempre se puede consultar el menú desplegable.**
It has wiped my file!	**¡Ha borrado mi fichero!**
This disk is corrupted.	**Este disco está degradado.**

Leisure & sport

16a Leisure

activity   la actividad
amateur   el amateur, el aficionado
book   el libro
boring   aburrido
camera   la cámara
I can   puedo
card   la tarjeta
card game   el juego de cartas
card table   la mesa de juego
casino   el casino
chess   el ajedrez
cinema/movie house   el cine
closed   cerrado
club   el club
I collect   colecciono
coin   la moneda
collection   la colección
collectors-fair   la feria de
   colecciones
connoisseur   el entendido, el
   conocedor
crossword puzzles   el crucigrama
I decide   decido
discotheque   la discoteca

DIY/do it yourself   hágalo usted
   mismo
energetic   enérgico
energy   la energía
enthusiasm   el entusiasmo
entrance   la entrada
entry fee   la tarifa de entrada
excitement   la excitación
exciting   excitante, divertido
excursion   la excursión
exit   la salida
fair   la feria
fascinating   fascinante,
   encantador
finished   terminado, finalizado
free time   el tiempo libre
fun   la diversión
I gamble   apuesto
I go out   salgo
guide   el guía
guided tour   el viaje con guía
hobby/pastime   el hobby, la
   afición, el pasatiempo
holiday   las vacaciones

– What is your favourite/favorite
pastime?
– Well, I used to go for a drive in
the country every Sunday, but I
have no time for hobbies
nowadays. Sometimes I go fishing.

I can meet you at the swimming
pool or, if you prefer, at the gym.

– ¿Cuál es tu pasatiempo
favorito?
– Bueno, solía ir a conducir por el
campo todos los domingos pero
ahora no tengo tiempo para
pasatiempos. Algunas veces voy
a pescar.

Puedo quedarme contigo
[Podemos vernos] en la piscina,
o si prefieres, en el gimnasio.

interest   **el interés, la afición**
interesting   **interesante**
I join   **me uno**
leisure   **el ocio**
I like (dis-)   **(no) me gusta**
I listen to   **escucho, oigo**
I look   **miro, veo**
market   **el mercado**
 antiques market   **el mercado de antigüedades**
 flea market   **el mercadillo, el mercado de la pulga**
I meet   **veo a, quedo con, me reúno con**
meeting place   **el punto de encuentro**
member   **el miembro**
membership   **la calidad de socio**
nightclub   **el club nocturno**
open   **abierto**
organization   **la organización**
I organize   **organizo**
photograph   **la fotografía**
picnic   **el picnic, la comida en el campo**
place   **el lugar**
I play   **juego**
pleasure   **la satisfacción, el placer**
politics   **la política**
I prefer   **prefiero**
private   **privado**

public   **público**
queue/line   **la cola**
I queue/get in line   **hago cola**
I read   **leo**
season   **la estación**
season ticket   **el billete de abono, [el tiquete de temporada]**
secluded   **aislado**
slide   **la diapositiva**
spectator   **el espectador**
I start (doing)   **comienzo, empiezo**
I stop (doing)   **termino**
I stroll   **paseo**
subscription   **la suscripción**
television   **la televisión, el televisor**
ticket   **el billete, la entrada, [el boleto, el tiquete]**
time   **el tiempo**
theatre/theater   **el teatro**
tour   **el viaje turístico, la excursión**
vacation   **las vacaciones**
I visit   **visito**
visit   **la visita**
I walk   **ando, camino**
I watch   **observo, miro**
youth club   **el club juvenil**
zoo   **el zoo, el (jardín/parque) zoológico**

– What do you like doing on a rainy day?
– Perhaps playing cards but not with my brother: he cheats!

– Shall we take the children to the zoo? – Good idea. If we take Eve's children and their school friends as well we can have a group reduction.

– **¿Qué te gusta hacer en un día lluvioso?**
– **Quizás, jugar a las cartas, pero no con mi hermano: ¡hace trampas!**

– **¿Llevamos a los niños al zoológico? – Buena idea. Si llevamos a los niños de Eva y a sus amigos del colegio también, nos harán un descuento de grupo.**

16b Sporting activity

against **contra**
I aim **apunto**
archer **el arquero**
athlete **el atleta**
athletic **atlético**
ball **la pelota, el balón**
bathtowel **la toalla de baño**
bet **la apuesta, la postura**
boat **la barca, el bote**
I bowl **juego al boliche, juego a las bolas**
boxer **el boxeador**
captain **el capitán**
I catch **cojo, recojo**
champion **el campeón**
championship **el campeonato**
changing/locker room **el vestuario**
I climb **escalo**
climber **el escalador**
coach **el entrenador**
cup (trophy) **la copa**
cycle **el ciclismo**
I cycle **hago ciclismo**
defeat **la derrota**
I dive **buceo**
I do (sport) **practico**
draw (tie) **el empate**
I draw (tie) **logro el empate**
effort **el esfuerzo**
endurance **la resistencia**
equipment **el equipo**
I exercize **hago ejercicio**

fall **la caída**
I fall **me caigo**
field **el campo**
finals **la final, las finales**
fit **en forma**
fitness **estar en forma**
I get fit **me pongo en forma**
game **el juego**
goal **el gol**
ground/stadium **el terreno, el estadio**
gym(nasium) **el gimnasio**
hit **el golpe**
I hit **golpeo**
ice-rink **la pista de patinaje**
I ice skate **patino sobre hielo**
injury **la herida, la lesión**
instructor **el instructor**
I jog **troto**
jogger **el atleta**
jump **el salto**
I jump **salto**
lawn **el césped**
league **la liga**
I lift weights **levanto pesas**
locker room **el vestuario**
I lose **pierdo**
marathon **el maratón**
match **el partido**
medal **la medalla**
gold/silver/bronze **de bronce/ de oro/de plata**

Without sponsorship, I won't be able to train using the best facilities. I cannot then compete at the highest level.

Sin patrocinio no podré entrenar con las mejores instalaciones. Por lo mismo, no podré competir al más alto nivel.

– Did you watch the match?
– No, I had to leave before the end. Who won?
– We lost 3-1.

– ¿Has visto el partido?
– No, me tuve que ir antes del final. ¿Quién ganó?
– Perdimos 3 a 1.

muscle   **el músculo**
Olympics Games (Winter)   **los Juegos Olímpicos (de invierno)**
opponent   **el adversario**
pedal   **el pedal**
pentathlon   **el pentatlón**
physical   **físico**
I pitch   **lanzo**
pitcher   **el lanzador**
player   **el jugador**
I play   **juego**
point   **el punto**
professional (adj)   **profesional**
race   **la carrera**
I race   **participo en una carrera**
referee   **el árbitro**
rest   **el descanso**
result   **el resultado**
I ride   **monto a caballo**
riding-school   **la escuela ecuestre**
I row   **remo**
run   **la carrera**
I run   **corro**
runner   **el corredor**
sail   **la vela**
I sail   **navego**
sailing school   **la escuela de náutica/navegación**
score   **el tanteo, el resultado, el puntaje**
I score (a goal)   **marco**
I shoot (ball, puck)   **chuto, tiro**
I shoot (at a target)   **tiro**
I shoot pool   **juego al billar**

show   **el espectáculo**
I ski   **esquío**
ski-lift   **el remonte, la telesilla**
skier   **el esquiador**
sponsor   **el patrocinador**
sponsorship   **el patrocinio**
sport   **el deporte**
sports field/pitch   **el campo de deportes**
sprint   **el sprint**
stadium   **el estadio**
stamina   **el vigor, la resistencia**
strength   **la fuerza**
supporter   **el seguidor, el hincha**
I swim   **nado**
team   **el equipo**
team sports   **el deporte de equipos**
touch-down   **el tocado en tierra**
I throw   **lanzo**
tournament   **el torneo**
track   **la pista**
I train   **me entreno**
trainer   **el entrenador**
training   **el entrenamiento**
triumph   **el triunfo**
trophy   **el trofeo**
I am unfit   **no estoy en forma**
victory   **la victoria**
I win   **gano**
work-out   **el entrenamiento, la preparación**
world championship   **el campeonato del mundo**
world cup   **la copa del mundo**

I still cannot understand how such a capable team could lose so disastrously after a brilliant season.
All sports commentators agree that they were particularly unlucky when the referee insisted on the penalty kick.

**Todavía no puedo entender cómo un equipo tan bueno pudo perder tan desastrosamente tras una magnífica temporada.
Todos los comentaristas deportivos están de acuerdo en que tuvieron muy mala suerte cuando el árbitro insistió en el penalty.**

16c Sports & equipment

Sports

aerobics **el aeróbic**
archery **el tiro con arco**
athletics **el atletismo**
badminton **el bádminton**
baseball **el béisbol**
basketball **el baloncesto**
bowling **la bolera, los bolos**
 ten-pin bowling/tenpins **el boliche**
boxing **el boxeo**
climbing **el montañismo, el alpinismo**
 free climbing **la escalada libre**
 rock climbing **la escalada en rocas**
crew **el equipo**
cricket **el cricket, el críquet**
cycling **el ciclismo**
decathlon **el decathlon**
diving **el buceo**
 deep water diving **el buceo en aguas profundas**
football **el fútbol**
handball **el balonmano**
hockey **el hockey**
horse-racing **las carreras de caballos**
horse-riding **montar a caballo**
ice-hockey **el hockey sobre patines**
ice-skating **el patinaje sobre hielo**
jogging **el footing**

motor racing **el automovilismo, las carreras de coches**
paragliding **el planeador**
polo **el polo**
pool **el billar**
racing **las carreras**
riding **montar a caballo**
roller-skating **el patinaje sobre ruedas**
rugby **el rugbi, el rugby**
sailing **la navegación**
skiing **el esquí**
 water skiing **el esquí acuático**
 cross-country skiing **el esquí nórdico**
 down-hill skiing **el esquí alpino**
snooker **el snooker**
soccer **el fútbol**
swimming **la natación**
table tennis **el tenis de mesa, el pinpón, el ping-pong**
volleyball **el voleibol**
water-polo **el polo acuático**
weight training **el entrenamiento con pesas**
windsurfing **el windsurf**

Leisure wear and sport clothes

anorak **el anorak**
bathing suit **el traje de baño**
boots **las botas**
cycling shorts **los pantalones de ciclista**
dancing shoes **los zapatos de**

The most popular sports in North America are baseball, (American) football, basketball and (ice) hockey. In South America, soccer is the major passion.

Los deportes más populares en Norteamérica son el béisbol, el fútbol americano, el baloncesto y el hockey sobre hielo. En Sudamérica la pasión es el fútbol.

baile
gardening gloves **los guantes de jardinería**
leotard **los leotardos**
parka **la parka**
salopette **el mono de esquiar**
swimsuit **el bañador [el vestido de baño] de mujer**
swimming trunks **el bañador [el vestido de baño] de hombre**
rugby shirt **la camiseta de rugbi**
track suit **el chandal**
trainers **las zapatillas de deporte**
walking boots **las botas para andar**
waterproof jacket **el chaleco impermeable**
Wellington boots **las botas de agua**
wet suit **el traje de buceo**

Leisure and sport equipment

arrow **la flecha**
ball **la pelota, el balón**
bat **el bate, la maza, la paleta**
binoculars **los anteojos, los prismáticos**
bow **el arco**
boxing gloves **los guantes de boxeo**
camera **la cámara**
crash helmet **el casco**
equipment **el equipo, el material**
exercise bike **la bicicleta de ejercicio, la bicicleta estática**
fishing rod **la caña de pescar**

headphone **el auricular**
hi-fi **hi-fi, (de) alta fidelidad**
knapsack **la mochila**
knitting needles **las agujas de hacer punto**
javelin **la javalina**
mountain bike **la bicicleta de montaña**
net **la red**
outrigger **el portarremos, el bote con portarremos exterior**
puck **el disco, el puck**
racket **la raqueta**
rifle **el rifle**
roller skates **los patines de ruedas**
rowing machine **el aparato de remo**
rowing boat **el bote de remo**
rucksack **la mochila**
sailing-boat **el barco de vela**
sewing kit **el costurero**
secateurs **las tijeras de podar, la podadora**
skate **el patín**
skis **los esquís**
ski boots **las botas de esquí**
ski sticks/poles **los bastones de esquí**
spinning wheel **la rueca**
sports bag **la bolsa de deporte**
stick *(hockey)* **el palo**
surf board **la tabla de surf**
weights **las pesas**
yacht **el yate**
zoom lens **el zoom**

In the final minutes, the goalminder made a spectacular save with his stick to flick the puck off the line and out of the goal.

En los últimos minutos, el portero impidió un gol de una manera espectacular con el palo quitando el puck de la línea y echándolo lejos de la portería.

The Arts

17a Appreciation and criticism

abstract **abstracto**
abstruse **abstruso**
action **la acción**
aesthete **el esteta**
aesthetics **la estética**
I appreciate **aprecio**
appreciation **la apreciación**
art **el arte**
artist **el artista**
artistic **artístico**
atmosphere **la atmósfera**
atmospheric **atmosférico**
author **el autor**
award **el premio**
I analyze **analizo**
avant-garde *(adj)* **en vanguardia**
believable **creíble**
character **el personaje**
characterization **la caracterización**
characteristic **característico**
climax **el clímax, el punto culminante**
it closes **cierra**
comic **cómico**
commentary **el comentario**
conflict **el conflicto**
contemporary **contemporáneo**
contrast **el contraste**
it creates **crea**
creativity **la creatividad**
credible **creíble, verosímil**
critic **el crítico**
criticism **el criticismo**
cultivated **cultivado**
culture **la cultura**
it deals with **trata de**
it describes **describe**
it develops **desarrolla**
development **el desarrollo**

device **la estratagema, el mecanismo**
dialogue **el diálogo**
disturbing **inquietante**
empathy **la empatía**
ending **el final, el fin**
it ends **finaliza, termina**
entertaining **divertido, entretenido**
entertainment **el divertimiento, el entretenimiento**
epic *(n)* **la épica**
event **el acontecimiento, el suceso**
eventful **memorable**
example **el ejemplo**
exciting **excitante**
I explain **explico**
explanation **la explicación**
it explores **explora**
it expresses **expresa**
fake **falso**
fantastic **fantástico**
fantasy **la fantasía**
figure **la figura**
funny **gracioso, divertido**
image **la imagen**
imaginary **imaginario**
imagination **la imaginación**
inspiration **la inspiración**
inspired by **inspirado por**
intense **intenso**
intensity **la intensidad**
invention **la invención**
inventive **inventivo, imaginativo**
ironic **irónico**
irony **la ironía**
issue **la cuestión, el problema**
life **la vida**
long-winded **prolijo, extenso**

lyrical **lírico**
modern **moderno**
mood **el humor, la atmósfera**
moral **moral**
morality **la moralidad**
moving **conmovedor**
mystery **el misterio**
mysterious **misterioso**
mystical **místico**
nature **la naturaleza**
obscure **oscuro, obstruso**
obscene **obsceno**
obscenity **la obscenidad**
opinion **la opinión**
optimism **el optimismo**
optimistic **optimista**
parody **la parodia**
passion **la pasión**
passionate **apasionado**
pessimistic **pesimístico**
pessimism **el pesimismo**
it portrays **describe, representa**
portrayal **el retrato, la representación**
precious **valioso, precioso**
protagonist **el protagonista**
I read **leo**
reader **el lector**

realistic **realista**
reference **la referencia**
I reflect **reflejo**
reflection **la reflexión, el pensamiento**
relationship **la relación, la conexión**
review **la revisión, el análisis**
sad **triste**
satire **la sátira**
it satirizes **satiriza**
satirical **satírico**
style **el estilo**
in the style of **al estilo de**
stylish **con estilo, elegante**
subject **el tema, el contenido**
technique **la técnica**
tension **la tensión**
theme **el tema**
tone **el tono**
tragedy **la tragedia**
tragic **trágico**
true **verdadero, auténtico**
vivid **vívido**
viewpoint **el punto de vista**
witty **ingenioso**
work of art **la obra de arte**

Artistic styles & periods

Art Nouveau **art nouveau**
Aztec **azteca**
Baroque **barroco**
Classical period **el período clásico**
Enlightenment **el Siglo de las luces**
existentialist **esistencialista**
expressionist **expresionista**
Futuristic **futurístico**
Georgian **georgiano**
Gothic **gótico**
Greek **griego**
medieval **medieval**
naturalistic **naturalístico**

Norman **normando**
Persian **persa**
poetic **poético**
post-modernist **pos-modernista**
realism **el realismo**
Renaissance **el Renacimiento**
Rococo **rococó**
Romanesque **románico**
romantic **romántico**
structuralist **estructuralista**
surrealist **surrealista**
symbolist **simbolico**
Twentieth century **el siglo veinte**
Victorian period **el período victoriano**

17b Art & architecture

antique	**antiguo**
antiquity	**la antigüedad**
architect	**el arquitecto**
art	**el arte**
artefact	**el artefacto**
artist	**el artista**
art student	**el estudiante de arte**
auction sale	**la subasta**
auctioneer	**el subastador**
balance	**el equilibrio**
baroque	**barroco**
beam	**la viga**
bronze	**el bronce**
brush	**el pincel**
I build	**construyo**
building	**la construcción, el edificio**
bust	**el busto**
caricature	**la caricatura**
I carve	**esculpo, tallo**
I cast	**fundo**
ceramics	**la cerámica**
charcoal	**el carbón, el carboncillo**
chisel	**el cincel**
chiselled	**cincelado**
classical	**clásico**
clay	**la arcilla**
collage	**el collage**
decorated	**decorado**
decoration	**la decoración**
decorative arts	**las artes decorativas**
I design	**diseño**

design	**el diseño**
dimension	**las medidas, la dimensión**
I draw	**dibujo**
drawing	**el dibujo**
easel	**el caballete**
elevation	**la elevación**
enamel	**el esmalte**
I engrave	**grabo**
engraving	**el grabado**
I etch	**grabo al aguafuerte**
etching	**el aguafuerte**
exhibition	**la exposición**
figure	**la figura**
figurine	**la figurilla**
filigree	**la filigrana**
fine arts	**las bellas artes**
flamboyant	**rimbombante, llamativo**
form	**la forma**
free-hand	**hecho a pulso**
fresco	**el fresco**
frieze	**el friso**
genre	**el género**
graphic arts	**las artes gráficas**
gravity	**la gravedad**
holograph	**elológrafo, el olograma**
interior	**interior, interno**
intricate	**intrincado**
ironwork	**el herraje**
landscape	**el paisaje**
landscape gardener	**el arquitecto**

We have a very good view of the cupola from this terrace. Look, in the foreground you can see the monastery, which dates back from 1679 and which is such a good example of religious architecture, and in the background the medieval towers are still visible.

La vista de la cúpula desde esta terraza es muy buena. Mira, al fondo puedes ver el monasterio que fue construido en 1679 y es un buen ejemplo de la arquitectura religiosa y detrás pueden verse todavía las torres medievales.

de jardines
landscape painter **el paisajista**
large-scale works **las obras a gran escala**
later works **las últimas obras**
light **la luz**
light *(adj)* **luminoso**
lithography **la litografía**
luminosity **luminosidad**
luminous **luminoso**
masterpiece **la obra maestra**
metal **el metal**
miniature **la miniatura**
model **el modelo**
monochrome **monocromo, de un solo color**
moorish **árabe**
mosaic **el mosaico**
museum **el museo**
oil painting **la pintura al óleo**
ornate **ornado, florido**
I paint **pinto, dibujo**
paint **la pintura**
painting **el cuadro, la pintura**
pastel **el pastel**
portrait **el retrato**
potter **el ceramista**
pottery **la cerámica**
it represents **representa**
representation **la representación**
reproduction **la reproducción**
restoration **la restauración**
I restore **restauro**
restored **restaurado**
restorer **el restaurador**

roughcast **el esbozo**
school **la escuela**
I sculpt **esculpo**
sculptor **el escultor**
sculpture **la escultura**
seascape **el paisaje marino, la marina**
shadow **la sombra**
shape **la forma**
I shape **doy forma, moldeo**
sketch **el boceto**
I sketch **hago un boceto**
sketching **el dibujo, el boceto**
stained-glass **la vidriera**
statuary **el estatuario**
statue **la estatua**
still-life **el bodegón, la naturaleza muerta**
I stipple **punteo**
studio **el estudio**
style **el estilo**
surrealism **el surrealismo**
tapestry **el tapiz**
tempera **la témpera, la pintura al temple**
town-planning **el urbanismo**
traditional **tradicional**
translucent **translúcido**
transparent **transparente**
visual arts **las artes visuales**
water-colour/color **la acuarela**
wood **la madera**
wood-carving **la talla de madera**
woodcut **la incisión**

I have just been to the exhibition at the Royal Academy, which has already attracted thousands of visitors. There is the most wonderful collection of drawings and sculptures of the Italian artist. Two of the paintings have been very skillfully restored.

Acabo de visitar una exposición en la Real Academia que ya ha atraído a miles de visitantes. Tiene la mejor colección de dibujos y esculturas del artista italiano. Dos de los dibujos han sido muy bien restaurados.

THE ARTS

17c Literature

autograph **el autógrafo**
book **el libro**
bookshop/store **la librería**
bookseller **el librero**
character **el personaje**
  main character **el personaje principal, el protagonista**
  secondary character **el personaje secundario**
comic **cómico**
dialogue/dialog **el diálogo**
fictional **ficticio**
hardback **la cubierta dura**
I imagine **imagino**
imagination **la imaginación**
inspiration **la inspiración**
inspired by **inspirado por**
it introduces **introduce**
introduction **la introducción**
I leaf through **hojeo un libro**
librarian **el bibliotecario**
library **la biblioteca**
  public library **la biblioteca pública**
  reference library **la biblioteca de consulta**

literal(ly) **literal(mente)**
map **el mapa**
myth **el mito**
mythology **la mitología**
it narrates **narra**
narrative **la narrativa**
narrator **el narrador**
note **la nota**
page **la página**
paperback **la cubierta rústica**
paragraph **el párrafo**
poem **el poema**
poetic **poético**
poetry **la poesía**
punctuation **la puntuación**
quote **la cita**
I quote **cito**
I read **leo**
I recount **cuento, refiero**
rhyme **la rima**
it is set in **está situado en**
table **la tabla**
text **el texto**
title **el título**
verse **el verso**

– What are you reading at the moment?
– A spine-chilling story with a tragic conclusion.
It is set in contemporary London.

¿Qué leyes ahora?

Una historia escalofriante con un final trágico.
Está situado [Tiene lugar] en el Londres actual.

It is a vivid account of life in the Thirties. The writer explores the theme of lost innocence.

Es un retrato vivo de la vida de los años treinta. El autor explora el tema de la inocencia perdida.

Types of books

adventure story   **la historia de aventuras**

atlas   **el átlas**

autobiography   **la autobiografía**

biography   **la biografía**

children's literature   **la literatura infantil**

comic novel   **la novela cómica**

cookery book   **el libro de cocina**

crime novel   **la novela policíaca de crimen**

diary   **el diario**

dictionary   **el diccionario**

bilingual   **el diccionario bilingüe**

monolingual   **el diccionario monolingüe**

encyclopedia   **la enciclopedia**

epic poem   **el poema épico**

essay   **el ensayo**

fable   **la fábula**

fairy tale   **el cuento de hadas**

feminist novel   **la novela feminista**

fiction   **la ficción, la narrativa**

Greek tragedy   **la tragedia griega**

horror story   **la historia/el cuento de terror**

letters   **las cartas**

manual   **el manual**

memoirs   **las memorias**

modern play   **el teatro moderno**

mystery play   **la obra de misterio**

non-fiction   **la literatura no novelesca**

novel   **la novela**

picaresque novel   **la novela picaresca**

poetry   **la poesía**

reference book   **el libro de consulta**

restoration comedy   **la comedia de la restauración**

satirical poem   **el poema satírico**

science fiction story   **la historia de ciencia ficción**

short story   **el cuento, la historia corta**

spy story   **la historia de espionaje**

teenage fiction   **la literatura juvenil**

travel book   **el libro de viajes**

war novel   **la novela de guerra**

A collection of modern foreign fiction.

Una colección de narrativa extranjera actual.

My novel deals with changes in 19th century Spanish rural society.

Mi novela trata de los cambios de la vida rural española en el siglo diecinueve.

It opens with a lyrical description of the valley. It ends with the last entry in the hero's diary.

Comienza con una descripción lírica del valle. Termina con lo último que el héroe escribió en su diario.

17d Music & dance

acoustics	**la acústica**
adjudicator	**el juez del concurso**
agent	**el agente**
album	**el álbum**
ampifier	**el amplificador**
audience	**el público, la audiencia**
audition	**la audición**
auditorium	**el auditorio**
ballet	**el balet**
band leader	**el director de la banda**
baton	**la batuta**
brass band	**la banda, la charanga**
cassette tape	**la cinta de cassete**
cassette-deck	**el cassete**
chamber music	**la música de cámara**
chart/hit parade	**la lista de éxitos**
choir	**el coro**
choral	**la coral**
chorale	**coral**
choreography	**la coreografía**
chorister	**el corista**
chorus	**el coro, el estribillo**
compact disc/disk	**el compact disc, el disco compacto**
competition	**el concurso**
compilation	**la recopilación**
I compose	**compongo**
composer	**el compositor**
composition	**la composición**
concert	**el concierto**
concert hall	**la sala de conciertos**

I conduct	**dirijo**
conductor	**el director de orquesta**
dance	**la danza**
I dance	**danzo**
dancer	**el danzarín**
dance music	**la música de danza**
discotheque	**la discoteca**
disc jockey	**el disc jockey**
drummer	**el batería**
ensemble	**el conjunto, la agrupación**
euphony	**la eufonía**
folk music	**la música folk, la música popular**
gig	**la actuación**
group	**el grupo**
harmony	**la armonía**
harmonic	**la armónica**
hit (song)	**la canción de éxito**
I hum	**canturreo**
instrument	**el instrumento**
instrumental music	**la música instrumental**
instrumentalist	**el instrumentalista**
I interpret	**interpreto**
interpretation	**la interpretación**
jazz	**el jazz**
juke-box	**la máquina de música**
key	**la clave**
lesson	**la lección**
I listen to	**escucho, oigo**
listening	**la audición**
microphone	**el micrófono**

– There is a concert at the Students' Union.
– What is the name of the band?
– I don't know. Their lyrics are quite good but the music is dreadful.

Rehearsals will be held in the cathedral on Friday evening

– **Hay un concierto en el Sindicato de Estudiantes.**
– **¿Cómo se llama el grupo?**
– **No lo sé. La letra es bastante buena pero la música es malísima.**

Los ensayos se harán el viernes por la tarde en la catedral.

music   la música
musically   musicalmente
musician   el músico
musicologist   el musicólogo
note   la nota
orchestra   la orquesta
orchestration   la orquestación
it is performed   es tocado, es
   representado
performance   la representación
performed by   representado por,
   ejecutado por
performer   el ejecutor
pianist   el pianista
piano   el piano
piece   la pieza musical
I play   toco
player   el músico
portable   portátil
I practise/practice   practico
promotional video   el vídeo
   promocional
I put on a record   pongo un disco
recital   el recital
record   el disco, la grabación
I record   grabo
recording   la grabación
recording studio   el estudio de
   grabación
refrain   el estribillo
I rehearse   ensayo
rehearsal   el ensayo
repertoire   el repertorio
rhythm   el ritmo

rhythmic   rítmico
rock   el rock
show   el espectáculo
I sing   canto
singer   el cantante
solo   el solo
soloist   el solista
song   la canción
song-writer   el autor de canciones
string   la cuerda
string orchestra   la orquesta de
   instrumentos de cuerda
symphony   la sinfonía
tape   la cinta
tour   la gira
   on tour   de gira
tune   el tono
   in tune   entonado, [afinado]
   out of tune   desentonado,
   [desafinado]
I tune   entono
tuner (of instruments)   afinador de
   instrumentos
tuning fork   el diapasón
violin maker   el fabricante de
   violines
vocal music   la música vocal
voice   la voz
I whistle   silbo
whistling   el silbido
wind band   la orquesta de
   instrumentos de viento
wind instruments   los
   instrumentos de viento

– Do you play an instrument?
– I play the viola.
– I never learnt to play an
instrument but I have just bought
an electric guitar.

The conductor was greeted by a
standing ovation.

– ¿Tocas algún instrumento?
– Toco la viola.
– Nunca he aprendido a tocar un
instrumento pero acabo de
comprar una guitarra eléctrica.

El público aplaudió en pie al
director.

17e Theatre & cinema/Theater & the movies

act   la actuación
I act   actúo
acting school   la escuela de teatro
actor   el actor
actress   la actriz
I applaud   aplaudo
applause   el aplauso
audience   el público
auditorium   el auditorio
I book   reservo
box   el palco
box-office   la taquilla
cabaret   el cabaret, el
   espectáculo de variedades
camera   la cámara
camera crew   los operadores de
   cámara
cameraman   el cámara, el
   camarógrafo
cartoons   los dibujos animados
choreographer   el coreógrafo
cinema/movies   el cine
cinema/movie buff   el cinéfilo
circle   la galería
circus   el circo
I clap   aplaudo
clapping   el aplauso
cloakroom   el guardarropa
comedian   el comediante, el actor
   cómico
comedienne   la comediante, la

   actriz cómica
curtain   el telón
I design   diseño
designer   el diseñador
I direct   dirijo
director   el director
drama   el drama, el teatro
dress rehearsal   el ensayo general
dubbed   doblado
dubbing   el doblaje
effect   el efecto
expectation   la expectación
farce   la farsa
farcical   farsesco, absurdo
film/movie   la película
film/movie maker   el cineasta
film/movie star   la estrella de cine
film/movie producer   el productor
   de cine
first night   el estreno
floor-show   el espectáculo de
   variedades/de cabaret
flop   el fracaso
gaffer   el iluminista
intermission   el intervalo, el
   descanso
interval   el descanso
lights   las luces, los focos
in the limelight   en candelero
lobby   el pasillo, el vestíbulo
location work   los exteriores, el

It does not transfer well on the screen.	No se transfiere bien en la pantalla.
Foreign films are usually dubbed, but some cinema clubs show them in the original language.	Las películas extranjeras generalmente se doblan, pero algunos clubs de cine las dan en el idioma original.
Stuntpersons have been used for the most dangerous scenes.	Se han usado dobles para les escenas más peligrosas.

rodaje fuera del estudio
I make a film/movie **hago una película**
masterpiece **la obra maestra**
matinée **la función de tarde**
melodrama **el melodrama**
mime **el mimo**
movie **la película**
music-hall **la sala de fiestas**
off-stage **entre bastidores**
opening night **el estreno**
ovation **la ovación**
pantomime **la pantomima**
performance **la actuación, la ejecución**
photography **la fotografía**
play **la obra de teatro**
I play **actúo**
playwright **el dramaturgo**
premiere **el estreno**
I produce **produzco**
producer **el productor**
production **la producción**
public **el público**
retrospective **la retrospectiva**
role **el papel**
row **la fila**
scene **la escena**
scenery **el escenario**
screen **la pantalla**
screen test **la prueba de proyección, la toma**
screening **la proyección**

script **el guión**
scriptwriter **el guionista**
seat **la butaca**
sequel **la continuación, el desenlace**
sequence **la secuencia**
it is shot **está filmado**
I show (a film/movie) **muestro**
sold-out **vendido**
sound-track **la banda sonora**
special effects **los efectos especiales**
stage (theatre/theater) **el escenario, la escena**
stage (cinema/movies) **el escenario, el decorado**
stage directions **la acotación**
stage effects **los efectos escenográficos, los efectos teatrales**
stage-fright **el miedo al público**
stalls **las butacas**
stunt person **el doble que realiza las escenas peligrosas**
trailer **el tráiler, el avance**
understudy (theatre/theater) **el suplente**
understudy (cinema/movies) **el doble**
usherette **la acomodadora**
walk-on part **el papel de figurante**
I zoom **capto, doy un golpe de zoom**

Sci-fi films were popular in the Sixties.

Las películas de ciencia-ficción eran populares en los años sesenta.

I want to see the latest production of her three-act play. All the critics will be there.

Quiero ver la última producción de su obra de teatro en tres actos. Toda la crítica acudirá.

He is playing one of the most demanding roles of his career.

Está jugando uno de los papeles más difíciles de su carrera.

18 The Media

18a General terms

admission	**la admisión**
I admit	**admito**
I analyze	**analizo**
analysis	**el análisis**
I appeal to	**apelo a, recurro a**
I argue	**discuto**
argument	**el argumento**
attitude	**la actitud**
biased	**parcial**
campaign	**la campaña**
censorship	**la censura**
cogent	**lógico, convincente, fuerte**
comment	**el comentario**
conspiracy	**la conspiración**
criticism	**la crítica**
critique	**la crítica**
cultural	**cultural**
culture	**la cultura**
cultured	**cultivado**
current events	**los sucesos de actualidad**
declaration	**la declaración**
it declares	**declara**

detailed	**detallado**
it discriminates	**discrimina**
disaster	**el desastre**
disinformation	**la desinformación**
educational	**educativo**
I entertain	**divierto, entretengo**
ethical	**ético**
event	**el suceso, el acontecimiento**
example	**el ejemplo**
expectations	**las expectativas**
I exploit	**exploto**
fallacious	**engañoso, falaz**
fallacy	**la falacia, el engaño**
freedom	**la libertad**
full/detailed	**detallado, extenso**
gullible	**crédulo, simplón**
hidden	**escondido, oculto**
homophobic	**homofóbico**
ignorance	**la ignorancia**
I ignore	**ignoro, desconozco**
influential	**influyente, prestigioso**
information	**la información**
informative	**informativo**

During the recent elections it was difficult to find an example of unbiased reporting.

Durante las recientes elecciones fue difícil encontrar un ejemplo de información objetiva en los medios de comunicación.

interview **la entrevista**
it intrudes **se entromete, obstruye**
intrusion **la intrusión, la intromisión**
intrusive **intruso**
issue *(problem)* **el problema, el asunto, la cuestión**
I keep up with *(news)* **estoy al día con**
libel **la difamación, la calumnia**
libellous **difamante, calumnioso**
likely **probable**
it is likely **es probable**
local interest news **las noticias de interés local**
(mass) media **los medios (masa) de comunicación**
material **el material**
meddling **entrometido**
news **las noticias**
news item **la noticia, el asunto**
partisan **partidario**
persuasive **persuasivo**
prejudice **el prejuicio**
political **político**
politics **la política**
press **la prensa**
privacy **la intimidad, la privacidad**
privacy law **la legislación para la protección de la intimidad**

problem **el problema**
review **el análisis de las noticias**
I review **analizo**
scoop **la exclusiva, la primicia informativa**
sensational **sensacional**
sensationalism **el sensacionalismo**
sexism **el sexismo**
sexist **sexista**
silence **el silencio**
silent **silencioso**
social **social**
society **la sociedad**
specious **especioso**
summary **el sumario**
   summary *(adj)* **sumario**
it takes place **tiene lugar**
trust **la confianza**
I trust **confío**
trustworthy **fiable**
truth **la verdad**
truthful **verdadero**
unbiased **objetivo**
untrustworthy **no fiable**
up to date **actualizado**
violent **violento, agresivo**
violence **la violencia**
weekly **semanal**

I am a freelance journalist specializing in investigative journalism.

Soy periodista independiente, especializado en periodismo investigativo.

In recent years many war correspondent have lost their lives while reporting from the front or have been taken as hostages.

En años recientes, muchos corresponsales de guerra han perdido la vida informando desde el frente, o han sido hecho [tomados como] rehenes.

➤ ADVERTISING 18d

18b The Press

agony aunt   **el columnista del consultorio sentimental**
article   **el artículo**
back page   **la última página**
barons   **los magnates de la prensa**
broadsheet   **el periódico sábana/de gran formato**
cartoon   **el tebeo, la caricatura**
chief editor   **el jefe de edición**
circulation   **la circulación**
colour/color supplement   **el suplemento en color**
column   **la columna**
comic   **el cómic, el tebeo**
correction   **la corrección**
correspondent   **el corresponsal**
foreign correspondent   **el corresponsal extranjero**
crossword puzzle   **el crucigrama**
daily newspaper   **el diario**
I edit   **edito, redacto**
edition   **la edición, la tirada**
editor   **el editor, el redactor, el director**
editorial   **editorial**
forgotten   **olvidado**
front page   **la primera página, la portada**
glossy magazine   **la revista de lujo**
gutter press   **la prensa basura, la**

prensa amarilla, **la prensa sensacionalista**
headline   **el titular**
heading   **el título, el encabezamiento**
illustration   **la ilustración**
it is published   **está publicado**
journalist   **el periodista**
layout   **la distribución, la diagramación**
leader   **el editorial, el artículo de fondo**
local paper   **el periódico local**
magazine   **la revista**
monthly   **la revista mensual**
national newspaper   **el periódico nacional**
newsagent   **la tienda de prensa**
newspaper   **el periódico**
news stand   **el kiosco de prensa, el quiosco de prensa**
page   **la página**
pamphlet   **el panfleto**
periodical   **la revista/la publicación periódica**
power   **el poder**
powerful   **poderoso**
press agency   **la agencia de prensa**
press conference   **la conferencia**

European current affairs are not always reported in the British press, though all quality papers have foreign correspondents in all the European capitals.

Las noticias de actualidad europea no siempre aparecen en la prensa británica, a pesar de que todos los periódicos de calidad tienen corresponsales en todas las capitales europeas.

The gutter press has a surprisingly high readership.

La prensa sensacionalista tiene una surprendente cantidad de lectores.

de prensa
I print **imprimo**
print **la impresión**
print room **la sala de impresión**
problem page **el consultorio**
I publish **publico**
publisher **el dueño de la casa
editorial**
publishing company **la casa
editora, la editorial**
quality press **la prensa de
calidad**
reader **el lector**
I report **informo**
report **el reportaje**
reporter **el reportero**

short news item **las noticias
breves, las breves**
small ad **los anuncios por
palabras**
special correspondent **el
corresponsal especial**
special issue **la edición especial**
sports page **la página de
deportes**
I subscribe to **me suscribo a**
subscription **la suscripción**
tabloid **la prensa sensacionalista**
type(face) **el tipo de letra, el
formato de la letra**
weekly **el semanario**

Newspaper sections

Announcements **anuncios**
Arts **arte**
Economy **economía**
Editorial **editorial**
Entertainment **ocio**
Finance **finanzas**
Food and Drink **gastronomía**
Games **pasatiempos**
Gossip column **la columna rosa**
Home news **noticias
nacionales**
Horoscope **horóscopo**

International news **noticias
internacionales**
Letters to the editor **cartas al
director**
Obituary **necrológicas,
obituario**
Problems page **consultorio**
Property **propiedad
inmobiliaria**
Sport **deportes**
Travel **viajes**
Women **mujer**

Media barons have dominated the press in many western countries.

Los magnates de la prensa dominan la prensa en muchos paises occidentales.

When is the colour/color supplement published?

¿Cuándo se publica el suplemento en color?

What a scoop! I guess the circulation of the paper has increased significantly in the last two weeks.

¡Qué primicia! Supongo que la circulación del periódico ha subido mucho en las dos últimas semanas.

18c Television & radio

aerial   **la antena**
anchorman   **el presentador**
anchorwoman   **la presentadora**
announcer   **el presentador, el locutor**
audience   **el público, la audiencia**
I broadcast   **emito**
broadcasting station   **la emisora**
cable TV   **la televisión por cable**
cameraman   **el cámara, el camarógrafo**
channel   **el canal**
commercial   **el anuncio de televisión**
couch potato   **el haragán del sofá**
dubbed   **doblado**
earphones   **los auriculares, [los audífonos]**
episode   **el episodio**
goggle box   **la caja boba, la caja tonta**
high frequency   **la alta frecuencia**
interactive   **interactivo**
listener   **el oyente**
live broadcast   **la emisión en**

directo
live coverage/commentary   **el reportaje en directo**
loudspeaker   **el altavoz**
low frequency   **la baja frecuencia**
microphone   **el micrófono**
newsreader   **el locutor**
personal stereo   **el walkman®**
production studio   **el estudio de producción**
program(me)   **el programa**
radio   **la radio**
on radio   **en la radio**
I record   **grabo**
recording   **la grabación**
remote control   **el mando a distancia, el control remoto**
I repeat   **repito**
repeat   **repetir**
satellite dish   **la antena parabólica**
satellite TV   **la televisión por satélite**
screen   **la pantalla**
I show   **presento, muestro**
signal   **la señal**

– What! Still glued to the set? You have been watching the box all evening! You have become a real couch potato!

– I'm just going to record this film/movie then I'll join you. Have you got any blank videocassettes?

Until recently most TV spots portrayed women in exclusively traditional roles.

– ¡Qué! ¿Todavía pegado a la televisión? Has estado viendo la caja boba toda la tarde. Te has convertido en un verdadero haragán de la televisión.

– Voy a grabar esta película y voy contigo. ¿Tienes alguna cinta de vídeo en blanco?

Hasta hace muy poco tiempo, en los anuncios de televisión las mujeres aparecían exclusivamente en papeles tradicionales.

station   **la estación**
subtitles   **los subtítulos**
I switch off   **apago**
I switch on   **enciendo**
teletext   **el teletexto**
television   **la televisión**
   on television   **en televisión**
telly/TV   **la tele**
I transmit   **retransmito**
TV set   **el aparato de televisión**

TV studio   **el estudio de televisión**
video clip   **el videoclip**
videogame   **el videojuego**
video library   **la videoteca**
video recorder   **el aparato de vídeo**
viewer   **el teleespectador, el televidente**
I watch   **veo**

TV and radio program(me)s

cartoons   **los dibujos animados**
children's program(me)   **el programa infantil**
comedy   **la comedia**
current affairs   **la actualidad**
drama   **el drama**
documentary   **el documental**
education program(me)s   **los programas educativos**
feature film/movie   **el largometraje**
light entertainment   **el programa de variedades**

news   **las noticias**
quiz program(me)s   **los programas concurso**
regional news   **las noticias regionales**
soap   **la telenovela**
school broadcasting   **la emisión escolar**
science program(me)   **el programa científico**
sports program(me)   **el programa deportivo**
weather forecast   **el pronóstico del tiempo**

Was the Pink Floyd concert broadcast live from Venice?

There should be a programme/program on students grants on this channel but perhaps the children would prefer watching the cartoons. Where is the TV listings?

During the summer the traffic bulletin is broadcast every hour in four languages for the benefit of foreign visitors.

¿El concierto de Pink Floyd se emitió en directo desde Venecia?

Debería haber un programa sobre becas para estudiantes en este canal, pero quizás los niños preferirían ver los dibujos animados. ¿Dónde está el programa [la programación] de la televisión?

Durante el verano el boletín de información del tráfico se emite cada hora en cuatro idiomas como servicio a los visitantes extranjeros.

18d Advertising

I advertise **anuncio**
advertisment **el anuncio**
advertising **la publicidad**
advertising industry **la industria de la publicidad**
appeal **el atractivo**
it appeals to **atrae, tiene atractivo para**
billboard **la cartelera, la valla publicitaria**
brand **la marca**
brochure **el folleto**
campaign **la campaña publicitaria**
catalog(ue) **el catálogo**
it catches the eye **se mete por los ojos**
commercial **el anuncio comercial**
competition (rival) **la competencia**
competition (game) **el concurso**
consumer **el consumidor**
consumer society **la sociedad de consumo**
copywriter **el escritor de material publicitario**
I covet **codicio, deseo**

it creates a need **crea una necesidad**
demand **la demanda**
disposable income **la renta disponible**
distributor **el distribuidor, el concesionario**
ethical **ético**
goods **los bienes**
hidden persuasion **la persuasión oculta**
image **la imagen**
junk mail **la propaganda de buzón**
I launch **lanzo**
life-style **el estilo de vida**
market **el mercado**
　　down-market **inferior, la sección popular del mercado**
　　up-market **superior, la sección superior del mercado**
market research **el análisis de mercados**
materialism **el materialismo**
model **el modelo**

– Do you think that TV adverts are more effective than adverts in newspapers?

– National TV reaches many more potential consumers but is extremely expensive.

This image will reach about a million potential consumers.

This has been his least successful campaign: next time we will use another agency or perhaps a freelance copywriter.

– ¿Piensas que los anuncios de la televisión son más eficaces que los anuncios de los periódicos?
– La televisión nacional llega a muchos más consumidores potenciales, pero es muy caro.

Esta imagen llegará a un millón de consumidores potenciales.

Esta ha sido su campaña de menos éxito; la próxima vez usaremos otra agencia, o quizás un periodista independiente.

I motivate **motivo**
need **la necesidad**
persuasion **la persuasión**
poster **el póster, el afiche**
product **el producto**
I promote **promociono**
promotion **la promoción**
publicity **la publicidad**
I publicize **doy publicidad a, anuncio**
public relations **las relaciones públicas**
purchasing power **el poder adquisitivo**
radio advertisements **los anuncios de la radio**
it sells **vende**
slogan **el eslogan, el lena**
status symbol **el símbolo del estatus**
stunt **el truco publicitario**
I target **mi objetivo es, me dirijo a**
target group **el grupo objeto**
I tempt **tiento**
trend **la tendencia**
trendy **muy al día**
truthful **verdadero**
TV advertisements **los anuncios de televisión**
unethical **no ético**

Small ads

accommodation **el alojamiento**
appointments **citas**
births **natalicios, nacimientos**
courses and conferences **cursos y conferencias**
deaths **necrológicas, obituario**
engagements **compromisos**
exchange **divisas**
exhibitions **exposiciones**
for sale **se vende**
health **salud**
holidays **vacaciones**
lonely hearts **encuentros**
marriages **bodas**
personal services **servicios personales**
property **propiedad inmobiliaria**
travel **viajes**
wanted **se quiere, se requiere**

The buildings are covered in ugly publicity billboards.

Los edificios están cubiertos con vallas publicitarias feas.

This publicity can be offensive to some ethnic groups.

Esta publicidad puede ser ofensiva para algunos grupos étnicos.

SPECIAL OFFER! For one week only! Buy 2 and get 1 free! Plus 20% discount on your next purchase!

¡OFERTA ESPECIAL! ¡Durante una semana nada más! ¡Compre 2 y te regalamos 1! ¡Más 20% de descuento en tu próxima compra!

Travel

19a General terms

I accelerate/speed up **acelero**
accident **el accidente**
adult **el adulto**
announcement **el anuncio**
arrival **la llegada**
I arrive (at) **llego (a)**
assistance **la ayuda, la asistencia**
I ask for assistance **pido ayuda**
bag **la bolsa**
baggage **el equipaje**
I book **reservo**
booking office **la oficina de reservas**
briefcase **el maletín**
business trip **el viaje de negocios**
I buy a ticket **compro un billete**
I call at **paso (por), hago escala en**
I cancel **cancelo**
I carry **llevo**
I catch **cojo**
I check (tickets) **confirmo**
child **el niño, la niña**
class **la clase**
I confirm **confirmo**
connection **el transbordo**
I cross **cruzo**
delay **el retraso**
I am delayed **tengo retraso, voy con retraso, [estoy retrasado]**
I depart **salgo**
departure **la salida**
destination **el destino**
direct **directo**
direction **la dirección**
disabled **el inválido**
distance **la distancia**

documents **los documentos**
driver (car) **el conductor**
early **temprano, pronto**
emergency **la emergencia, la urgencia**
emergency call **la llamada de emergencia/urgencia**
emergency stop **la parada de emergencia**
I enquire **pregunto, pido información**
enquiry **la pregunta, la consulta**
en route **en ruta**
entrance **la entrada**
exit **la salida**
extra charge **el recargo, el suplemento**
fare **la tarifa**
  fare reduction **la reducción de tarifa**
  reduced fare **la tarifa reducida**
fast **rápido, veloz**
I fill a form **relleno un formulario**
free **gratis**
from **de**
information **la información**
information office **la oficina de información**
insurance **el seguro**
help **la ayuda, el socorro**
helpful **útil**
late **tarde**
I leave (place) **salgo**
I leave (person/object) **dejo**
I leave at **salgo a**
left-luggage/baggage check office **la consigna**

lost **perdido**
lost property/lost and found office **la oficina de objetos perdidos**
loudspeaker **el altavoz, el altoparlante**
luggage/baggage **el equipaje**
message **el mensaje, el recado, la nota**
I miss **pierdo**
money **el dinero**
non-smoker **no-fumador**
notice **el aviso**
nuisance **la molestia**
occupied **ocupado**
on board **a bordo**
on time **a tiempo**
I pack **hago la maleta**
passenger **el pasajero**
porter **el mozo**
porter (hotel) **el portero, el conserje**
perfect timing **el horario perfecto**
reduction **el descuento, la rebaja**
rescue **el rescate**
reservation **la reserva**
I reserve **reservo**
I return **vuelvo**
return **la vuelta**
return/round-trip ticket **el billete de ida y vuelta**
safe **seguro**
safety **la seguridad**
seat **el asiento**
seatbelt **el cinturón de seguridad**
I set off **salgo**
signal **la señal**
single/one-way ticket **el billete de ida**
slow **lento**
I slow down **reduzco la velocidad**
smoking **fumar**
speed **la velocidad**
staff **el personal**
I start from **salgo de**

stop **la parada**
I stop **paro**
on strike **de huelga**
I take (bus, train) **cojo**
ticket **el billete**
ticket desk **la ventanilla de billetes, el despacho de billetes, la taquilla**
ticket office **la oficina de billetes, la taquilla**
timetable **el horario**
toilet/restroom **los servicios**
I travel **viajo**
travel **el viaje**
travel agent **el agente de viajes**
travel agency **la agencia de viajes**
travel documents **los documentos**
travel information **la información de viajes**
travel pass **el pase de viaje, el pasaporte**
travel sickness (car) **el mareo**
traveller **el viajero, el pasajero**
tunnel **el túnel**
turn **el giro, la vuelta**
I turn **giro**
unhelpful **inútil**
I unpack **deshago la maleta**
valid **válido**
via/through **a través, pasa por**
visitor **el visitante**
warning **el aviso**
way in **la entrada**
way out **la salida**
weekdays **los días de la semana**
week-end **el fin de semana**
Welcome! **¡Bienvenido!**
welcoming **acogedor**
window **la ventana**
window seat **el asiento al lado de la ventana**

19b Going abroad & travel by boat

Going abroad

I cross (the English Channel)
atravieso/cruzo (el canal de la Mancha)
currency **la moneda**
currency exchange office **la oficina de cambio de moneda**
customs **la aduana**
customs control **el control de aduanas**
customs officer **el oficial de aduana**
customs regulations **la legislación/el reglamento de aduanas**
declaration **la declaración**
I declare **declaro**
duty **el derecho, el impuesto**
duty-free goods **los productos libres de impuestos**
duty-free shop **la tienda de productos libres de impuestos**
English Channel **la Mancha**
Channel Tunnel **el túnel del canal**

exchange rate **la tasa de cambio**
expired **caducado, vencido**
foreign currency **la moneda extranjera**
frontier **la frontera**
I go through customs **paso la aduana**
I go through passport control **paso el control de pasaportes**
immigration office **la oficina de inmigración**
immigration rules **el reglamento de inmigración**
passport **el pasaporte**
I pay duty on **pago el impuesto de**
smuggler **el contrabandista**
smuggling **el contrabando**
visa **la visa**

Travel by boat

boat **el barco**
bridge **el puente**
cabin **el camarote**
calm sea **el mar calmado, el mar en calma**

– Here are my documents. My final destination is Santiago.
– Thank you. Have a nice trip!

– Aquí están mis documentos. Mi destino final es Santiago.
– Gracias. Buen viaje.

– I have nothing to declare. This is for my personal use.
– What! All forty bottles of whisky and 100 cartons of cigarettes?

– No tengo nada a declarar. Es para mi uso personal.
– ¡Qué! ¿Cuarenta botellas de whisky y 100 cajas de cigarillos?

For your comfort and safety, please fasten your seatbelts.

Por su comodidad y seguridad, por favor, abróchense los cinturones de seguridad.

captain **el capitán, el comandante**
car-ferry **el ferry**
coast **la costa**
crew **la tripulación**
crossing **la travesía**
cruise **el crucero**
deck **la cubierta**
  lower deck **la cubierta inferior**
  upper deck **la cubierta superior**
deck chair **la butaca de cubierta**
I disembark **desembarco**
disembarkation **el desembarco**
dock **el muelle**
I embark **embarco**
embarkation card **la tarjeta de embarque**
I go on board **entro a bordo**
harbour/harbor **el puerto**
lifejacket **el chaleco salvavidas**
lifeboat **el bote de salvamento**
lounge **la sala**
ocean **el océano**
off-shore **el mar abierto, la alta mar**
on board **a bordo**

overboard **por la borda**
port **(a) babor**
port (of call) **el puerto (de escala)**
quay **el muelle**
reclining seat **el asiento reclinable**
sea **el mar**
  calm sea **el mar en calma**
  choppy sea **el mar empicado, el mar picado/agitado**
  heavy sea **el mar grueso**
  stormy sea **el mar borrascoso**
sea-sickness **el mareo**
seaman **el marino, el marinero**
ship **el buque**
shipping forecast **el pronóstico del mar**
shipyard **el astillero**
smooth **la calma**
starboard **(a) estribor**
storm **la tormenta**
tide **la marea**
waves **las olas**
wind **el viento**
windy **ventoso**
yachting **la navegación en yate, el deporte de la vela**

From which quay does the ship leave?

– Have you got any remedy against sea-sickness?
– Yes, I have some pills in my cabin. Meet me on C deck in 10 minutes.
– Thanks, but I don't think I'll survive that long.

Is passport control carried out on board?

¿De qué muelle sale el barco?

– **¿Tiene algo para el mareo?**

– **Sí, tengo pastillas en mi camarote. Le veo en la cubierta C dentro de 10 minutos.**
– **Gracias, pero no creo que sobrevivo tanto tiempo.**

– **¿Se controlan los pasaportes a bordo?**
[¿El control de pasaportes se lleva a cabo a bordo?]

access   **el acceso**
I allow   **permito**
articulated lorry/truck   **el camión articulado/a remolque**
automatic   **automático**
I back up/reverse   **doy marcha atrás**
bike/bicycle   **la bicicleta**
black ice   **el hielo invisible en la carretera**
bottleneck   **el embotellamiento**
breathalyzer   **el respirador para la prueba de alcoholemia, el alcoholímetro**
breathalyzing test   **la prueba de alcoholemia**
breakdown   **la avería**
breakdown service   **el servicio de avería**
I breakdown   **tengo avería**
broken   **roto**
bus   **el autobús, [el guagua]**
bus fare   **la tarifa del autobús**
bus stop   **la parada del autobús**
car   **el coche, [el guagua, el carro]**
car hire/rental   **el alquiler de coche**
car park/parking lot   **el aparcamiento de coches, el estacionamiento, el párking, [el parqueadero]**
multistorey/multistoried   **de muchos pisos**
car parts   **las piezas del coche**
car wash   **el lavado de coches, el autolavado**
caravan/trailer   **la caravana**
caution   **la prudencia**
caution (legal)   **la amonestación**
I change gear   **cambio de marcha**
chauffeur   **el chófer**
check   **el control**
I collide   **me estrello, choco**
collision   **la colisión, el choque**

company car   **el coche/[el carro] de la empresa**
competent   **competente**
conductor (bus)   **el cobrador**
I cross   **cruzo, atravieso**
dangerous   **peligroso**
detour/diversion   **la desviación**
diesel   **el diesel**
I do 30 mph   **voy a 30 millas por hora**
I drive   **conduzco**
drive/driving   **la conducción**
driver   **el conductor**
driving instructor   **el profesor de conducir**
driving lesson   **la lección de conducir**
driving licence/driver's license   **el carné/carnet de conducir**
driving school   **la autoescuela, [la escuela de conducción]**
driving test   **el examen de conducir**
drunken driving   **la conducción bajo los efectos del alcohol**
engine trouble   **el problema del motor**
I fasten (seatbelt)   **me ajusto**
I fill up   **lleno**
filling station   **la gasolinera, la estación de servicio/de gas, [la bomba]**
fine   **la multa**
I fix/repair   **arreglo**
forbidden   **prohibido**
for hire/rent   **en/para alquiler**
garage   **el garaje**
gear   **la marcha**
 in gear   **en marcha**
 in first gear   **en primera (marcha)**
 in neutral   **en punto muerto, [en neutro]**
 in reverse   **en marcha atrás, en reversa**

I get in the car **me monto en el coche, subo al coche**

I get in lane **me meto en el carril**

I get out **salgo**

I give way **doy paso**

highway **la carretera**

Highway Code **el código de la circulación**

highway police **la policía de carreteras**

I hire/rent **alquilo**

hired/rental car **el coche alquilado**

I hitchhike **hago autoestop**

hitchhiker **el autoestopista**

hitchhiking **el autoestop**

I am insured **estoy asegurado**

insurance **el seguro**

insurance policy **la póliza del seguro**

jack **el gato**

it is jammed **está bloqueado**

I keep my distance **guardo mi distancia**

keys **las llaves**

key-ring **el llavero**

kilometre **el kilómetro**

learner driver **el conductor novato**

line of cars **la fila de coches**

logbook **los documentos del coche**

lorry/truck **el camión [el carro]**

lorry/truck driver **el conductor de camiones, el camionero**

make of car **la fabricación de coches**

MOT/vehicle inspection **la ITV (Inspección Técnica de Vehículos)**

mechanic **la mecánica**

mechanical **mecánico**

motel **el motel**

motor caravan **la caravana**

motor show **la exposición de coches/de automóviles**

one-way only **la dirección única, [una sola vía]**

I overtake/pass **adelanto, doblo**

overtaking/passing **el adelantamiento, el paso**

I park **aparco, estaciono, [parqueo]**

parking **el aparcamiento**

parking ban **la prohibición de aparcar**

parking meter **el contador de aparcamiento/[parqueadero]**

parking ticket **el ticket/la multa de aparcamiento/estacionamiento**

I pass **paso**

passenger **el pasajero**

pedestrian **el peatón**

petrol/gasoline **la gasolina**

leaded **con plomo**

four-star **súper**

two star **normal**

unleaded/lead-free **sin plomo**

picnic area **la zona de picnic**

police **la policía**

policeman **el policía**

policewoman **la mujer policía**

police station **la comisaría/ [estación] de policía**

position **la posición**

private car **el coche particular**

public transport **el transporte público**

puncture/flat **el pinchazo**

ramp **la rampa**

registration papers **los papeles de inscripción**

rental charge **el precio de alquiler**

repair **la reparación**

I repair **reparo**

I reverse **doy marcha atrás, doy reversa**

(in) reverse **(en) marcha atrás, (en) reversa**

right of way **la preferencia**

road **la carretera**

road accident **el accidente de carretera**

road block **el bloqueamiento de la carretera**

road hog   **el loco del volante**
road map   **el mapa de carreteras**
road sign   **la señal de tráfico**
road works   **las obras de la carretera**
route   **la ruta**
I run over   **atropello**
rush hour   **la hora punta, [la hora pico]**
seatbelt   **el cinturón de seguridad**
second-hand car   **el coche de segunda mano**
self-service   **el autoservicio**
service   **el servicio**
service area   **el área de servicio**
I set off   **salgo**
signal   **la señal**
signpost   **el poste de señales, el poste indicador**
slippery   **resbaladizo**
slow   **lento**
I slow down   **reduzco la velocidad**
I sound the horn/honk   **toco la bocina, [pito]**
speed   **la velocidad**
I speed up   **acelero**
speed limit   **el límite de velocidad**
spot fine   **la multa**

I start (engine)   **enciendo**
I switch off/on   **apago/enciendo**
taxi/cab   **el taxi**
taxi/cab driver   **el taxista**
taxi rank   **la parada de taxis**
I test   **compruebo**
toll   **el peaje**
I tow away   **quito remolcando, retiro a remolque**
town plan   **el plano de la ciudad**
town traffic   **el tráfico urbano**
traffic   **el tráfico, la circulación**
traffic jam   **el atasco de tráfico, [el trancón]**
traffic light   **el semáforo**
traffic offence/violation   **el incumplimiento de las normas de tráfico**
traffic news   **el informe del tráfico**
traffic police   **la policía de tráfico**
traffic-free zone   **la zona libre de tráfico, la zona peatonal**
trip   **el viaje corto**
I turn left   **giro a la izquierda**
I turn right   **giro a la derecha**
I turn off at   **giro a**
I turn off (engine)   **apago**
underground   **subterráneo**

I have a puncture/flat tire and the lights are not working. Could you also have a look at the clutch?

Tengo una rueda pinchada y las luces no funcionan. ¿Puede echarle un vistazo al embrague también?

Fill it up with unleaded, please.

Lleno. Gasolina sin plomo, por favor.

I had to stop on the hard shoulder. Thankfully, emergency phones are found on all motorways/ expressways.

Tuve que parar en el arcén de la autopista. Afortunadamente, hay teléfonos de emergencia en todas las autopistas.

This new model has a very low petrol/gas consumption. It also has excellent handling around corners.

Este nuevo modelo consume muy poca gasolina. También se maneja muy bien en las curvas.

U-turn **el giro en U**
vehicle **el vehículo**
I wait **espero**
warning **el aviso**
witness **el testigo**

Roads

alley **el callejón**
avenue **la avenida**
bend/curve **la curva**
bridge **el puente**
built-up area **la zona edificada, la zona urbanizada**
bump **el badén, el bache**
bypass **la carretera de circunvalación**
central reservation **la mediana**
closed *(road)* **cerrada**
corner **la esquina**
crossing **el cruce**
crossroad **el cruce de carreteras**
cul-de-sac **la calle sin salida**
hard shoulder **el arcén**
inside lane **el carril interior**
intersection **el cruce, la intersección**
junction **el cruce**
lane **el carril**

lay-by **el apartadero**
level crossing **el paso a nivel**
main street **la calle principal**
motorway/expressway **la autopista**
entry **la entrada, el acceso**
exit **la salida**
junction **el cruce**
one-way street **la calle de dirección única**
outside lane **el carril exterior**
pavement/sidewalk **el pavimento**
pedestrian crossing **el cruce de peatones**
pedestrian island **la isleta de peatones**
ring road **la carretera de circunvalación**
road **la carretera**
roundabout **la rotonda**
side street **la calle lateral**
slip road **el carril de acceso**
square **la plaza**
street **la calle**
underground passage **el pasaje subterráneo**
white/yellow line **la raya blanca/amarilla**

Because of black ice on the roads, there is a risk of collision: so keep your distance.

Debido al hielo invisible en la carretera, hay riesgo de choque: así que guarda la distancia.

There has been a serious accident on the motorway/expressway A1 between junction 7 and 8. A lorry travelling towards Madrid has crashed against the central barrier. Three vehicles are involved and one of the drivers is seriously injured. I have put on the hazard lights. Send an ambulance immediately.

Ha habido un accidente grave en la autopista A1 entre los cruces 7 y 8. Un camión viajando a Madrid ha chocado contra la barrera central. Otros tres vehículos han sufrido y uno de los conductores está gravemente herido. He encendido la luz de emergencia. Mande una ambulancia inmediatamente.

19d Travel by air

aeroplane/airplane **el avión**
aircraft **la nave aérea**
air hostess/stewardess **la azafata**
airline **la aerolínea**
airline desk **la ventana de la línea aérea**
air travel **el viaje de avión**
airport **el aeropuerto**
I am airsick **estoy mareado**
baggage **el equipaje**
body search **el registro personal, la requisa**
I board a plane **subo a bordo de un avión**
boarding card **la tarjeta de embarque**
business class **la clase de ejecutivo**
by air **por avión**
cabin **la cabina**
cancelled flight **el vuelo cancelado**
carousel **la cinta de equipaje**
charter flight **el vuelo chárter**
I check in **facturo**
check-in operations **las**

operaciones de facturación
control tower **la torre de control**
co-pilot **el copiloto**
crew **la tripulación**
desk **la ventana**
direct flight **el vuelo directo**
domestic flight **el vuelo interior/interno**
during landing **durante el aterrizaje**
during take-off **durante el despegue**
during the flight **durante el vuelo**
duty-free goods **los productos libres de impuestos**
economy class **la clase económica**
emergency exit **la salida de emergencia**
emergency landing **el aterrizaje de emergencia**
excess baggage **el exceso de equipaje**
I fasten **ajusto**
flight **el vuelo**

Can I make a connection to Zaragoza? Do I have to change flight?

– I have some excess luggage.
– Have you packed your luggage yourself?

There is some turbulence in the Andes.
The expected landing time is now 11:40, local time.

¿Puedo hacer un transbordo para Zaragoza? ¿Tengo que cambiar el vuelo?

– Tengo exceso de equipaje.
– ¿Ha hecho su equipaje usted mismo?

Hay algunas turbulencias en los Andes.
La hora de aterrizaje está prevista para las 11.40, hora local.

flight attendant   **el asistente de vuelo**
I fly   **vuelo**
I fly at a height of   **vuelo a una altura de**
flying   **la aviación**
fuselage   **el fuselaje**
gate   **la puerta**
instructions   **las instrucciones**
hand luggage   **el equipaje de mano**
headphones   **los auriculares**
highjacker   **el secuestrador (aéreo)**
immigrant   **el inmigrante**
immigration   **la inmigración**
immigration rules   **las normas de inmigración**
I land   **aterrizo**
landing   **el aterrizaje**
landing lights   **las luces de aterrizaje**
Ifejacket   **el chaleco de salvavidas**
no-smoking sign   **la señal de no fumar**
non-stop   **sin parada**

on board   **a bordo**
parachute   **el paracaídas**
passenger   **el pasajero**
passengers lounge   **la sala de pasajeros**
passport control   **el control de pasaportes**
pilot   **el piloto**
plane   **el avión**
refreshments   **los refrescos**
runway   **la pista de aterrizaje**
security measures   **las medidas de seguridad**
security staff   **el personal de seguridad**
steward   **el auxiliar de vuelo**
stewardess   **la azafata**
I take off   **despego**
take off   **el despegue**
terminal   **la terminal**
tray   **la bandeja**
turbulence   **la turbulencia**
view   **la vista, el panorama**
window   **la ventana, la ventanilla**
window seat   **el asiento junto a la ventana**

– Will Mr/Ms Bosé travelling on flight IB 131 to Alicante please contact the information desk immediately.
– Where do I check-in for flight IB 131?

– El señor/la señora Bosé viajando en el vuelo IB 131 para Alicante por favor preséntense en el mostrador de información.
– ¿Dónde facturo para el vuelo IB 131?

This is the last call for passengers travelling on flght IB 881 to Buenos Aires.

Última llamada para los pasajeros del vuelo IB 881 para Buenos Aires.

How long is the delay?

¿Cuánto dura el retraso?

My luggage has not yet been unloaded.

Mi equipaje no ha sido descargado todavía.

What is the flight number?

¿Cuál es el número del vuelo?

19e Travel by rail

announcement   el anuncio
barrier   la barrera
buffet   el menú
buffet-car   el vagón-cafetería, el coche-comedor
coach   el vagón
compartment   el compartimiento
connection   la conexión, el transbordo
dining-car   el vagón restaurante
exemption   la exención
fare   la tarifa
inspector   el inspector, el revisor
I lean out   me asomo
level crossing   el paso a nivel
luggage rack   la reja de equipaje, la baca
I miss   pierdo
non-refundable   sin devolución
(non-)smokers compartment   el compartimiento de (no) fumadores
occupied   ocupado
on time   a tiempo
platform   el andén, [la plataforma]
porter   el portero
I punch (ticket)   perforo
rail station   la estación de tren
rail tracks   el raíl, la vía, la carrilera
railway/railroad   la red ferroviaria
   elevated railway   el ferrocarril elevado
ramp   la rampa
reduction   el descuento
reservation   la reserva
reserved   reservado
sleeper   el coche cama
smokers   fumadores
speed   la velocidad
stairs   las escaleras
station master   el jefe de estación

A special announcement:
On Sundays and (Bank) Holidays the service to Valencia does not operate and on weekdays after 9 a.m. fares are subject to supplementary charges.
In addition, reservations are required for seats in the non-smoking compartments on the Gijón service. We apologize for any inconvenience.

Un anuncio especial:
Los domingos y festivos no sale el servicio para Valencia y en los días laborales después de las nueve de la mañana las tarifas están sujetas a cargos suplementarios. Además, se necesitan reservas para los compartimientos para no-fumadores en el servicio para Gijón. Pedimos disculpas por los inconvenientes.

The 11.45 to Lima is now leaving from platform 10.

El tren de las 11.45 para Lima sale del andén 10.

The underground/subway is closed until 7 am.

El metro está cerrado hasta las 7 de la mañana.

stop **la parada**
subway/underground **el metro**
supplement **el suplemento**
taxi rank **la parada de taxis**
ticket **el billete, [el tiquete, el boleto]**
  first class **de primera clase**
  group **de grupo**
  second class **de segunda clase**
  single/one-way **de ida**
  return/round-trip **de ida y vuelta**
ticket collector **el revisor de billetes, [el controlador de boletos]**
ticket office **la oficina/el despacho de billetes, la taquilla**
timetable **el horario**
  summer timetable **el horario de verano**
  winter timetable **el horario de invierno**
timetable changes **los cambios de horario**
track **la vía**
traveller **el viajero**
train **el tren**
  direct train **el tren directo**
  express train **el tren expreso, el rápido**
  Intercity train **el tren interurbano/de largo recorrido**
  local train **el tren local**
  night train **el tren nocturno**
trolley **el carrito**
underground/subway **el metro**
user **el usuario**
I wait **espero**
waiting-room **la sala de espera**
warning **el aviso**
window **la ventana**

Where do I have to change?

¿Dónde tengo que cambiar?

When is the first train?

¿Cuándo es el primer tren?

Excuse me, this a non-smoking compartment.

– Perdone, este es un compartimiento para no fumadores.

Is this the Intercity to Barcelona?

¿Es este el servicio de largo recorrido para Barcelona?

There are no facilities for disabled travellers on this train.

No hay servicios para pasajeros inválidos en este tren.

This is a public announcement for all passengers travelling to Seville. We are sorry to announce that this service is subject to delays. There will also be a platform change.

Anuncio para los pasajeros viajando a Sevilla. Sentimos anunciar que este servicio tiene retraso. También se hará un cambio de andén [plataforma].

Holidays/Vacation

20a General terms

abroad **el extranjero**
accommodation **la vivienda, la estancia, el alojamiento**
alone **solo**
area **el área, la zona**
arrival **la llegada**
available **disponible**
beach **la playa**
camera **la cámara**
clean **limpio**
climate **el clima**
closed **cerrado**
clothes **la ropa**
cold **frío**
comfort **el confort, la comodidad**
comfortable **confortable, cómodo**
congested **congestionado, lleno**
cost **el costo, el precio**
country **el país**
countryside **el campo**
dirty **sucio**
disadvantage **la desventaja**
disorganized **desorganizado**
exchange **el cambio**
fire **el fuego**
folding chair **la silla plegable**
folding table **la mesa plegable**
food **la comida**
free **gratis**
full **lleno**
full-up **lleno, completo**
I get brown **me bronceo**
I go **voy**
group **el grupo**
group travel **el viaje en grupo**
guide **el guía**
guide book **el guía**
guided tour **el viaje con guía**
guided walk **la visita con guía**
holidays/vacation **las vacaciones**

land **el país, la tierra**
landscape **el paisaje**
journey **el viaje**
mild *(climate)* **templado**
money **el dinero**
open **abierto**
organization **la organización**
I organize **organizo**
organized **organizado**
plan *(town)* **el plano**
I plan **planeo**
portable **portátil**
I return *(to a place)* **vuelvo**
rucksack/knapsack **la mochila**
sea **el mar**
seascape **el paisaje marino**
seaside resort **punto de veraneo en la playa, el lugar de veraneo**
show **el espectáculo**
I show **muestro, demuestro, exhibo**
sight **la vista**
I spend time **paso tiempo**
stay **la estancia**
I stay **estoy en**
sun **el sol**
sunny **soleado**
I sunbathe **tomo el sol**
tour **la gira, el viaje, la excursión**
tourism **el turismo**
tourist **el turista**
tourist menu **el menú turístico**
tourist office **la oficina de turismo**
town **la ciudad, el pueblo**
town plan **el mapa de la ciudad**
travel **el viaje**
I travel **viajo**
travel adaptor **el adaptador de viaje**
trip **el viaje corto**

I understand **entiendo**
I unpack **deshago la maleta**
visit **la visita**
I visit **visito**
visiting hours **las horas de visita**
visitors **los visitantes**
welcome **la bienvenido**
worth seeing **visita recomendada**

Holiday activities

beach holiday/vacation **en la playa**
boating holiday/vacation **las vacaciones en barco**
camping **el camping**
canoeing **el viaje en canoa**
coach holiday/vacation **las vacaciones en autobús**
cruise **el crucero**
cycling **el ciclismo**
fishing **la pesca**
fruit picking **la recolección de fruta**

home exchange **el intercambio de casa**
hunting **la caza**
motoring holiday/vacation **las vacaciones en coche/[carro]**
mountain climbing **el montañismo, la escalada de una montaña**
rock climbing **la escalada en rocas**
sailing **la navegación**
shopping **las compras**
sightseeing **el excursionismo**
skiing **el esquí**
study holiday/vacation **las vacaciones de estudio**
sunbathing **el baño de sol**
volunteer work **el trabajo voluntario**
walking **caminar, andar**
wine tasting **la cata de vinos**

Dear all at work

Having a wonderful holiday. The weather is hot (I've a great tan), the campsite is clean and the local food is excellent.

The kids are having a great time too, enjoying the water sports, building sandcastles and making lots of friends.

I'm not looking forward to coming home!
Best wishes, María.

Mis queridos colegas

Me estoy divirtiendo en estas vacaciones. Hace calor (estoy muy bronceada), el camping es limpio, y la comida regional es excelente.

Los chicos están pasándolo bien, disfrutando de las actividades acuáticas, haciendo castillos de arena, y haciendo muchos amigos.

¡No tengo ganas de volver!

Un afectuoso saludo de María.

➤ TRAVEL 19; HOBBIES 16a; ON THE BEACH App.20a; WEATHER 24d

20b Accommodation & hotel

Accomodation

apartment **el apartamento**
bed & breakfast **la pensión**
campsite **el camping, la zona de camping**
caravan/trailer **la caravana**
farm **la granja**
full board **la pensión completa**
half board **la media pensión**
home exchange **el intercambio de casa**
hotel **el hotel**
mobile home **la caravana**
inn **la posada, la fonda, el mesón**
self-catering **el piso con cocina propia**
villa **la villa**
youth hostel **el albergue juvenil**

Booking & payment

affordable **asequible, razonable**
all included **todo incluido**
bill **la cuenta**
I book/reserve **reservo**
brochure **el folleto**
I cash **hago efectivo, cobro**
cheap **barato**
cheque/check **el cheque**
cost **el costo, el coste**
credit **el crédito**
credit card **la tarjeta de crédito**
economical **económico**
Eurocheque **el eurocheque**
expensive **caro**

excluding **excluido**
exclusive **exclusivo**
extra charge **el suplemento, el recargo**
evening meal **la cena**
fee **el precio**
I fill in **relleno, lleno**
form **el impreso, el formulario**
free **gratis**
inclusive **completo, que incluye**
I pay **pago**
payment **el pago**
price-list **la lista de precios**
receipt **el recibo**
reduction **el descuento, la rebaja**
refund **la devolución, el reembolso**
reservation **la reserva**
I reserve **reservo**
I sign **firmo**
signature **la firma**
traveller's cheque/traveler's check **el cheque de viaje/viajero**
VAT/sales tax **el IVA**

Hotel

air-conditioning **el aire acondicionado**
amenities **los servicios**
balcony **el balcón**
bath **el baño**
bed **la cama**
bed linen/bedding **la ropa de cama**
bedspread **el cubrecama, el**

I'd like to reserve a room with a double bed and en-suite bathroom for three days from March 5th.

Quisiera reservar una habitación doble con baño para tres días desde el cinco de marzo.

We are checking out now. I shall collect the luggage at 10:30.

Ahora pagamos. Recogeré el equipaje a las 10.30.

Do not disturb

No molestar

cobertor, **la colcha**
bed and breakfast **la pensión (desayuno incluido)**
billiard/pool room **la sala de billar**
board **la pensión**
full board **pensión completa**
half board **media pensión**
breakfast **el desayuno**
broken **roto, estropeado**
business meeting **la reunión de negocios**
call **la llamada**
I check in/out **facturo/me retiro**
coathanger **la percha, el perchero**
comfortable **cómodo, confortable**
I complain **me quejo, reclamo**
complaint **la queja, el reclamo**
conference **la conferencia**
conference facilities **el salón de conferencias**
damage **el daño, el perjuicio**
dining-room **el comedor**
early morning call **la llamada por la mañana temprano**
en-suite bathroom **el baño adjunto**
facilities **los servicios**
fire exit **la salida de incendios**
fire extinguisher **el extintor de fuego, el extinguidor**
guest **el huésped**
hairdresser **el peluquero**
hairdryer **el secador de pelo**
heating **la calefacción**
hotel **el hotel**
key **la llave**

laundry **la lavandería**
laundry service **el servicio de lavandería**
lift/elevator **el ascensor**
meal **la comida**
night porter **el portero de noche**
noisy **ruidoso**
nuisance **la molestia**
overnight bag **el maletín de fin de semana**
parking space **el espacio para aparcar**
plug **el enchufe**
porter **el portero**
privacy **privacidad, intimidad**
private toilet **el wáter particular, el baño privado**
reception **la recepción**
receptionist **el recepcionista**
room **la habitación**
double room **la habitación doble**
family room **la habitación familiar**
twin-bedded room **la habitación con camas gemelas**
room service **el servicio a la habitación**
shower **la ducha**
shower-cap **el gorro de ducha**
stay **la estancia**
I stay **estoy en, me alojo en**
trouser/pants-press **la prensa de pantalones**
view **la vista**
water **el agua**

I'd like to complain. The hot water tap does not work and the elevator is out of order. There is only one coathanger in the wardrobe and I asked for a room with a view.

Quiero hacer un reclamo. Ni el grifo de agua caliente ni el ascensor funcionan. Solo hay una percha en el armario y había pedido una habitación con vista.

Press the button

Apriete el botón

➤ ROOMS 8a; FURNITURE & FURNISHINGS 8c; EATING OUT 10a

20c Camping & self-catering/service

air bed **el colchón inflable**
antihistamine cream **la crema antihistamínica**
ants **las hormigas**
barbeque **la barbacoa**
battery **la pila**
I camp **acampo**
camp bed **la cama de camping**
camper **el campista**
camping **el camping**
camping equipment/gear **el equipo de camping**
camping gas **el camping gas**
campsite **el camping**
caravan/trailer **la caravana**
connected **conectado**
cooking facilities **la posibilidad de cocinar**
disconnected **desconectado**
drinking water **el agua potable**
dustbin/trashcan **el bote/la caneca de la basura**
extension lead **la extensión**
forbidden **prohibido**

fun **la diversión**
gas cooker/stove **la cocina de gas**
gas cylinder **la bombona de gas**
ground-sheet **la tela impermeable**
guy rope **el viento de la tienda**
launderette **la lavandería**
I make friends **hago amigos**
medicine box **el botiquín**
mosquito bite **la picadura de mosquito**
mosquito net **la red contra los mosquitos, el mosquitero**
mosquitos **los mosquitos**
pan **la sartén, el cazo, la cacerola, la cazuela**
peg **la estaca**
I pitch/put up my tent **pongo mi tienda de campaña**
registration **la inscripción**
services **los servicios**
sheet **la sábana**
site **el emplazamiento, el sitio**
sleeping bag **el saco de dormir**
space **el espacio**

– Where shall we put up the tent?

– Away from the main block.
– I'll pitch it in the shade.
– No, it is a bit damp there. This is better here and there are no mosquitos.

– Where's the torch/flashlight? It's not in the tent.
– It was in the rucksack/knapsack just now.
– Keep your voice down, please, we are trying to sleep!

Do you have a few spare pegs?

– **¿Dónde ponemos la tienda de campaña?**

– **Lejos del bloque principal.**
– **La montaré en la sombra.**
– **No, está un poco húmedo allí. Está mejor aquí, y no hay mosquitos.**

– **¿Dónde está la linterna? No está en la tienda de campaña.**
– **Justo ahora estaba en la mochila.**
– **Baja la voz por favor, estamos tratando de dormir.**

¿Tienes algunas estacas que me podrías dejar?

➤ GENERAL TERMS 20a; SHOPPING 9; COOKING 10d; FOODSTUFFS 9b

I take down (tent)   **quito (la tienda de campaña)**
tent   **la tienda de campaña**
tin opener   **el abrelatas**
toilet   **el servicio, el baño**
torch/flashlight   **la linterna, la antorcha**
uncomfortable   **incómodo, poco confortable**
vehicles   **los vehículos**
washing facilities   **las duchas**
water filter   **el filtro de agua**

Self-catering/service

agency   **la agencia**
agreement   **el acuerdo**
amenities   **las facilidades**
apartment   **el apartamento**
I clean   **limpio**
I cook   **cocino**
damaged   **dañado, estropeado**
damages   **los daños, los perjuicios**
dangerous   **peligroso**
electricity   **la electricidad**
equipment   **el equipo**

farm   **la granja**
maid   **la criada**
meter   **el contador**
owner   **el dueño, el propietario**
rent   **el alquiler, la renta**
I rent   **alquilo, arriendo**
I rent out   **doy en alquiler**
repair   **la reparación**
I repair   **reparo**
I return *(give back)*   **devuelvo**
ruined   **en ruinas, estropeado, dañado**
self-service   **el autoservicio**
set of keys   **el juego de llaves**
I share   **comparto**
shutters   **las contraventanas**
smelly   **oloroso, que huele**
spare keys   **las llaves de repuesto**
water supply   **el suministro de agua**
well   **el pozo**
well kept   **bien guardado**

I'm making a packed lunch. | **Estoy preparando un almuerzo empaquetado.**

The apartment is close to the town centre/center, just a few kilometres/kilometers from the nearest shops/stores and convenient for the swimming pool. | **El apartamento está cerca del centro de la ciudad, a sólo unos kilómetros de las tiendas más cercanas, y cerca de la piscina.**

You will find the electricity meter under the stairs. | **El contador de electricidad está debajo de las escaleras.**

There are no blankets, the cooker/stove doesn't work and there is a frog in the bathroom. | **No hay mantas, no funciona el horno, y hay una rana en el baño.**

Is there no more water? | **¿No queda agua?**
Beware of the dog! | **Perro peligroso!**

Language

21a General terms

---

accuracy **la exactitud**
accurate **exacto**
I adapt **adapto**
I adopt **adopto**
advanced **avanzado**
aptitude **la aptitud**
artificial language **el lenguaje artificial**
based on **basado en**
bilingual **bilingüe**
bilingualism **el bilingüismo**
borrowing **el préstamo**
branch **la rama**
classical languages **las lenguas clásicas**
it derives from **se deriva de, viene de**
development **el desarrollo**
difficult **la dificultad**
easy **fácil**
error **el error**
foreign language **el idioma extranjero**
I forget **olvido, me olvido de**
grammar **la gramática**

grammatical **gramatical**
I improve **mejoro**
influence **la influencia**
known **conocido**
language **el idioma, la lengua**
  language course **el curso de idiomas**
  language family **la familia de idiomas**
  language school **la escuela de idiomas**
  language skills **las aptitudes para los idiomas**
Latin **el latín**
I learn **aprendo**
learning **el aprendizaje**
level **el nivel**
linguistics **la lingüística**
link **el nexo**
living **vivo**
major languages **los idiomas principales**
it means **significa, quiere decir**
I mime **represento con gestos**
minor languages **los idiomas**

Lesser languages may disappear; however, thanks to the oral tradition in some communities, some have been preserved.

Los idiomas secundarios podrían desaparecer, sin embargo gracias a la tradición oral en algunas comunidades, algunos se han preservado.

---

secundarios
mistake **el error**
modern languages **las lenguas modernas**
monolingual **monolingüe**
mother tongue **la lengua madre, la lingua materna**
mutation **la mutación, el cambio**
name **el nombre, el sustantivo**
nation **la nación**
national **nacional**
native **el nativo**
natural **natural**
official **oficial**
offshoot **el ramal**
origin **el origen**
phenomenon **el fenómeno**
I practise/practice **practico**
preserved **preservado**
question **la pregunta**
register **el registro**
self-assessment **la autoevaluación**
separate **separararado, independiente**
sign language **el lenguaje de señas**
survival **la supervivencia**
it survives **sobrevive**
I teach **enseño**
teacher **el profesor**
teaching **la enseñanza**

test **la prueba, el examen**
I test **evalúo, corrijo un examen, ensayo**
I translate **traduzco**
translation **la traducción**
I understand **entiendo, comprendo**
unknown **desconocido**
widely **ampliamente**
witticism **la agudeza**

Words & vocabulary

antonym **el antónimo**
colloquial **familiar**
consonant **la consonante**
dictionary **el diccionario**
expression **la expresión**
idiom **la expresión idiomática**
idiomatic **idiomático**
jargon **la jerga**
lexicographer **el lexicógrafo**
lexicon **el léxico**
phrase **la frase, la oración**
phrase book **el libro de frases**
sentence **la frase, la oración**
slang **el argot**
syllable **la sílaba**
synonym **el sinónimo**
vocabulary **el vocabulario**
vowel **la vocal**
word **la palabra**
word play **el juego de palabras**

I am not very good at languages but my sister is a gifted linguist.

No soy muy bueno para los idiomas, pero mi hermana es una dotada para las lenguas.

She learned French and Italian in school, then she travelled extensively and picked up Bulgarian and Urdu while working as a volunteer.

Aprendió francés e italiano en el colegio, y ha viajado mucho y aprendió un poco de búlgaro y de urdú mientras trabajaba como voluntaria.

Speaking & listening

accent **el acento**
   regional accent **el acento regional**
articulate **elocuente**
I articulate **articulo**
clear **claro**
I communicate **comunico**
conversation **la conversación**
I converse **converso, hablo**
dialect **el dialecto**
diction **la dicción**
I express myself **me expreso**
fluent **la fluidez, la soltura, la facilidad**
fluently **con fluidez, con soltura, con facilidad**
I interpret **interpreto**
interpreter **el intéprete**
intonation **la entonación**
lisp **el ceceo**
I lisp **ceceo**
I listen **escucho, oigo**
listener **el oyente**
listening **la audición**
listening skills **las aptitudes de audición**
I mispronounce **pronuncio mal**
mispronunciation **el error de pronunciación**
oral(ly) **oral(mente), verbal(mente)**
I pronounce **pronuncio**
pronunciation **la pronunciación**
rhythm **el ritmo**
sound **el sonido**
I sound **sueno**
I speak **hablo**
speaker **el hablante**
speaking **el habla**
speaking skills **las aptitudes para hablar, las aptitudes verbales**
speech **el discurso**
speed **la velocidad**
spoken **hablado**
spoken language **el lenguaje hablado**
stress **la entonación**
stressed (un-) **(in)acentuado**
I stutter/stammer **tartamudeo, balbuceo**
unpronounceable **impronunciable**
verbally **verbalmente**

– I have no difficulty in reading Spanish, but I don't understand it when people speak very fast or with a strong regional accent.

– Do you practise Spanish with a native speaker?
– No, I prefer to attend a class.

Don't worry about spelling mistakes for the moment.

– No tengo dificultad para leer el español, pero no lo entiendo cuando la gente habla muy rápido o con un acento regional fuerte.

– ¿Practicas español con un nativo?
– No, prefiero ir a clase.

No te preocupes por los errores de ortografía de momento.

Writing & reading

accent   **el acento**
   acute accent   **el acento agudo**
   tilde   **la tilde**
alphabet   **el alfabeto**
alphabetically   **alfabéticamente**
in bold   **en negrita, en negrilla**
Braille   **el Braille**
character   **el carácter**
code   **el código**
I correspond (with)   **estoy en correspondencia (con)**
correspondence   **la correspondencia**
I decipher   **descifro**
graphic   **gráfico**
handwriting   **la escritura a mano, la letra**
ideogram(me)/ideograph   **el ideograma**
illiterate   **analfabeto**
italic   **en bastardilla**
I italicize   **pongo en bastardilla**
letter *(alphabet)*   **la letra**
literate   **alfabetizado, que sabe leer y escribir**
literature   **la literatura**
note   **la nota**

paragraph   **el párrafo**
philology   **la filología**
philologist   **el filólogo**
pictograph   **pictográfico**
I print   **imprimo**
I read   **leo**
reading   **la lectura**
reading skills   **las aptitudes de lectura**
I re-write   **escribo de nuevo**
scribble   **los garabatos**
I scribble   **garrapateo, hago garabatos**
sign   **el signo**
I sign   **firmo**
signature   **la firma**
I spell   **deletreo**
spelling   **la ortografía**
text   **el texto**
I transcribe   **transcribo**
transcription   **la transcripción**
I underline   **subrayo**
I write   **escribo**
writing   **la escritura**
writing skills   **las aptitudes para la escritura**
written language   **el lenguaje escrito**

Which languages have a Slavonic alphabet?

¿Qué idiomas tienen un alfabeto eslavo?

Portuguese spoken here.

Aquí se habla portugués.

Do you have any previous knowledge of Russian?

¿Tienes algún conocimiento previo de ruso?

– Which is the easiest language to learn for an English speaker? – Spanish, of course!

– ¿Cuál es el idioma más fácil de aprender para un hablante inglés? – ¡El español, por supuesto!

Education

22a General terms

achievement **el éxito, el logro**
admission **la admisión**
   I am admitted to school **estoy admitido en el colegio**
absent **ausente**
age group **el grupo etario, [el grupo de la misma edad]**
I am away **estoy ausente**
aptitude **la aptitud, la facilidad**
I analyze **analizo, estudio**
answer **la respuesta**
I answer (someone) **respondo, contesto (a alguien)**
   I answer (a question) **respondo (a una pregunta)**
I ask **pregunto**
I attend (a school) **voy (al colegio)**
boring **aburrido**
career **la carrera, la profesión**
careers advice **el asesoramiento sobre la profesión**
careers teacher **el profesor encargado del asesoramiento profesional de los alumnos**
careers education **la guía vocacional/profesional**
caretaker **el cuidador, el bedel, el vigilante, el conserje**
I catch up **me pongo al día**
chapter **el capítulo**
cheat **el tramposo, el petardista**
class **la clase**
class council **la reunión de delegados de clase**
class representative **el delegado de la clase**
class teacher **el profesor**
class trip **el viaje escolar, el viaje con la clase**

club **el club, el grupo**
I complete **completo**
comprehension **la comprensión**
compulsory schooling **el colegio obligatorio**
computer **el ordenador, [el computador]**
concept **el concepto**
I copy (out) **copio**
copy **la copia**
course **el curso**
deputy head **el subdirector**
detention **la detención**
   I am in detention **estoy castigado**
difficult **difícil**
discuss **la discusión**
easy **fácil**
education **la educación**
educational system **el sistema educativo**
I encourage **aliento, doy ánimo**
essay **la redacción, el ensayo**
example **el ejemplo**
excellent **excelente**
favourite/favorite **el favorito**
favourite/favorite subject **la asignatura favorita**
I forget **olvido**
governing body **la junta directiva**
holidays **las vacaciones**
headteacher/principal **el director**
homework **la tarea, los deberes**
instruction **la instrucción, la enseñanza**
interesting **interesante**
I learn **aprendo**
I leave **salgo, dejo**
lesson **la lección, la clase**

lesson *(chapter)* **la lección**
lessons **las lecciones**
I listen **escucho, oigo**
local education authority **la delegación/la administración/el consejo local de educación**
I look at **miro, considero**
I misunderstand **entiendo mal, no entiendo bien, malinterpreto**
mixed ability group **el grupo de alumnos con capacidades diversas**
modular **modular**
module **el módulo**
oral **oral**
outdoor **exterior**
out of school activity **la actividad fuera del colegio**
parents' evening **la tarde de reunión de los padres**
pastoral care **la tutoría**
I play truant **hago rabona, hago novillos, me ausento**
I praise **alabo**
principal **principal**
project **el proyecto**
punctual **puntual**
I punctuate **escribo los signos de puntuación**
punctuation mark **el signo de interrogación**
I punish **castigo**
punishment **el castigo**
pupil **el alumno**
qualification **el título, los requisitos**
I qualify **saco un título, lleno los requisitos**
question **la pregunta**
I question **pregunto**
I read **leo**
reading **la lectura**
I repeat a year **repito un curso**
report **las notas, el certificado escolar**
research **la investigación**

I research **investigo**
resources centre/center **el centro de servicios escolares/de recursos**
scheme of work **el esquema de trabajo, el plan de trabajo**
school book **el libro escolar**
school council **el consejo escolar**
school-friend/pal **el amigo del colegio**
set **el grupo**
school sets **los grupos, las clases**
skill **la aptitud**
specialist teacher **el profesor especializado**
spelling **la ortografía**
staff **el personal**
I stay in **me quedo en casa**
I stay down *(year)* **repito curso**
strict **estricto**
I study **estudio**
sum **la suma**
I summarize **resumo, sumarizo**
I swot **empollo**
task **el deber, la tarea**
I teach **enseño**
teacher **el profesor, el maestro**
teaching **la enseñanza**
term/semester **el trimestre**
I train **preparo, entreno**
training **la preparación**
I translate **traduzco**
translation **la traducción**
tutor **el tutor**
I understand **entiendo, comprendo**
understanding **el entendimiento, la comprensión**
unit (of work) **la unidad de trabajo**
I work **trabajo, estudio**
I work hard **estudio mucho**
work experience **la experiencia laboral**
I write **escribo**
written (work) **escrito**

22b School

blackboard   **la pizarra**
black-out   **el bloqueo**
book   **el libro**
break   **el recreo**
briefcase   **la maleta del colegio, el maletín**
canteen   **el bar del colegio, la cantina del colegio**
cassette (audio/video)   **la cinta**
cassette recorder   **la grabadora**
classroom   **la clase**
computer   **el ordenador, [el computador]**
desk   **el pupitre**
dormitory   **el dormitorio**
gym(nasium)   **el gimnasio**
headphone   **el auricular, [el audífono]**
interactive TV   **la televisión interactiva**
laboratory   **el laboratorio**
(language) laboratory   **el laboratorio (de idiomas)**
library   **la biblioteca**
lunch-hour   **el descanso para comer, la hora de almuerzo**
note   **la nota**
office   **la oficina**
playground   **el patio de juego**
radio   **la radio**
ruler   **la regla**
slide   **la diapositiva**

satellite TV   **la television por satélite**
school hall   **la sala**
schoolbag/satchel/bookbag   **la maleta del colegio**
sports field   **el campo de deportes**
sports hall   **el polideportivo**
staffroom   **el cuarto de profesores**
studio   **el estudio**
timetable   **el horario**
video   **el vídeo**
  video (adj)   **de vídeo**
video camera   **la cámara de vídeo**
video cassette   **la cinta de vídeo**
video recorder   **el aparato de vídeo**
workshop   **el taller**

Type of school

boarding school   **el internado**
boarder   **el interno**
comprehensive school   **el colegio de enseñanza secundaria**
day school   **el colegio (que no es internado)**
further education   **la formación profesional, la educación media**
grammar school   **el colegio de segunda enseñanza, el instituto**
infant/nursery school   **el colegio infantil, ia guardería**

– At what age do children start school?
– They have to go to school when they are six.

Our son already goes to the kindergarten and is looking forward to school.

– **¿A qué edad empiezan los niños la escuela?**
– **Tienen que ir a la escuela a la edad de seis años.**

Nuestro hijo ya va al jardín de infancia, y tiene ganas de ir a la escuela.

playgroup **el grupo de juego**
primary **primario**
primary/elementary school **el colegio de enseñanza primaria**
school **el colegio, la escuela**
school type **el tipo de colegio**
of school age **en edad escolar**
secondary **secundario**
secondary school/junior high school **el colegio de enseñanza secundaria**
secondary modern school/senior high school **el colegio de enseñanza secundaria**
sixth form/senior year **el último curso de la enseñanza secundaria**
special school **el colegio especial**
technical school **el colegio técnico**

Classroom commands

Answer the question! **¡Contesta la pregunta!**
Be careful! **¡Ten cuidado!**
Be quiet! **¡Cállate!**
Be quick! **¡Sé rápido!**
Bring me your work! **¡Tráeme tu cuaderno!**
Clean the blackboard! **¡Limpia la pizarra!**
Close the door! **¡Cierra la puerta!**
Come here! **¡Ven aquí!**
Come in! **¡Entra!**

Copy these sentences! **¡Copia estas frases!**
Do your homework! **¡Haz la tarea!**
Don't talk/chatter! **¡No charles!**
Go out! **¡Salte fuera!, ¡Fuera!**
Learn by heart! **¡Aprende de memoria!**
Listen carefully! **¡Escucha con atención!, ¡Escucha atentamente!**
Make less noise! **¡No hagas tanto ruido!**
Make notes! **¡Toma apuntes!, ¡Coge apuntes!**
Open the window! **¡Abre la ventana!**
Pay attention! **¡Atiende!**
Read the text! **¡Lee el texto!**
Show me your book! **¡Enséñame tu cuaderno!**
Sit down! **¡Siéntate!**
Stand up! **¡Levántate!**
Tick the boxes! **¡Rellena los cuadrados!**
Work in pairs! **¡Trabajad en parejas!**
Work in groups! **¡Trabajad en grupos!**
Write it down! **¡Escribe esto!**
Write out in rough! **¡Escribe en sucio!, ¡Escribe en borrador!**
Write out in neat/neatly! **¡Escribe con buena letra!, ¡Escribe claramente!**

Our daughter goes to the primary school/elementary school. She reads to her teacher every day and can read well now.

Nuestra hija va a la escuela primaria. Lee a su maestra todos los días y ya sabe leer bien.

– Do you move up a class every year?
– No, last year I had to stay down a year.

– ¿Subes una clase todos los años [un grado cada año]?
– No, el año pasado tuve que repetir el curso.

22c School subjects & examinations

Subjects

arithmetic **la aritmética**
art **el arte**
biology **la biología**
business studies **los estudios empresariales/de negocios**
careers education **la formación profesional**
chemistry **la química**
commerce **el comercio**
compulsory subject **la asignatura obligatoria**
computer studies **la informática**
design technology **la tecnología de diseño**
economics **la economía**
English **el inglés**
foreign language **el idioma extranjero**
geography **la geografía**
gymnastics **la gimnasia**
history **la historia**
home economics **la economía doméstica**
information technology **la informática**

Italian **el italiano**
Latin **el latín**
law **el derecho**
main subject **la asignatura principal**
mathematics **las matemáticas**
metalwork **el trabajo con metal**
music **la música**
option(al subject) **la asignatura optativa**
philosophy **la filosofía**
physical education **la educación física**
physics **la física**
religious education **la educación religiosa**
science **la ciencia, las ciencias**
sex education **la educación sexual**
social studies **los estudios sociales**
sociology **la sociología**
Spanish **el español**
sport **el deporte**
    type of sport **el tipo de deporte**
subject **la asignatura**

– Which school do you go to?
– I go to the comprehensive/high school. I enjoy it a lot. There are lots of clubs and activities.
– Which is your favourite subject?
– I like maths/math, but prefer physics.
My favourite/favorite subject is PE.

I don't like history, it is so boring.

I'm good at English, since I did an exchange.
I work very hard at it.

– **¿A qué escuela vas?**
– **Voy al instituto. Me gusta mucho. Hay muchos clubs y actividades.**
– **¿Qué asignatura prefieres?**
– **Me gustan las matemáticas, pero prefiero la física.**
Mi asignatura preferida es la educación física.

No me gusta la historia, es tan aburrida.

Estoy fuerte en inglés, desde que hice un intercambio.
Trabajo mucho en inglés.

subsidiary subject   **la asignatura secundaria**
technical drawing   **el dibujo técnico**
technology   **la tecnología**
textiles   **los estudios textiles**
woodwork   **el trabajo con madera**

Examinations

I assess   **evalúo, corrijo**
assessment   **la evaluación**
certificate   **el certificado, las notas**
degree   **el grado**
diploma   **el diploma, el título**
dissertation   **el proyecto de fin de carrera, [la tesis]**
distinction   **la matrícula de honor**
doctorate   **el doctorado**
examination   **el examen**
   external   **externo, exterior**
   final   **final**
grade   **la nota**
I grade   **califico, doy nota a**
graduate (engineer)   **el licenciado (en ingeniería)**
listening comprehension   **la comprensión de escucha**
mark   **la nota**
mark system   **el sistema de notas**

masters   **el título de master**
merit   **el mérito**
oral   **oral**
point   **el punto**
post-graduate course   **el curso de post-licenciado, [el curso de posgrado]**
reading comprehension   **la comprensión de textos**
I pass (an exam)   **apruebo**
I sit/take an exam   **me presento a un examen**
I test   **examino**
test   **el examen, el test, la prueba**
thesis   **la tesis**
trainee   **el aprendiz, el estudiante**
written test   **el examen escrito**

Marks

very good   **sobresaliente**
good   **notable**
satisfactory   **bien, satisfactorio**
pass   **aprobado**
poor   **insuficiente**
uncertified   **muy deficiente**

Here are your marks!
Well done! Isabel, you have done excellent work.
Teodoro, you will need to work harder. Your spelling is very poor.

Anna, this is very satisfactory, but please improve your handwriting. Your work is so sloppy.

Next month we are having another test. It will count towards your final grade.

¡Aquí tenéis vuestras notas!
¡Bravo! Isabel, tu trabajo es sobresaliente.
Teodoro, tendrás que trabajar más. Tu ortografía es muy deficiente.

Ana, esto es muy satisfactorio, pero haz lo que puedas para mejorar tu escritura. Tu trabajo es tan descuidado.

El mes que viene haremos otra prueba/evaluación. Se incluirá en vuestra nota final.

EDUCATION

22d Further and higher education

adult **de adultos**
adult education **la educación de adultos**
alumni **los alumnos**
apprentice **el aprendiz**
apprenticeship **el aprendizaje**
chair *(university)* **la cátedra**
college **el colegio universitario**
 college of further education **el colegio de formación profesional**
 college of higher education **el colegio universitario**
course of study **el curso**
diploma **el diploma, el título**
faculty **la facultad**
further education **la formación profesional**
hall of residence/residence hall **la residencia de estudiantes**
in-service training **el cursillo de formación de profesorado**
lecture **la clase, la conferencia**
lecture hall **el aula, el salón de conferencias**

lecturer **el profesor universitario**
masters degree **el título de master**
part-time education **la educación a tiempo parcial/de medio tiempo**
polytechnic **el politécnico**
postgraduate/graduate **licenciado**
practical **la clase práctica**
principal **el director**
professor/college professor **el profesor universitario, el catedrático**
quota *(for university entry)* **el cupo**
research **la investigación**
retraining **la reeducación, la recapacitación**
I retrain **hago un curso de reeducación**
scholarship *(grant)* **la beca, la ayuda escolar**
seminar **el seminario**
student **el/la estudiante**

We have increased the number of universities and are aiming for a broader provision.

Hemos aumentado el número de universidades, y aspiramos a conseguir una provisión más amplia.

The technical colleges now belong to the university sector and we now speak of a comprehensive university.

Los colegios técnicos ya pertenecen al sector universitario, y ahora nos referimos a una universidad abierta.

The length of course is four years (eight semesters).

La duración del curso es de cuatro años.

Financial support is of the greatest importance. Many students get a state grant.

El apoyo económico es muy importante. Muchos estudiantes reciben una beca del estado.

Many students apply for places but they can not all be admitted.

Muchos estudiantes solicitan puestos, pero no se les puede admitir a todos.

student council   **la junta de delegados de clase**
student grant   **la beca de estudios**
student union   **el sindicato de estudiantes, la asociación de estudiantes**
teacher training college   **la escuela de magisterio**
technical college   **el colegio técnico**
university/college   **la universidad**
university entrance qualification   **el certificado de selectividad, [el exámen de clasificación]**

Faculties & departments

accountancy/accounting   **la contabilidad**
architecture   **la arquitectura**
business management   **la organización de negocios**
catering   **la hostelería**
classics   **las clásicas, los clásicos**
civil engineering   **la ingeniería civil**
commerce   **el comercio**
construction   **la construcción**

education   **la educación**
electronics   **la electrónica**
electrical engineering   **la ingeniería eléctrica**
economics   **las ciencias económicas**
engineering   **la ingeniería**
environmental sciences   **las ciencias del medioambiente**
history of art   **la historia del arte**
hotel management   **la dirección hotelera**
languages   **los idiomas**
law   **el derecho**
leisure and tourism   **el turismo**
literature   **la literatura**
mechanical engineering   **la ingeniería mecánica**
medicine   **la medicina**
pharmacy   **la farmacia**
nuclear science   **la ciencia nuclear**
office skills   **el secretariado**
philosophy   **la filosofía**
psychology   **la psicología**
sociology   **la sociología**
theology   **la teología**

There is now an entrance restriction.

Ahora la entrada tiene restricciones.

The right to a place depends on marks in the COU exams.

El derecho a un puesto depende de las notas obtenidas en los exámenes de COU.

They require particularly high marks/grades for medicine.

Se exigen notas especialmente altas para poder estudiar Medicina.

Our results are always outstanding.

Nuestros resultados siempre son sobresalientes.

Many students want vocational/job qualifications.

Muchos estudiantes quieren sacar títulos profesionales.

They can easily transfer between courses.

Pueden cambiar fácilmente los cursos.

Science: the changing world

23a Scientific study & life sciences

Scientific study

academic paper   **el artículo académico, [la ponencia]**
I analyze   **analizo**
analysis   **el análisis**
authentic   **auténtico**
Bunsen burner   **el mechero Bunsen**
I challenge   **desafío**
I check   **compruebo, reviso**
classification   **la clasificación**
I classify   **clasifico**
control   **control**
I discover   **discubro**
discovery   **el discubrimiento**
(electron) microscope   **el microscopio (electrónico)**
experiment   **el experimento**
I experiment   **experimento**
flask   **el frasco, el matraz**
hypothesis   **la hipótesis**
I identify   **identifico**
I investigate   **investigo**
I invent   **invento**

invention   **el invento**
laboratory   **el laboratorio**
material   **el material**
I measure   **mido**
measurement   **la medición**
I observe   **observo**
origin   **el origen**
pipette   **la pipeta**
process   **el proceso**
research   **la investigación**
I research   **investigo**
result   **el resultado**
I solve *(problem)*   **resuelvo**
test   **la prueba**
I test   **compruebo**
test-tube   **el tubo de ensayo**
theory   **la teoría**
I transfer   **transfiero**

Biology

bacteria   **la bacteria**
botanical   **botánico**
I breathe   **respiro**
cell   **la célula**

The researcher took a sample, mounted it on a slide and put it under the microscope for examination.

La investigadora tomó una muestra, la fijó en una platina y la puso debajo del microscopio para examinarla.

All the results from the experiments support her hypothesis.

Todos los resultados de los experimentos apoyan su hipótesis.

chlorophyll **la clorofila**
it circulates **circula**
decay **la decadencia**
decline **el descenso, la disminución**
it declines **desciende**
it excretes **excreta**
excretion **la excreción**
it feeds **alimenta**
food chain **el ciclo alimenticio, la cadena alimenticia**
gene **el gen, el gene**
genetic **genético**
genetic disorder **la alteración genética**
it grows **crece**
growth **el crecimiento**
habitat **el hábitat**
it inherits **hereda**
membrane **la membrana**
it mutates **se transforma, cambia**
nucleus **el núcleo**
organic **orgánico**
organism **el organismo**
photosynthesis **la fotosíntesis**
population **la población**
it reproduces **se reproduce**
respiration **la respiración**
sensitivity **la sensibilidad**
survival **la sobrevivencia**
it survives **sobrevive**
virus **el virus**

Medical science & research

cosmetic/plastic surgery **la cirugía plástica**
DNA **el ADN**
donor **el donante**
embryo **el embrión**
embryo research **la investigación embrionaria**
ethical consideration **la consideración ética**
experiments on animals **los experimentos con animales**
hereditary illness **la enfermedad hereditaria**
IVF (in vitro fertilisation) **FIV (la fertilización/fecundación in vitro)**
I justify **justifico**
microorganism **el microorganismo**
organ transplant **el transplante de órgano**
pacemaker **el marcapasos**
I permit **permito**
recipient **el recipiente**
I reject *(organ)* **rechazo**
risk **el riesgo**
I risk **me arriesgo**
survival rate **la tasa de sobrevivencia**
test-tube baby **el niño probeta**
transplant **el transplante**
X-ray **el rayo X**

A girl of seventeen was today given a new heart in a transplant operation which lasted ten hours.

A una chica de diecisiete le dieron hoy un nuevo corazón, en una operación de transplante que duró diez horas.

Research on human embryo tissue is likely to remain highly controversial.

Los trabajos de investigación sobre los tejidos de embrión humano probablemente serán siempre una cuestión muy controvertida.

23b Physical sciences

Chemistry	Physics & mechanics
acid **el ácido**	it accelerates **acelera**
air **el aire**	acceleration **la aceleración**
alkali **el álcali**	acoustics **la acústica**
alkaline **alcalino**	artificial **artificial**
I analyze **analizo**	automatic **automático**
I calculate **calculo**	ball-bearing **la bola**
chemical **químico**	boiling-point **el punto de**
compound **el componente**	**ebullición**
composition **la composición**	circuit **el circuito**
it dissolves (in water) **se disuelve**	cog **el diente, la rueda dentada**
(en agua)	conservation **la conservación, la**
element **el elemento**	**preservación**
emulsion **la emulsión**	density **la densidad**
equation **la ecuación**	dial **la esfera, el dial**
gas **el gas**	distance **la distancia**
inorganic **inorgánico**	energy **la energía**
insoluble **insoluble**	it expands **se expande**
liquid **el líquido**	fibre/fiber **la fibra**
liquid (adj) **líquido**	force **la fuerza**
Litmus paper **el papel de tornasol**	it freezes **se congela**
matter **la materia**	formula **la fórmula**
metal **el metal**	freezing-point **el punto de**
natural gas **el gas natural**	**congelación**
opaque **opaco**	friction **la fricción, el rozamiento**
it oxydizes **oxida**	gauge (measuring) **el calibrador,**
periodic table **la tabla periódica**	**el indicador**
physical **físico**	gear **el engranaje**
pure **puro**	gravity **la gravedad**
it reacts **reacciona**	I heat **caliento**
reaction **la reacción**	heat **el calor**
salt **la sal**	heat loss **la pérdida de calor**
solid **el sólido**	laser **ei láser**
solid (adj) **sólido**	laser beam **el rayo láser**
soluble **soluble**	lever **la palanca**
solution **la solución**	light **la luz**
stable **estable**	light beam **el rayo de luz, el haz**
substance **la sustancia**	**de luz**
transparent **transparente**	lubricant **el lubricante**

Water has a boiling point of 100 degrees centigrade.	**El agua tiene un punto de ebullición de 100 grados centígrados.**

machinery **la maquinaria, el mecanismo**
magnetism **el magnetismo**
magneto **la magneto**
mass **la masa, el peso**
mechanics **la mecánica**
mechanical **mecánico**
mechanism **el mecanismo**
metallurgy **la metalurgia**
microwave **la microonda**
mineral **el mineral**
missile **el misil**
model **el modelo**
motion **el movimiento**
observation **la observación**
I operate *(machinery)* **manejo**
operational **operacional**
optics **la óptica**
pressure **la presión**
property **la propiedad**
proportional **proporcional**
ray **el rayo**
reflection **la reflexión**
refraction **la refracción**
relativity **la relatividad**
resistance **la resistencia**
resistant **resistente**
robot **el robot, el autómata**
I sort **clasifico**
sound **el sonido**
speed **la velocidad**
structure **la estructura**
synthetic **sintético**
temperature **la temperatura**
theory **la teoría**
time **el tiempo**
transmission **la transmisión**
turbine **la turbina**
vapour/vapor **el vapor**
it vibrates **vibra**
vibration **la vibración**

wave **la onda**
long waves **las ondas largas**
medium/short waves **las ondas medias/cortas**
wavelength **la longitud de onda**
it works **funciona**

Electricity

battery *(large)* **la batería**
battery *(small)* **la pila**
charge **la carga**
I charge the battery **cargo la batería**
current **la corriente**
electrical **eléctrico**
electricity **la electricidad**
electrode **el electrodo**
electron **el electrón**
electronic **electrónico**
electronics **la electrónica**
positive **positivo**
negative **negativo**
voltage **el voltaje**

Nuclear physics

atom **el átomo**
atomic **atómico**
it emits **emite**
fission **la fisión, la escisión**
fusion **la fusión**
molecular **molecular**
molecule **la molécula**
neutron **el neutrón**
nuclear **nuclear**
nuclear energy **la energía nuclear**
nucleus **el núcleo**
particle **la partícula**
proton **el protón**
quantum theory **la teoría cuántica**
radiation **la radiación**
reactor **el reactor**

What's the voltage of this equipment?

¿Cuál es el voltaje de este aparato?

23c The earth & space

Geology & minerals

bauxite **la bauxita**
carbon-dating **la prueba del carbono**
chalk **la creta**
chalky **cretoso**
clay **la arcilla**
diamond **el diamante**
I excavate **excavo**
exploration **la exploración**
geologist **el geólogo**
geology **la geología**
gemstone **la gema**
granite **el granito**
graphite **el grafito**
layer **la capa**
lime **la cal**
limestone **la piedra caliza**
loam **la marga**
marble **el mármol**
mine **la mina**
I mine **trabajo en la mina**
ore **la mena, el mineral**
quartz **el cuarzo**
quarry **la cantera**
raw materials **las materias primas**
sand **la arena**
sandstone **la piedra arenisca**
sediment **el sedimento**
silica **la sílice**
slate **la pizarra**
soil **la tierra, el suelo**
stalactite **la estalactita**
stalagmite **la estalagmita**

Energy & fuels

atomic energy **la energía atómica**
coal **el carbón**
concentration **la concentración**
coolant **el refrigerante**
energy **la energía**
energy conservation **la conservación de la energía**
energy consumption **el consumo de energía**
energy needs **las necesidades energéticas**
energy saving **el ahorro de energía**
energy source **la fuente de energía**
fossil fuels **el combustible fósil**
fuel **el carburante, el combustible**
fuel consumption **el consumo de combustible**
it generates **genera, produce**
geothermal energy **la energía geotérmica**
hydro-electric dam **la presa hidroeléctrica**
hydro-electric power **la fuerza hidroeléctrica**
natural gas **el gas natural**
nuclear energy **la energía nuclear**
nuclear power station **la central nuclear**
nuclear reactor **el reactor nuclear**
oil **el petróleo**
oil production **la producción de petróleo**
oil-producing countries **los países productores de petróleo**
ozone layer **la capa de ozono**
petroleum **el petróleo**
solar cell **la célula solar**
solar energy **la energía solar**
I strike oil **descubro un yacimiento de petróleo**
thermal energy **la energía térmica**
wave power **la energía de las ondas**
tidal power station **la planta colectora de energía de las mareas**
wind energy/power **la energía eólica**

➤ PRECIOUS STONES App.9c; ELECTRICITY 23b; POLLUTION 24e

Space

asteroid   **el asteroide**
big-bang theory   **la teoría del big-bang**
black hole   **el agujero negro**
eclipse   **el eclipse**
it eclipses   **eclipsa**
galactic   **galáctico**
galaxy   **la galaxia**
gravitational pull   **la fuerza de atracción planetaria, la fuerza de gravedad**
the heavens   **los cielos**
light year   **el año luz**
meteorite   **el meteorito**
moon   **la luna**
   full moon   **la luna llena**
   new moon   **la luna nueva**
nova   **la nova**
orbit   **la órbita**
planet   **el planeta**
shooting-star   **la estrella fugaz**
solar system   **el sistema solar**
solstice   **el solsticio**
space   **el espacio**
star   **la estrella**
sun   **el sol**
sunspot   **la mancha solar**
universe   **el universo**

Space research & travel

antenna   **la antena**
astrologer   **el astrólogo**
astronomer   **el astrónomo**
astronaut   **el astronauta**
cosmonaut   **el cosmonauta**
dish antenna   **la antena parabólica**
I launch   **lanzo**
launch pad   **la plataforma de lanzamiento**
lunar module   **el módulo lunar**
moon-buggy   **el vehículo lunar**
moon-walk   **el paseo sobre la superficie lunar**
observatory   **el observatorio**
orbit   **la órbita**
planetarium   **el planetario**
it re-enters   **vuelve a entrar, reentra**
relativity   **la relatividad**
rocket   **el cohete**
rocket fuel   **el combustible del cohete**
satellite   **el satélite**
   communications   **de comunicaciones**
   spy   **espía**
   weather   **meteorológico**
sky lab   **el laboratorio espacial**
space flight   **el vuelo espacial**
space probe   **la prueba espacial**
space shuttle   **el transbordador espacial**
space walk   **el paseo espacial**
spacecraft   **la nave espacial**
spacesuit   **el traje de astronauta**
stratosphere   **la estratosfera**
telescope   **el telescopio**
time-warp   **el salto en el tiempo**
touchdown on land   **el aterrizaje**
   on sea   **el amerizaje**
   on moon   **el alunizaje**
zodiac   **el zodíaco**

By studying the light received from stars many millions of light years away, scientists hope to discover the origins of the universe.

Los científicos esperan descubrir el orígen del universo por medio de sus estudios de la luz que nos llega de estrellas que están a muchos millones de años luz.

The Environment: the natural world

24a Geography

archipelago **el archipiélago**
area **el área, la zona**
bank (river) **la ribera (del río)**
bay **la bahía**
beach **la playa**
bog **el pantano, la ciénaga**
bottom **el fondo**
canyon **el cañón**
clean **limpio**
cliff **el acantilado, el precipicio**
coast **la costa**
coastline **el litoral**
continent **el continente**
coppice/copse **el soto, el bosquecillo**
country **el país**
    in the country **en el campo**
countryside **el campo**
creek **la cala, la ensenada**
dangerous **peligroso**
deep **profundo**
delta **el delta**
desert **el desierto**
dirty **sucio**
dune **la duna**
earth tremor **el temblor de tierra**
earthquake **el terremoto**
equator **el ecuador**
equatorial **ecuatorial**
eruption **la erupción**
it erupts **erupciona**
escarpment **la escarpa**
estuary **el estuario**
field **el campo**
fjord **el fiordo**
flat **plano, llano**
it flows **fluye, discurre**
foothills **las estribaciones**
forest **el bosque**
friendly **no perjudicial**

geographical **geográfico**
geography **la geografía**
geyser **el geiser**
globe **el globo terráqueo, la esfera terrestre**
gradient **la pendiente, la inclinación**
hemisphere **el hemisferio**
high **alto**
hill **la colina**
incline/slope **la inclinación, la pendiente**
it is situated **está situado**
island **la isla**
jungle **la jungla**
lake **el lago**
land **la tierra**
it is located **está situado, se localiza en**
location **la situación, la localización**
map **el mapa**
marsh **el pantano, la ciénaga, la marisma**
meridian **el meridiano**
mountain **la montaña**
mountain range **la cordillera**
national **nacional**
national park **el parque nacional**
nature **la naturaleza**
nice/pleasant **agradable**
ocean **el océano**
ocean floor **el fondo del mar**
peaceful **tranquilo, silencioso**
peak **el pico, la cumbre**
peninsula **la península**
plateau **la meseta, el altiplano**
pole **el polo**
province **la provincia**
reef **el arrecife**

region   **la región**
regional   **regional**
ridge   **la sierra, la cresta**
river   **el río**
riverbed   **el lecho del río**
rockpool   **la charca entre rocas**
sand   **la arena**
scenery   **el escenario, la vista**
sea   **el mar**
seaside   **el borde del mar**
shore   **la orilla del mar**
spring   **la fuente, el manantial**
steep   **escarpado, empinado**
steppe   **la estepa**
stream   **el arroyo, la corriente**
summit   **la cima, la cumbre**
tall   **alto, elevado**
territory   **el territorio**
top   **la cima, la cumbre**
the tropics   **los trópicos**
tundra   **la tundra**
unfriendly   **perjudicial**
valley   **el valle**
volcano   **el volcán**
water   **el agua** *(f)*
   fresh water   **el agua fresca/
   limpia**
   salt water   **el agua salada**
   sea water   **el agua de mar**
waterfall   **la catarata, el salto**
wood   **la madera, el bosque**

woodland   **el bosque, la región
   boscosa**
zenith   **el zénit**
zone   **la zona**

Man-made features

aqueduct   **el acueducto**
bridge   **el puente**
canal   **el canal**
capital (city)   **la capital**
city   **la ciudad**
country road   **la carretera
   secundaria, el camino**
dam   **la presa, la represa, el
   dique**
embankment   **el terraplén**
factory   **la fábrica**
farm   **la granja**
farmland   **las tierras de labranza**
hamlet   **la aldea, el caserío**
harbour/harbor   **el puerto**
industry   **la industria**
marina   **el puerto deportivo**
oasis   **el oasis**
reclaimed land   **la tierra ganada al
   mar**
reservoir   **el pantano, el embalse**
town   **la ciudad, el pueblo**
track   **el camino**
village   **la aldea, el pueblo**
well   **el pozo, el manantial**

The area was marshy and
unsuitable for development.

La zona no era apta para el
desarrollo por ser pantanosa.

The village is situated in a valley
about five kilometers/kilometers
north of a small provincial Chilean
town.

El pueblo está situado en un
valle a unos cinco kilómetros al
norte de una pequeña ciudad
provincial chilena.

The inhabitants of the small towns
at the foot of Everest were among
the poorest people in the world
before 1950.

Los habitantes de los pequeños
pueblos al pie del Everest
figuraban entre la gente más
pobre del mundo antes de 1950.

24b The animal world

Animals

animal   **el animal**
it barks   **ladra**
it bites   **muerde**
it bounds   **salta hacia delante**
it breeds   **cría**
budgerigar   **el periquito**
burrow   **la madriguera**
cage   **la jaula**
carnivore   **el carnívoro**
cat   **el gato**
it crawls   **anda a gatas**
den   **la guarida, la madriguera**
dog   **el perro**
I feed   **doy de comer, alimento**
it feeds   **alimenta**
food   **la comida, el alimento**
gerbil   **el gerbo**
goldfish   **el pez de colores**
guinea pig   **el conejo de indias, el curí**
habitat   **el hábitat**
hamster   **el hámster**
herbivore   **el herbívoro**
it hibernates   **hiberna**
it howls   **aúlla**
hut/hutch   **la conejera**
I keep a cat   **tengo un gato**
kitten   **el gatito**
lair   **el cúbil, la guarida**
it leaps   **salta**
litter   **la camada**

mammal   **el mamífero**
it miaows   **hace miau**
mouse   **el ratón**
omnivore   **el omnívoro**
pack   **la manada, la jauría**
predator   **el depredador**
prey   **la presa**
pet   **el animal doméstico**
puppy   **el perrito**
rabbit   **el conejo**
rabies   **la rabia**
reptile   **el reptil**
it roars   **ruge**
safari park   **el parque de safari**
it squeaks   **chilla**
I stroke   **acaricio**
tortoise   **la tortuga**
I walk *(the dog)*   **paseo**
wildlife park   **la reserva natural**
zoo   **el (jardín/parque) zoológico**

Birds

bird   **el pájaro**
it flies   **vuela**
flock   **la bandada**
it hovers   **permanece inmóvil en el aire**
it migrates   **migra, emigra**
nest   **el nido**
it nests   **anida**
it pecks at   **pica**
it sings   **canta**

Guinea pigs and hamsters are popular pets in Britain.	**Los conejillos de indias y los hámsteres figuran entre los animales domésticos más populares en Gran Bretaña.**
The campaign to save the whale is increasing in popularity.	**La campaña para salvar la ballena está ganando popularidad.**

Sealife/Waterlife

alligator	**el caimán**
anemone	**la anémona**
angling	**la pesca con caña**
coral	**el coral**
crab	**el cangrejo**
crocodile	**el cocodrilo**
dolphin	**el delfín**
fish	**el pez**
I fish	**pesco**
harpoon	**el arpón**
hook	**el anzuelo**
marine	**marino, marítimo**
mollusc	**el molusco**
net	**la red**
octopus	**el pulpo**
plankton	**el plancton**
rod	**la caña de pescar**
seal	**la foca**
shark	**el tiburón**
shoal	**el banco**
starfish	**la estrella de mar**
it swims	**nada**
turtle	**la tortuga marina**
whale	**la ballena**
whaling	**la pesca de ballenas**

Insects

ant	**la hormiga**
bee	**la abeja**
queen bee	**la abeja reina**
worker bee	**la abeja obrera**
bedbug	**el chinche**
beetle	**el escarabajo**

bug	**el insecto, el bicho**
butterfly	**la mariposa**
it buzzes	**zumba**
caterpillar	**la oruga**
cocoon	**el capullo**
cockroach	**la cucaracha**
cricket	**el grillo**
dragonfly	**la libélula**
flea	**la pulga**
fly	**la mosca**
grasshopper	**el chaltamontes, [el chapulín]**
hive	**la colmena**
insect	**el insecto**
invertebrate	**el invertebrado**
ladybird	**la mariquita**
larva	**la larva**
locust	**la langosta**
it metamorphoses	**metamorfosea**
mosquito	**el mosquito**
moth	**la polilla**
scorpion	**el escorpión**
silkworm	**el gusano de seda**
slug	**la babosa**
snail	**el caracol**
spider	**la araña**
it spins (a web)	**teje (una tela)**
it stings	**pica**
termite	**la termita**
tick	**la garrapata**
web	**la red**
wasp	**la avispa**
worm	**el gusano**

The panda is in danger of extinction in the wild, because the bamboo which it eats inexplicably dies away every 50 years.

Don't forget to walk the dog, feed the cat, and talk to the goldfish!

El panda corre riesgo de extinción en la selva, pues el bambú que come desaparece por completo cada 50 años sin que nadie sepa por qué.

¡No olvides de llevar al perro de paseo, de dar de comer al gato y de hablar al pez de colores!

24c Farming & gardening

Farm animals

bull **el toro**
cattle **el ganado**
chicken **el pollo**
cock/rooster **el gallo**
cow **la vaca**
it crows **canta, cacarea**
dairy *(adj)* **lácteo**
duck **el pato**
it eats **come**
feed **el alimento**
it feeds **se alimenta**
foal **el potro**
fodder **el pienso, el forraje**
food *(for animals)* **el alimento de los animales**
it gallops **galopa**
goat **la cabra**
goose **el ganso**
it grazes **pace, pasta**
it grunts **gruzñe**
horse **el caballo**
horseshoe **la herradura**
it kicks **da patadas**
kid **la cría**
I milk **ordeño**
it moos **muge**
it neighs **relincha**
ox **el buey**
it pecks **picotea**
pig **el cerdo**
pony **el poni, el caballito**
poultry **las aves**
produce **los productos agrícolas**
it quacks **hace cua-cua**
I ride *(a horse)* **monto**

I shear **esquilo**
sheep **la oveja**
sheep dog **el perro pastor de ovejas**
I slaughter **mato, sacrifico**
stallion **el semental**
it trots **trota**

On the farm

agricultural **agrario**
arable **arable, cultivable**
barn **la granja**
combine harvester **la coseadora, la segadora**
crop **el cultivo**
dairy **la quesería**
farm **la granja**
farmhouse **la casa de la granja**
farm labourer/laborer **el granjero**
farmyard **el patio de la granja**
fence **la valla, el seto, la cerca**
I groom **cepillo al caballo**
harvest **la cosecha**
I harvest **cosecho**
hay **el heno**
haybale **la bala de heno**
I irrigate **riego**
milk churn **la lechera**
milking machine **la ordeñadora**
pasture **el pasto**
pen **el corral**
pigsty **la porqueriza, la pocilga**
silage **el silo**
slaughterhouse **el matadero**
stable **el establo**
stud farm **la caballeriza**

In the developing countries, arable land is often owned by rich landlords.

En los países en desarrollo, la tierra cultivable a menudo es propiedad de propietarios ricos.

Agriculture & gardening

acorn **la bellota**
agriculture **la agricultura**
barley **la cebada**
it blooms **florece**
bloom **la flor**
bouquet **el ramo, el bouquet**
branch **el ramo**
bud **el capullo**
bulb **el bulbo**
bush **el arbusto**
cactus **el cactus**
compost **el abono**
corn **el trigo**
corn *(US)*/maize **el maíz**
I cultivate **cultivo**
cutting **el esqueje**
I dig **cavo**
ear **la espiga**
I fertilize **abono**
fertilizer **el fertilizante, el abono**
fir **el abeto**
flower **la flor**
it flowers **florece**
flowerpot **el tiesto, la maceta, [la malera]**
foliage **el follaje**
garden/yard **el jardín**
I gather **recojo**
grain **el grano**
grass **la hierba**
I grow **planto, cultivo**
it grows **crece**
hedge **el seto**
horticulture **la horticultura**
lawn **corto el césped**
leaf **la hoja**
maize **el maíz**

I mow **corto la hierba**
oats **la avena**
orchard **la huerta**
petal **el pétalo**
I pick **cojo, recojo**
pine **el pino**
pine-forest **el bosque de pinos**
I plant **planto**
plant **la planta**
pollen **el polen**
I reap **cosecho, recojo**
ripe **maduro**
it ripens **madura**
root **la raíz**
rotten **podrido**
rye **el centeno**
sap **la savia**
seed **la semilla**
sorghum **el sorgo**
species **la especie**
stalk **el tallo, la caña**
stamen **el estambre**
stem **el tallo**
thorn **la espina**
I transplant **transplanto**
tree **el árbol**
trunk **el tronco**
undergrowth **la maleza, el monte bajo**
vegetable(s) **las verduras**
vegetation **la vegetación**
I water **riego**
weeds **las malas hierbas**
I weed **mato las malas hierbas**
wheat **el trigo**
wild flower **la flor salvaje, la flor silvestre**
it wilts **se marchita**

Let's go for a walk in the country and stop at the old farmhouse. We'll probably see some new-born lambs in the fields.

Vámonos a dar un paseo en el campo hasta el cortijo viejo. Probablemente veremos unos corderos recién nacidos en los campos.

24d Weather

anticyclone **el anticiclón**
avalanche **la avalancha**
average temperature **la temperatura media**
bad weather **el mal tiempo**
bright **despejado, claro**
bright period **el periodo despejado**
centigrade **centígrado**
changeable **variable**
climate **el clima**
climatic **climático**
cloud **la nube**
clouded over **cubierto**
cloudless **despejado, sin nubes**
cloudy **nuboso**
cold **frío**
it is cold **hace frío**
cold front **el frente frío**
it is cool **hace fresco**
cyclone **el ciclón**
damp **húmedo**
degree **el grado**
   above zero **sobre cero**
   below zero **bajo cero**
depression **la depresión**

drizzle **el chirimiri, [la llovizna]**
it drizzles **llovizna**
drought **la sequía**
dry **seco**
dull weather **el tiempo gris**
it's fine **hace buen tiempo**
flash **el relámpago**
fog **la niebla**
it is foggy **está nuboso**
it's freezing **está helando**
frost **la helada, la escarcha**
frosty **helado**
gale **el vendaval, el ventarrón**
gale warning **el aviso de tormenta**
it's hailing **está granizando**
hailstones **el granizo**
heat **el calor**
heatwave **la ola de calor**
high pressure **la presión alta**
highest temperature **la temperatura máxima**
it's hot **hace calor**
ice **el hielo**
Indian summer **el verano de San Martín**
lightning **el relámpago, el rayo**

It will be cold over the whole country tomorrow, maximum temperatures 4-6 Celsius (39-43 Fahrenheit).

Mañana hará frío en todo el país, con una temperatura máxima de entre 4 y 6 grados Celsius.

Freezing fog patches in the Ebro valley should clear by midday.

Las zonas de niebla helada que se encuentran en la Cuenca del Ebro desaparecerán con toda probabilidad antes de mediodía.

Outlook for the weekend – very warm and sunny.

El pronóstico para el fin de semana – sol y mucho calor.

The whole country will be affected by rain, turning to sleet in the mountains.

El país entero será afectada por la lluvia, que caerá como aguanieve en las zonas montañosas.

low pressure **la presión baja**
lowest temperature **la temperatura mínima**
mild **suave**
mist **la bruma**
misty **brumoso**
monsoon **el monzón**
moon **la luna**
occluded front **el frente ocluso**
rain **la lluvia**
it's raining **está lloviendo**
rainy **lluvioso**
shade **la sombra**
it shines **brilla**
shower **el chaparrón**
snow **la nieve**
snowball **la bola de nieve**
snowdrift **la ventisca de nieve**
snowfall **la nevada**
snowflake **el copo de nieve**
snowman **el muñeco de nieve**
snow report *(for skiing)* **el pronóstico de la nieve**
it's snowing **está nevando**
snowstorm **la tormenta de nieve**
star **la estrella**
storm **la tormenta**
stormy **tormentoso**

sultry **bochornoso**
sun/sunshine **hace sol**
sunny day **un día de sol**
(daily) temperature **la temperatura diurna**
thunder **el trueno**
it's thunder **hay truenos**
thunderbolt **el rayo**
thunderstorm **la tormenta eléctrica/de rayos**
torrent **el torrente**
torrential **torrencial**
tropical **tropical**
warm **cálido**
warm front **el frente cálido**
weather **el tiempo**
weather conditions **las condiciones climáticas**
weather forecast **el pronóstico del tiempo**
weather report **el informe del tiempo**
wet **mojado, húmedo**
What's the weather like? **¿Cómo es el tiempo?**
wind **el viento**
windy **ventoso**

The monsoon is now well established over southeast Asia.

El monzón ya está establecido en la zona sureste de Asia.

The south of the country will be affected by tropical storms later tonight.

Durante la noche la zona sur del país se verá afectada por tormentas tropicales.

– Did you have a good holiday/vacation?
– Yes, apart from the weather.
– I thought it was always hot and sunny on the Mediterranean.
– So did I. We must have chosen the one week when it was cold and rainy.

– ¿Lo pasaste bien en tus vacaciones?
– Sí, aparte del tiempo.
– Creía que siempre hacía sol y calor en el Mediterráneo.
– Yo también. Sin duda escogimos la única semana en que hizo frío y llovió.

24e Pollution

balance of nature **el equilibrio natural**

it becomes extinct **se agota, se extingue**

conservation **la conservación, la preservación**

conservationist **el conservacionismo**

I conserve **conservo, preservo**

corrosion **la corrosión, la oxidación**

I consume **consumo**

consumption **el consumo**

I damage **daño, estropeo, perjudico**

damaging **perjudicial, dañoso**

danger (to) **peligro a**

I destroy **destruyo**

disaster **el desastre, el devastamiento**

disposal **el desecho**

I dispose of **desecho, [boto a la basura]**

I do without **no necesito, me arreglo sin**

ecology **la ecología**

ecosystem **el ecosistema**

emission **la emisión**

it emits **emite, desprende**

environment **el medioambiente**

exhaust pipe **el tubo de escape**

garbage/rubbish **la basura**

harmful **perjudicial**

I improve **mejoro**

industrial waste **los residuos industriales**

I insulate **aíslo**

litter **la basura, los desperdicios**

I poison **enveneno**

poison **el veneno, el tóxico**

pollutant **el contaminante**

I pollute **contamino**

pollution **la contaminación**

I predict **pronostico**

I protect **protejo**

recyclable **reciclable**

I recycle **reciclo**

recycled paper **el papel reciclado**

reprocessing **el reprocesamiento**

residue **el residuo**

it runs out **se agota, se acaba**

I throw away **tiro**

waste *(domestic)* **la basura**

waste disposal unit **el triturador de basuras**

waste products **los productos de desecho, los productos desechables**

The city council/municipality provides facilities for recycling glass, cans and newspapers.

El ayuntamiento [la alcadía] suministra facilidades para reciclar el vidrio, latas y periódicos.

Recent studies suggest the hole in the ozone layer will have serious consequences in the Northern Hemisphere.

Estudios recientes indican que el agujero en la capa de ozono tendrá consecuencias graves para el Hemisferio Norte.

On the earth

artificial fertilizer   **el fertilizante artificial**
bio-degradable   **biodegradable**
deforestation   **la deforestación**
natural resources   **los recursos naturales**
nature reserve   **la reserva natural, el parque natural**
nitrates   **los nitratos**
pesticide   **el pesticida**
radioactive   **radioactivo**
radioactive waste   **el residuo radioactivo**
rain forest   **la selva**
refuse   **el desperdicio, la basura, el desecho**
rubbish/garbage dump   **el vertedero de basura, [el relleno sanitario]**
scrap metal   **la chatarra**
soil erosion   **la erosión del suelo**
weedkiller   **el herbicida**

In the atmosphere

acid rain   **la lluvia ácida**
aerosol *(system)*   **el aerosol**
aerosol can   **el tubo de aerosol, la botella de aerosol**
air pollution   **la contaminación del aire**

atmosphere   **la atmósfera**
catalytic convertor   **el catalizador**
CFCs   **los clorofluorocarbonos**
emission (of gas)   **la emisión (de gas)**
incinerator   **el incinerador**
lead-free/unleaded petrol   **la gasolina sin plomo**
skin cancer   **el cáncer de piel**
I spray   **pulverizo, atomizo, rocío, riego**
waste gases   **los gases residuales**

In the rivers & seas

detergent   **el detergente**
drainage   **el drenaje, el desagüe**
drought   **la sequía**
flooding   **la inundación**
industrial effluent   **los residuos industriales**
oil slick   **la mancha de petróleo**
phosphates   **los fosfatos**
sea-level   **el nivel del mar**
sewage   **la depuración de las aguas**
water level   **el nivel del agua**
water supply system   **el sistema de abastecimiento de agua**
water supply   **el suministro de agua**

– Do you think this awful weather is normal? Don't you think it's because of global warming?

– Not really. It's just the normal cycle.
– Well, I think it's a combination of the greenhouse effect and nuclear testing in the last 40 years.

– **¿Crees que este tiempo horroroso es normal? ¿No crees que son resultado del recalentamiento mundial?**
– **No lo creo. Sólo se trata del ciclo normal.**
– **Bueno, yo creo que se trata de una combinación del efecto invernadero y de las pruebas nucleares que se hacen desde hace cuarenta años.**

Government & politics

25a Political life

I abolish **abolo, suprimo una ley**
act (of parliament) **la ley, la disposición parlamentaria**
administration **la administración**
I appoint **nombro, designo**
appointment **el nombramiento**
asylum-seeker **el solicitante de asilo político**
it becomes law **cobra fuerza de ley, entra en vigor**
bill **la proposición/el proyecto de ley**
I bring down **derroco, derribo**
citizen **el ciudadano**
civil disobedience **la resistencia pasiva**
civil servant **el funcionario público**
civil war **la guerra civil**
coalition **la coalición**
it comes into effect **entra en vigor, rige**
common **civil**
constitution **la constitución**
co-operation **la cooperación**
corruption **la corrupción**
county/region **la región**
coup **el golpe de estado**

crisis **la crisis**
debate **el debate**
decree **el decreto**
delegate **el delegado, el diputado**
I demonstrate **participo en la manifestación**
demonstration **la manifestación**
I discuss **discuto**
discussion **la discusión**
I dismiss **destituyo**
I dissolve **disuelvo**
I draw up *(a bill)* **redacto**
duty **el deber**
equality **la igualdad de oportunidades**
executive **el ejecutivo**
executive *(adj)* **ejecutivo**
foreign policy **la política exterior**
I form a pact with **pacto con**
freedom **la libertad**
freedom of speech **la libertad de expresión**
I govern **gobierno**
government **el gobierno**
I introduce (a bill) **presento (un proyecto de ley)**
judiciary **la judicatura**
law **el derecho, la ley**

The Prime Minister summoned the Cabinet to an emergency meeting.

El Primer Ministro convocó una reunión extraordinaria del Consejo de Ministros.

The Home Secretary/Minister of the Interior said the Government was determined to halt the rise in juvenile crime.

El Ministro del Interior dijo que el Gobierno estaba resuelto a parar la subida en el nivel del crimen juvenil.

➤ ELECTIONS 25b; INTERNATIONAL RELATIONS 27c; WAR 27a

I lead **lidero, encabezo**
legislation **la legislación**
legislature **la legislatura**
liberty **la libertad**
local affairs **los asuntos internos/locales**
local government **el gobierno local**
long-term **a largo plazo**
majority **la mayoría**
meeting **la reunión**
middle-class **la clase media**
ministry **el ministerio**
minority **la minoría**
nation **la nación**
national **nacional**
national flag **la bandera nacional**
Spanish national flag **la bandera roja y gualda**
I nationalize **nacionalizo**
I oppose **me opongo**
opposition **la oposición**
I organize **organizo**
I overthrow **derroco**
pact **el pacto**
I pass *(a bill)* **apruebo**
policy/politics **la política**
political **político**
power **el poder**
I privatize **privatizo**
I protest **protesto**
public **el público**
public *(adj)* **público**
public opinion **la opinión pública**
I ratify **ratifico**

reactionary **reaccionario**
I reform **reformo, dimito**
reform **la reforma**
I reject **rechazo**
I repeal *(an act)* **rechazo**
I represent **represento**
I repress **reprimo**
I resign **dimito**
responsible **responsable**
responsiblity **la responsabilidad**
reunification **la reunificación**
revolt **la revuelta, el levantamiento**
I rule **rijo, dispongo**
sanction **la sanción**
seat **el escaño**
short-term **a corto plazo**
solidarity **la solidaridad**
speech **el discurso**
state **el estado**
statesman **el hombre de estado**
I support **apoyo**
I take power **tomo el poder**
tax **el impuesto**
taxation **los impuestos**
term of office **la duración del cargo**
I throw out (a bill) **rechazo**
unconstitutional **inconstitucional**
unilateral **unilateral**
unity **la unidad**
veto **el veto**
I veto **veto**
welfare **el bienestar**
working class **la clase obrera**

The Lower House of Parliament/ Chamber voted on the question of immigration controls.

The Treasury promised to cut the proportion of national income taken in taxes to 30 per cent.

La Cámara Baja votó sobre la cuestión del control de inmigración.

El Ministerio de Hacienda prometió reducir a 30 por ciento la proporción de renta nacional recaudada en impuestos.

➤ SOCIAL ISSUES 12; THE ECONOMY 14

25b Elections & ideology

Elections

ballot **la votación**
ballot box **la urna electoral/de votos**
ballot paper **la papeleta de voto**
by-election **la elección parcial**
I hold an election **celebro una elección**
campaign **la campaña**
candidate **el candidato**
constituency **la circunscripción electoral**
count **el recuento, la cuenta**
I elect **elijo**
election **la elección**
electorate **el electorado**
I'm entitled to vote **tengo derecho a votar**
floating vote **el voto flotante**
general election **la votación general**
I go to the polls **voto**
I hold *(an election)* **celebro**
local elections **las elecciones regionales**
majority system **el sistema mayoritario**
opinion poll **el sondeo de opinión**
party **el partido**
poll **el sondeo**
primary **la primaria**
proportional system **el sistema proporcional**
recount **el recuento**

I recount **vuelvo a contar**
referendum **el referéndum**
right to vote **el derecho de voto, el derecho a votar**
seven-year term of office **el cargo de siete años de duración**
I stand for election **me presento a la elección**
suffrage **el sufragio**
swing **el desplazamiento, el movimiento**
universal suffrage **el sufragio universal**
vote **el voto**
I vote (for) **voto (por)**
voter **el votante**

Political ideology

anarchist **el anarquismo**
anarchy **la anarquía**
aristocracy **la aristocracia**
aristocratic **aristocrático**
capitalism **el capitalismo**
capitalist **capitalista**
centre/center ground **los partidos de centro**
communism **el comunismo**
communist **comunista**
conservatism **el conservadurismo, el conservatismo**
conservative **conservador**
democracy **la democracia**
democratic **democrático**

Presidential elections in the USA occur every four years.

Las elecciones presidenciales en los Estados Unidos se celebran cada cuatro años.

The voters went to the polls today; it was a record turn-out.

Los votantes acudieron a las urnas hoy; hubo un número récord de votantes.

dictator **el dictador**
dictatorship **la dictadura**
duke **el duque**
empire **el imperio**
emperor/empress **el emperador, la emperatriz**
extremist **extremista**
fascism **el fascismo**
fascist **fascista**
I gain independence **me independizo**
green party **el partido verde, el partido ecologista**
ideology **la ideología**
imperialism **el imperialismo**
imperialist **imperialista**
independence **la independencia**
independent **independiente**
king **el rey**
left **la izquierda**
left-wing **el ala izquierda**
liberal **liberal**
liberalism **el liberalismo**
marxism **el marxismo**
marxist **marxista**
monarchy **la monarquía**
nationalism **el nacionalismo**
nationalist **nacionalista**
patriotic **patriótico**
patriotism **el patriotismo**
prince **el príncipe**
princess **la princesa**
queen **la reina**
racism **el racismo**
racist **racista**
radicalism **el radicalismo**

radical **radical**
republic **la república**
republicanism **republicanismo**
revolutionary **el revolucionario**
right **la derecha**
right-wing **el ala derecha**
royal **real**
royalist **monárquico**
socialism **el socialismo**
socialist **el socialista**

Representatives & politicians

Chancellor **el canciller, el ministro**
congressman/woman **el diputado, la diputada, el/la congresista**
Foreign Minister/Secretary of State **el Ministro de asuntos exteriores**
head of state **el jefe del estado**
leader **el líder**
leader of the party/party leader **el líder del partido político**
mayor **el alcalde**
minister **el ministro**
Home Secretary/Minister of the Interior **el Ministro del interior**
politician **el político**
prefect **el subsecretario**
President **el presidente**
Prime Minister **el primer ministro**
senator **el senador**
Speaker **el presidente de la cámara/del Parlamento**
spokesperson **el/la portavoz**

An opinion poll gave the Democrats a two point lead over the Republicans.

Un sondeo atribuyó a los Demócratas una ventaja de dos puntos sobre los Republicanos.

In the local elections, the Socialist Party won a majority of seats on the town council.

En las elecciones locales, el Partido Socialista ganó una mayoría de escaños en el concejo municipal.

26 Crime & justice

26a Crime

accomplice   **el cómplice**
armed   **armado**
assault   **el asalto**
assault and battery   **el maltrato y la agresión física**
battered baby   **el bebé golpeado, el bebé maltratado**
burglar   **el ladrón**
burglary   **el robo, el allanamiento de morada**
I burgle/burglarize   **robo en la casa**
car theft   **el robo de coche**
 theft from car   **el robo desde el coche**
child abuse   **el abuso de menores**
I come to blows   **me peleo a golpes**
I commit   **cometo**
crime   **el crimen, el delito**
crime rate   **la tasa delictiva**
crime wave   **la ola de crimen, la ola criminal**
criminal   **el criminal, el delincuente**
 criminal *(adj)*   **criminal**
I deceive   **defraudo, engaño**

delinquency   **la delincuencia**
drug abuse   **el abuso de drogas**
drug addict   **el drogadicto**
drug barons   **los capos de la droga**
drug dealer/pusher   **el traficante de drogas, el camello**
drugs   **las drogas**
drug-trafficking   **el tráfico de drogas, el narcotráfico**
I embezzle   **desfalco, malverso**
embezzlement   **el desfalco, la malversación**
extortion   **la extorsión**
I fight   **peleo, lucho, riño**
fight   **la pelea, la lucha, la riña**
firearm   **el arma de fuego**
I forge *(banknote, signature)*   **falsifico**
forged   **falsificado**
forgery   **la falsificación**
fraud   **el fraude**
gang   **la banda**
gang warfare   **la guerra de las pandilllas**
grievous bodily harm   **los daños**

Members of the public have begun to give information to the police about the rape of two teenage girls by a gang in west Buenos Aires last week.

Miembros del público han empezado a dar información a la policía con respecto a la violación, la semana pasada, de dos chicas adolescentes por una pandilla en la zona del oeste de Buenos Aires.

---

corporales graves
gun **la pistola**
handbag snatching **el tirón del bolso**
handcuffs **las esposas**
Help! **¡Socorro!**
I hi-jack **secuestro (un avión)**
hi-jacker **el secuestrador aéreo**
hold-up **el atraco, el asalto**
hooker **la prostituta, la fulana**
hostage **el rehén**
illegal **ilegal**
I importune **importuno, molesto**
I injure/wound **hiero, causo heridas**
I joy ride **conduzco un coche robado**
joy riding **el robo de coches para la conducción temeraria**
I kidnap **rapto**
kidnapper **el raptor**
kidnapping **el rapto**
I kill **mato**
killer **el homicida**
knife **el cuchillo**
knifing **matar a cuchilladas**
legal **legal**
mafia **la mafia**
I mug **asalto**
mugger **el asaltador**
mugging **el asalto**
murder **el homicidio**
I murder **mato**

murderer **el asesino, el homicida**
I offend **cometo un delito**
pickpocket **el ratero, el carterista, el bolsista**
pickpocketing **el robo de cartera**
pimp **el proxeneta, el chulo, el alcahuete**
pimping **el proxenetismo, el chuleo**
poison **el veneno**
I poison **enveneno**
procuring **el proxenetismo, el chuleo**
prostitute **la prostituta, la fulana**
prostitution **la prostitución**
I rape **violo**
rape **la violación**
receiver **el receptador/receptor de bienes robados**
reprisals **la represalias**
shop-lifting **el hurto en las tiendas**
I steal **robo**
stolen goods **los bienes robados, las cosas robadas**
terrorist **el terrorista**
torture **la tortura**
thief **el ladrón**
trafficking **el tráfico ilegal**
I traffick **trafico**
underworld **los fondos bajos, los bajos fondos**
victim **la víctima**

Pablo Escobar, the world's most infamous drug baron, was killed in a shoot-out with police and the army in Medellín.

Pablo Escobar, el magnate narcotraficante más infame del mundo, resultó muerto en un tiroteo con la policía y el ejército en Medellín.

He was stopped by the police for speeding in a residential area of Lugo.

Fue detenido por la policía por exceso de velocidad en una zona residencial de Lugo.

➤ TRIAL 26b; PUNISHMENT, CRIME PREVENTION 26c

26b Trial

accusation **la acusación**
I accuse **acuso**
accused person **el acusado**
I acquit **absuelvo**
I acquit for lack of evidence
absuelvo por falta de pruebas
appeal **el recurso**
I appeal **recurro**
case for the defence **el discurso de la defensa**
compensation **la indemnización**
confession **la confesión**
I confess **confieso**
I convince **pruebo, convenzo**
costs **las costas**
counsel for the defendant/defense
el abogado defensor
court **el juzgado, el tribunal, la corte**
court of appeal **el juzgado de apelación, la corte de apelación**
courtroom **la sala de juicios**
criminal court **el juzgado criminal, el juzgado (de lo) penal**
I cross-examine **interrogo**
I debate **debato, discuto**
defence/defense **la defensa**
I defend **defiendo**
I defend (myself) **me defiendo**
defendant **el demandado, el acusado**

diminished responsibility **la culpabilidad reducida**
I disagree **disiento**
I discuss **discuto**
district attorney **el fiscal de distrito**
dock **el banquillo de los acusados**
I enquire **pregunto**
evidence **la prueba**
examining magistrate **el juez de instrucción**
extenuating circumstances **las circunstancias atenuantes**
eye-witness **el testigo ocular/presencial**
I find guilty **declaro culpable**
I give evidence **declaro**
for the defense **declaro en favor de la defensa**
for the prosecution **declaro en favor del cargo**
guilt **la culpa**
guilty **culpable**
high court of appeal **el tribunal supremo**
I impeach **acuso**
impeachment **la acusación**
indictment **el procesamiento**
indictment in court **el procesamiento ante el tribunal**
innocence **la inocencia**

The judge imposed a fine of 100,000 pesetas and ordered the accused to pay costs.

El juez impuso al acusado una multa de cien mil pesetas y le condenó con costas.

A man will appear in court today charged with the attempted murder of a 14-month old baby boy.

Un hombre comparecerá hoy en el tribunal acusado de tentativa de asesinato de un nene de 14 meses.

innocent **inocente**
judge **el juez**
juror **el miembro del jurado**
jury **el jurado**
jury-box **el estrado del jurado**
justice **la justicia**
lawsuit **el proceso civil, el pleito, el litigio**
lawyer **el abogado, el letrado**
leniency **la clemencia**
life imprisonment **la condena a cadena/reclusión perpetua**
litigation **la litigación**
magistrate **el magistrado**
magistrate's court **el juzgado correccional/de paz**
mercy **la misericordia**
minor offence **la falta menor**
miscarriage of justice **el error de la justicia**
motive **el móvil, el motivo**
not guilty **inocente**
oath **el juramento**
offence **el delito**
on remand **en prisión preventiva**
I pass judgement **pronuncio sentencia**
perjury **el perjurio**
plea **el argumento de la defensa**
plea bargaining **las negociaciones para los cargos**
I plead not guilty **me declaro inocente**
premeditation **la premeditación**

I prosecute **acuso**
prosecution **la acusación**
public prosecutor **el fiscal**
public prosecutor's office **la fiscalía**
I question **pregunto**
retrial **la revisión del proceso**
I reward **recompenso, indemnizo**
speech for the defence/defense **el alegato de la defensa**
I stand accused **estoy acusado**
I stand bail (for *someone*) **garantizo la fianza**
statement **la declaración**
I sue/I take to court **demando**
summons **la citación**
I suspect **sospecho**
suspect **la sospecha**
Supreme Court **el tribunal supremo, la corte suprema**
sustained! **¡confirmado!**
I swear **juro**
I take legal proceedings **empiezo un proceso**
trial **el juicio, el proceso**
unanimous **unánime**
verdict **el veredicto**
I witness **atestiguo**
witness **el testigo**
witness-box **el estrado de los testigos**
writ **la orden, el decreto, el mandato**

The case against the accused was dismissed on grounds of insufficient evidence.

El tribunal absolvió al acusado por falta de pruebas.

The accused had strong connections in the underworld.

El acusado tenía fuertes relaciones en el mundo del hampa.

26c Punishment

confinement   **la reclusión**
in solitary confinement   **en régimen de aislamiento**
I convict   **declaro culpable**
convict   **el convicto, el reo**
death penalty   **la pena de muerte**
I deport   **deporto**
I escape   **escapo**
fine   **la multa**
I fine   **multo**
I free   **libero**
hard labour/labor   **los trabajos forzados**
I imprison   **hago prisionero, meto en prisión**
jailbird   **el presidiario**
prison   **la prisión, la cárcel**
prisoner   **el prisionero**
I punish   **castigo**
punishment   **el castigo, la pena**
I release on bail   **salgo bajo fianza**
I reprieve a condemned prisoner   **indulto**
I sentence to death   **sentencio a muerte, condeno a muerte**
I serve a sentence   **cumplo una condena**
sentence   **la sentencia**

severity   **la severidad, la dureza**
suspended sentence   **la suspensión de sentencia**

The fight against crime

alarm   **la alarma**
burglar/car alarm   **la alarma antirrobo**
autopsy   **la autopsia**
arrest   **el arresto**
I arrest   **arresto**
baton   **la porra, el bastón**
chief of police   **el comisario de policía, el jefe de policía**
civil law   **el derecho civil**
clue   **la pista**
come quickly!   **¡venga!**
crime prevention   **la prevención del crimen**
criminal law   **el derecho penal**
criminal record   **los antecedentes penales**
customs   **la aduana**
customs officer   **el agente de aduana**
deportation   **la deportación**
detective   **el detective**
drugs raid   **la redada de drogas**

– What was the verdict in the trial?

– The defendant was sentenced to four years imprisonment.

– Will he serve that long?

– No, nothing like it. He'd already spent 8 months on remand/awaiting trial.

– Did he plead guilty?

– Yes, to manslaughter.

– **¿Cuál ha sido el veredicto en el proceso?**

– **El acusado fue condenado a cuatro años de cárcel.**

– **¿Servirá tanto tiempo en la cárcel?**

– **No, nada de eso. Ya había pasado 8 meses en prisión preventiva.**

– **¿Se confesó culpable?**

– **Sí. Se confesó culpable al homicidio sin premeditación.**

drugs squad   **la brigada antidrogas**
enquiry   **el interrogatorio**
error   **el error**
escape   **la escapada, el escape**
I escape (to)   **me escapo (a)**
examination   **el examen, la prueba**
I examine   **examino**
I extradite   **extradito**
extradition   **la extradición**
fingerprints   **las huellas dactilares/digitales**
fugitive   **el fugitivo**
guard dog   **el perro guardián**
handcuff   **la esposa**
identikit/photofit picture   **el retrato robot**
informer   **el informador, el confidente, el informante**
interview   **el interrogatorio**
I interview   **interrogo**
I investigate   **investigo**
investigation   **la investigación**
investigator   **el investigador**
   private investigator   **el investigador privado**
key   **la clave**
law   **el derecho, la ley**
law-breaking   **la contravención de la ley, el incumplimiento de la ley**

lock   **la cerradura**
I lock   **cierro con llave**
padlock   **el candado**
plain-clothes police   **el policía vestido de paisano**
police officer   **el policía**
police badge   **la placa policial**
police record   **el registro policial, los antecedentes penales**
   clean record   **sin antecedentes penales**
police station   **la comisaría [estación] de policía**
policeman   **el policía**
policewoman   **la mujer policía**
reward   **la recompensa**
riot police   **la policía antidisturbios [antimotines]**
security   **la seguridad**
speed trap   **el control de velocidad por radar**
traffic police   **la policía de tráfico**
truncheon   **la porra, [el bolillo]**
undercover   **secreto, clandestino**
warrant   **la orden**
   arrest warrant   **la orden de prisión**
   search warrant   **la orden de búsqueda**

He was convicted of breaking and entering and given a two year sentence.

Fue declarado culpable de allanamiento de morada y condenado a dos años de prisión.

The government recommends more custodial sentences for serious offenders.

El gobierno recomienda que haya más condenas a la cárcel para los que son culpables de delitos graves.

Overcrowding is a serious problem in many prisons.

La masificación [superpoblación] es un problema grave en muchas cárceles.

War & peace

27a War

I abduct **rapto, secuestro, plagio**	confrontation **la confrontación**
aerial bombing **el bombardeo aéreo**	I contaminate **contamino**
aggressor **el agresor**	conventional *(weapon/warfare)* **convencional**
air force **las fuerzas aéreas**	court-marshal **el consejo de guerra, el consejo militar**
I airlift **me transporto por avión**	cowardly **la cobardía**
air-raid **el ataque aéreo**	the plane crashes **el avión se estrella**
air-raid shelter **el refugio antiaéreo**	I crush *(opposition)* **estrello**
air-raid warning **la alarma antiaérea**	I declare *(war)* **declaro**
ambush **la emboscada**	defeat **la derrota**
anti-aircraft **antiaviones**	I defeat **derroto**
army **el ejército**	I am defeated **estoy derrotado**
I assassinate **asesino, mato**	defence/defense **la defensa**
assault **el asalto**	I defend **defiendo**
atomic **atómico**	I destroy **destruyo**
I attack **ataco**	I detain **detengo**
attack **el ataque**	I detect **detecto**
barracks **las barracas, el cuartel**	devastating **devastador**
battle **la batalla**	enemy **el enemigo**
battlefield **el campo de batalla**	espionage **el espionaje**
blast **la explosión**	ethnic cleansing **la limpieza étnica**
I blockade **bloqueo**	I evacuate **evacúo**
blockade **el bloqueo**	evacuation **la evacuación**
I blow up **vuelo, hago explotar**	I fight a battle **libro una batalla, lucho en una batalla**
bomb alert **el aviso de bomba**	I fight off **rechazo**
bombardment **el bombardeo**	I flee **huyo, escapo**
brave **valiente**	front **el frente**
war breaks out **el estallido de guerra**	guerrilla warfare **la guerra de guerilleros**
I call up **llamo a filas**	harmful **dañino**
camp **el campo**	headquarters **los cuarteles generales**
campaign **la campaña**	hostilities **las hostilidades**
I capture **capturo**	I interrogate **interrogo**
causes of war **las causas de la guerra**	interrogation **el interrogatorio**
I claim responsibility for **pido responsabilidad por**	I intervene **intervengo**
I commit *(an act)* **cometo**	
conflict **el conflicto**	

intervention **la intervención**
intimidation **la intimidación**
I invade **invado**
invasion **la invasión**
I issue an ultimatum **doy un ultimátum**
I liquidate **liquido**
manoeuvres/maneuvers **las maniobras**
massacre **la masacre**
missing in action **desaparecido en acción**
military service **el servicio militar**
mobilization **la movilización**
I mobilize **movilizo**
morale **la moral**
multilateral **multilateral**
navy **la armada, la marina de guerra**
nuclear **nuclear**
occupation **la ocupación**
I occupy **ocupo**
offensive **la ofensiva**
  offensive (adj) **ofensivo**
I patrol **patrullo**
peace **la paz**
propaganda **la propaganda**
I provoke **provoco**
battle rages **el furor de la batalla**
raid **el ataque, la incursión**
rank **la fila**
reinforcements **los refuerzos**
reprisals **las represalias**
I resist **resisto**
resistance **la resistencia**

I review (troops) **paso revista a, revisto**
I revolt **me rebelo, me sublevo**
revolution **la revolución**
riot **el motín, la sublevación**
rubble **el escombro**
security check **la inspección de seguridad**
shell **el obús, el proyectil, la granada**
shelter **el refugio**
I sink the ship **hundo el barco**
the ship sinks **el barco se hunde**
skirmish **la escaramuza**
I spy **espío**
I start a war **comienzo una guerra**
strategy **la estrategia**
striking power **el poder ofensivo, el poder de ofensiva**
the vessel submerges **la nave se sumerge**
the vessel surfaces **la nave emerge**
survival **la supervivencia**
tactics **las tácticas**
terrorist attack **el ataque terrorista**
I threaten **amenazo**
trench **la trinchera**
underground **bajo tierra, subterráneo**
war **la guerra**
war-mongering **el belicismo**
I win **gano**
wound **la herida**
I wound **hiero**

The Christmas truce was broken as hostilities broke out again in Bosnia.

La tregua de Navidad fue infringida cuando se reanudaron las hostilidades en Bosnia.

Civil wars are the bloodiest of all.

Las guerras civiles son las más sangrientas de todas las guerras.

Total war is a concept of the 20th century.

La guerra total es un concepto del siglo veinte.

27b Military personnel & weaponry

archer **el arquero**
assassin **el asesino**
casualty *(dead)* **la baja**
   casualty *(injured)* **el herido**
cavalry **la caballería**
civilian **el civil**
commandos **los comandos**
conscientious objector **el objetor de conciencia**
conscript **el conscripto**
convoy **el convoy**
deserter **el desertor**
division **la división**
foot soldier **el soldado de a pie**
general **el general**
guard **la guardia**
guerrilla **la guerrilla**
hostage **el rehén**
infantry **la infantería**
intelligence officer **el oficial de la inteligencia**
marines **la infantería de marina**
military personnel **el personal militar**
ministry of defence **el ministerio de defensa**
NCO **el suboficial**
officer **el oficial**
orderly **el ordenanza, el asistente**
parachutist **el paracaidista**
prisoner of war **el prisionero de guerra**
rebel **el rebelde**
recruit **el reclutamiento**

regiment **el regimiento**
seaman/sailor **el marino, el marinero**
secret agent **el agente secreto**
sentry **el centinela, el guardia**
sniper **el francotirador**
soldier **el soldado**
spy **el espía**
squadron **el escuadrón**
staff **el personal**
terrorist **el terrorista**
traitor **el traidor**
troops **las tropas**
victor **el vencedor**

Weaponry and its effects

I aim (at) **apunto (a)**
aircraft carrier **el portaviones, el portaeronaves**
ammunition **la munición**
armaments **los armamentos**
armoured/armored car **el coche blindado/acorazado**
arms **las armas**
arms race **la carrera de armas**
artillery **la artillería**
bacteriological **bacteriológico**
barbed wire **el alambre de púas**
bayonet **la bayoneta**
I bomb(ard) **bombardeo**
bomb **la bomba**
bombardment **el bombardeo**
bomber *(aircraft)* **el bombardero aéreo**

In Sarajevo today, a man was shot dead by a sniper.

The explosion was several miles away, but it knocked everyone to the ground. Then the alert sounded for chemical weapons.

Hoy en Sarajevo, un hombre fue matado por un francotirador.

La explosión se produjo a varias millas de distancia, pero derribó a todo el mundo. Luego sonó la alarma de armas químicas.

bullet   **la bala**
car bomb   **el coche bomba**
crossbow   **la ballesta**
chemical   **química**
destroyer *(ship)*   **el destructor**
I execute   **ejecuto**
I explode a bomb   **hago explotar una bomba**
explosive   **el explosivo**
fighter plane   **el caza**
I fire (at)   **disparo a**
frigate   **la fragata**
gas   **el gas**
gas attack   **el ataque de gas**
gun   **la pistola**
hand-grenade   **la granada de mano**
H-bomb   **la bomba H**
it hits   **da contra, impacta, alcanza**
jet *(plane)*   **el avión a reacción**
I kill   **mato**
knife   **el cuchillo, el puñal**
laser   **el láser**
launcher   **el lanzador**
letter-bomb   **la cartabomba**
machine-gun   **la ametralladora**
manufacturer   **el fabricante**
minefield   **el campo de minas**
mine-sweeper   **el dragaminas**
missile   **el misil**
mortar   **el mortero**
neutron bomb   **la bomba de neutrones**
nuclear test   **la prueba nuclear**
nuclear warhead   **la cabeza nuclear**

pistol   **la pistola**
poison gas   **el gas venenoso**
radar   **el radar**
radar screen   **la pantalla de radar**
radiation   **la radiación**
radiation sickness   **la enfermedad debida a la radiación**
radio-active   **radioactivo**
radioactive fallout   **el polvillo radioactivo**
revolver   **el revólver**
rifle   **el rifle**
rocket   **el cohete**
rocket attack   **el ataque con cohetes**
I sabotage   **hago sabotaje, saboteo**
shell   **el obús, el proyectil, la granada**
I shoot dead   **mato de un tiro, mato a tiros**
shotgun   **el tiro de pistola**
shrapnel   **la metralla**
siege   **el sitio, el asedio**
I stock-pile   **formo una reserva**
submachine-gun   **la metralleta**
submarine   **el submarino**
tank   **el tanque**
target   **el blanco, el objetivo**
torpedo   **el torpedo**
torpedo attack   **el ataque con torpedos**
I torpedo   **torpedeo**
warship   **el barco de guerra**
weapon   **el arma**

The missile, which had been shot down, scattered debris over a wide area.	**El misil que había sido derribado esparció escombros sobre un área extensa.**
Six people were wounded when a shell landed in the old town.	**Quedaron heridas seis personas al caer un proyectil sobre el barrio viejo del pueblo.**

➤ CRIME 26

27c Peace & international relations

Peace

I ban *(the bomb)*	**prohíbo**
cease-fire	**el cese al fuego**
control	**el control**
I declare peace	**declaro la paz**
I demobilize	**desmovilizo**
deterrent	**la fuerza disuasiva**
I diminish tension	**aminoro la tensión**
disarmament	**el desarme**
exchanges of information	**los intercambios de información**
free	**libre**
I free	**libero**
human rights	**los derechos humanos**
I mediate	**medio**
military service	**el servicio militar**
negotiable	**negociable**
negotiation	**la negociación**
neutral	**neutral**
neutrality	**la neutralidad**
pacifist	**el pacifista**
pacifism	**el pacifismo**
peace	**la paz**
peace plan	**el plan de paz**
peace protester	**el manifestante por la paz**
peace talks	**las conferencias de paz**
peace-keeping force	**las fuerzas para mantener la paz**
surrender	**el rendimiento, la rendición**
I surrender	**me rindo**
test ban	**la suspensión de pruebas**
treaty	**el tratado**
uncommitted	**no comprometido**
victory	**la victoria**

International relations

aid	**la ayuda, la asistencia**
ambassador	**el embajador**
arms reduction	**la reducción de armamentos**
attaché	**el agregado**
citizen	**el ciudadano**
citizenship	**la ciudadanía**
consul	**el cónsul**
consulate	**el consulado**
developing countries	**los países en desarrollo**
diplomacy	**la diplomacia**
diplomat	**el diplomático**
diplomatic immunity	**la inmunidad**

The Spanish government was in danger of being embroiled in a diplomatic row.	**El gobierno español corría el riesgo de enredarse en una disputa diplomática.**
The Ministry of Defence announced cuts in the military budget today.	**Hoy el Ministerio de defensa anunció una reducción en el presupuesto militar.**
Importers continue to take advantage of the low tariff rates.	**Los importadores continúan apovechándose de las tarifas bajas.**

diplomática
embassy **la embajada**
emergency aid **la asistencia de emergencia**
envoy **el enviado**
famine **el hambre**
foreign affairs **los asuntos exteriores**
foreign aid **la asistencia exterior**
foreigner **el extranjero**
I apply economic sanctions **empleo sanciones económicas**
I join *(organization)* **me afilio, me hago miembro de**
national security **la seguridad interior**
non-aligned **no alineado, neutral**
overseas **en ultramar, en el extranjero**
I ratify *(treaty)* **ratifico**
relief organization **la organización de beneficencia**
relief supplies **las provisiones de auxilio**
I represent **represento**
sanctions **las sanciones**
summit meeting **la cumbre**
Third World **el Tercer Mundo**
underdeveloped countries **los países subdesarrollados**

Trade

agricultural policy **la política agraria**
balance of payments **la balanza de pagos**
balance of trade **la balanza comercial**
Common market **el mercado común**
currency **la moneda, la divisa**
customs **la aduana**
customs union **la unión aduanera**
European Union **la unión europea**
exchange rate **el tipo de cambio**
exports **las exportaciones**
floating currency **la divisa flotante**
it floats **flota**
foreign investment **la inversión extranjera**
free-trade zone **la zona franca**
gap between rich and poor **la diferencia entre ricos y pobres**
GNP/gross national product **el producto nacional bruto/PNB**
import controls **el control de importaciones**
imports **las importaciones**
tariff barriers **las tarifas aduaneras**
tariffs **las tarifas**
trade gap *(negative)* **el déficit exterior**

A spokesman for the Spanish Interior Ministry revealed the European Commission is investigating alleged unfair trading practices/practises.

It is hoped that the gap between rich and poor will decrease with the lifting of international trade barriers.

Un portavoz del Ministerio del Interior anunció que la Comisión Europea está investigando presuntas prácticas comerciales injustas.

Se espera que la diferencia entre ricos y pobres disminuya al suprimir las barreras al comercio internacional.

C
APPENDICES

Appendices

3b Clocks & watches*

alarm clock   **el despertador**
clock   **el reloj**
cuckoo clock   **el reloj de cuco**
dial   **la esfera, la cara, el cuadrante**
digital watch   **el reloj digital**
egg-timer   **el cronómetro para huevos**
grandfather clock   **el reloj de pie, el reloj de caja**
hand (of a clock)   **la aguja del reloj**
  minute hand   **el minutero**
  hour hand   **el horario**
  second hand   **el segundero**
hour-glass   **el reloj de arena**
pendulum   **el péndulo**
stop-watch   **el cronógrafo**
sundial   **el reloj de sol**
timer (on cooker)   **el cronómetro de la cocina, el avisador**
watch   **el reloj de pulsera, el reloj de mano**
  watch strap   **la pulsera del reloj, la correa del reloj**
I wind up   **doy cuerda**

4d Mathematical & geometrical terms

acute   **agudo**
algebra   **el álgebra**
algebraic   **algebraico**
Arabic numerals   **los números arábicos**
arithmetic   **la aritmética**
arithmetical   **aritmético**
average   **el promedio**
axis   **el eje**
circumference   **la circunferencia**
complex   **complejo**
constant   **la constante**
cube   **el cubo**
cube root   **la raíz cúbica**
cubed   **al cubo**
decimal   **el decimal**
equality   **la igualdad**
factor   **el factor**
I factorize   **factorizo**
fraction   **la fracción, el quebrado**
function   **la función**
geometry   **la geometría**
geometrical   **geométrico**
imaginary   **imaginario**
integer   **el número entero**
irrational   **el número irracional**
logarithm   **el logaritmo**
mean   **la media**
median   **medio, el número medio, el punto medio**
multiple   **el múltiplo**
nine is to three as ...   **nueve es a tres como ...**
natural   **natural**
numerical   **numérico**
obtuse   **obtuso**
prime   **primo**
product   **el producto**
probability   **la probabilidad**
I raise to a power   **elevo a una potencia**
to the fifth power   **a la quinta potencia**
to the nth power   **a la enésima potencia**
radius   **el radio**
rational   **racional**
quotient   **el cociente**
real   **real**
reciprocal   **recíproco**
Roman   **romano**
set   **el conjunto**
square   **cuadrado**

* Appendices are numbered according to the most relevant Vocabulary.

square root **la raíz cuadrada**
symmetry **la simetría**
symmetrical **simétrico**
table(s) **las tablas**
tangent **la tangente**
trigonometry **la trigonometría**
variable **la variable**
vector **el vector**

5b Parts of the body

ankle **el tobillo**
arm **el brazo**
back **la espalda**
backbone **la columna vertebral**
bladder **la vejiga**
blood **la sangre**
blood pressure **la presión arterial**
body **el cuerpo**
bone **el hueso**
bowel **los intestinos**
brain **el cerebro**
breast **el pecho, el busto, el seno**
buttock **las nalgas**
cheek **la mejilla**
chest **el pecho**
chin **el mentón, la quijada**
ear **la oreja**
elbow **el codo**
eye **el ojo**
eyebrow **la ceja**
eyelash **la pestaña**
face **la cara**
finger **el dedo**
fingernail **la uña**
foot **el pie**
forehead **la frente**
genitalia **los genitales**
gland **la glándula**
hair **el pelo, el cabello**
hand **la mano**
head **la cabeza**
heart **el corazón**
hip **la cadera**
hormone **la hormona**
index finger **el dedo índice**
jaw **la mandíbula**

kidney **el riñón**
knee **la rodilla**
knuckle **el nudillo**
leg **la pierna**
lid **el párpado**
lip **el labio**
liver **el hígado**
lung **el pulmón**
mouth **la boca**
muscle **el músculo**
nape of neck **la nuca**
neck **el cuello**
nose **la nariz**
nostril **la ventana de la nariz**
organ **el órgano**
part of body **la parte del cuerpo**
penis **el pene**
sex organs **los órganos sexuales**
shoulder **el hombro**
skin **la piel**
stomach **el estómago**
thigh **el muslo**
throat **la garganta**
thumb **el pulgar**
toe **la punta del pie**
tongue **la lengua**
tooth **el diente**
vagina **la vagina**
waist **la cintura**
womb **la matriz**
wrist **la muñeca**

6a Human characteristics

absent-minded **despistado**
active **activo**
adaptable **adaptable, flexible**
affectionate **cariñoso**
aggression **la agresión**
aggressive **agresivo**
ambition **la ambición**
ambitious **ambicioso**
amusing **divertido**
anxious **ansioso, nervioso**
arrogant **arrogante**
artistic **artístico**
attractive **atractivo**

6a Human characteristics (cont.)

bad-tempered **mal humorado**
bad/evil **malo, malvado**
boring **aburrido**
brave **valiente**
care **la atención, el cuidado**
careful **atento, cuidadoso**
careless **descuidado**
charm **encanto**
charming **encantador**
cheeky **caradura, fresco**
cheerful **alegre**
clever **listo, espabilado**
cold **frío**
comic **gracioso**
confidence **la seguridad en sí mismo**
confident **seguro de sí mismo**
conscientious **meticuloso**
courage **el valor**
courtesy **la educación, la cortesía**
cowardly **cobarde**
creative **creativo, imaginativo**
critical **crítico, exigente**
cruel **cruel**
cruelty **la crueldad**
cultured **cultivado, educado**
cunning **astuto**
curiosity **la curiosidad**
decisive (in-) **(in)decisivo, firme, tajante, (vacilante)**
demanding **exigente**
dependence (in-) **la (in)dependencia**
dependent (in-) **(in)dependiente**
distrustful **desconfiado**
eccentric **excéntrico**
energetic **enérgico, activo, vigoroso**
envious **envidioso**
envy **la envidia**
extroverted **extrovertido**
faithful (un-) **(in)fiel**
faithfulness **la fidelidad**
friendly (un-) **simpático (antipático)**

frivolous **frívolo**
generosity **la generosidad**
generous **generoso**
gentleness **la amabilidad, la ternura**
good-tempered **amable**
greed **la avaricia**
greedy **avaricioso, avaro**
hard-working **trabajador, laborioso**
helpful **servicial**
honest (dis-) **(des)honesto, (poco) honrado**
honesty (dis-) **la (des)honestidad**
honour/honor **el honor**
humane (in-) **(in)humano**
humble **humilde, modesto**
humorous **gracioso**
hypocritical **hipócrita**
idealistic **idealista**
imagination **la imaginación**
imaginative **imaginativo, creativo**
individualistic **individualista, independiente**
innocence **la inocencia**
innocent **inocente**
inquisitive **inquisitivo**
intelligence **la inteligencia**
intelligent **inteligente**
introverted **introvertido**
ironic **irónico**
kind **amable**
kindness **la amabilidad**
laziness **la pereza, la holgazanería**
lazy **perezoso, holgazán**
liberal **liberal**
likeable **simpático, fácil**
lively **animado**
lonely **solitario**
loveable **encantador**
mad **loco**
madness **la locura**
malicious **malvado**
mature (im-) **(in)maduro**
mean/stingy **tacaño, agarrado**

modest **modesto**
moody **voluble**
moral (im-) **(in)moral**
naive **ingenuo**
natural **natural**
nervous **nervioso**
nice **amable, simpático**
obedience (dis-) **la (des)obediencia**
obedient (dis-) **(des)obediente**
openness **la franqueza**
optimistic **optimista**
originality **la originalidad**
patience (im-) **la (im)paciencia**
patient (im-) **(im)paciente**
pessimistic **pesimista**
pleasant **agradable**
polite **educado, cortés**
politeness **la educación, la cortesía**
possessive **posesivo**
prejudiced **lleno de prejuicios**
pride **el orgullo**
proud **orgulloso**
reasonable (un-) **(poco) razonable**
rebellious **rebelde**
reserved **reservado**
respect **el respeto**
respectable **respetable**
respectful **respetuoso**
responsible (ir-) **(ir)responsable**
rude **maleducado, descortés, grosero**
rudeness **la mala educación, la descortesía, la grosería**
sad **triste**
sarcastic **sarcástico**
scornful **despreciable**
self-confident **seguro de sí mismo**
self-esteem **la autoestima**
selfish (un-) **(no) egoísta**
selfishness **el egoísmo**
self-sufficient **autosuficiente**
sensible **sensible**
sensitive (in-) **(in)sensible**

serious **serio, formal**
shy **tímido**
silent **silencioso**
silly **tonto, bobo**
sincerity **la sinceridad**
skilful **hábil**
sociable (un-) **(in)sociable**
strange **raro, especial**
strict **estricto**
stubborn **cabezota, tenaz, testamudo, terco**
stupidity **la estupidez**
suspicious **suspicaz**
sweet **dulce, cariñoso**
sympathetic (un-) **comprensivo, simpático, (in)compasivo**
sympathy **la simpatía, la solidaridad**
tactful (-less) **(in)discreto**
talented **dotado**
talkative **hablador, charlatán**
temperamental **temperamental**
thoughtful **pensativo, considerado**
thoughtless **irreflexivo, desconsiderado**
tidy (un-) **(des)ordenado, limpio**
tolerance (in-) **la (in)tolerancia**
tolerant (in-) **(in)tolerante**
traditional **conservador, tradicional**
trust **la confianza**
trusting **confiado**
vain **vanidoso, engreído, vano**
vanity **la vanidad**
violent **violento, agresivo**
virtuous **virtuoso**
warm **cálido**
well-adjusted **equilibrado**
well-behaved **bueno, de buena conducta**
wisdom **la prudencia, la sabiduría**
wise **prudente**
wit **el ingenio**
witty **ingenioso, vivo, ocurrente**

8b Tools

axe/ax   **el hacha**
bit   **la barrena**
blade   **el filo**
bolt   **el tornillo**
bucket   **el cubo**
chisel   **el formón, el cincel**
crowbar   **la palanca**
drill   **el taladro**
file   **la lima**
garden gloves   **los guantes de jardinería**
garden shears   **las tijeras de jardín**
hammer   **el martillo**
hedge clippers   **las tijeras podadoras**
hoe   **la azada**
hose   **la manga**
ladder   **la escalera, la escala**
lawn-mower   **el cortacésped, [la segadora]**
mallet   **el mazo**
nail   **el clavo**
nut   **la tuerca**
paint   **la pintura**
paint brush   **la brocha, el pincel**
pickax(e)   **el pico, el zapapico**
plane   **el cepillo de carpintería**
pliers   **los alicates, las pinzas**
rake   **el rastrillo**
sandpaper   **el papel de lija**
saw   **la sierra**
screw   **el tornillo**
screwdriver   **el destornillador**
shovel   **la pala**
spade   **la pala**
spanner/wrench (adjustable)   **la llave (de tuercas)**
spirit level   **el nivel de aire**
stepladder   **la escalera doble/de tijera**
toolbox   **la caja de herramientas**
trowel   **el desplantador**
varnish   **el barniz**

vice   **el torno de banco**
weedkiller   **el herbicida**

9a Shops, stores & services

antique shop/store   **la tienda de antigüedades, el anticuario**
baker's/bakery   **la panadería**
bank   **el banco**
betting shop//bookmaker's   **la agencia de apuestas**
bookshop/store   **la librería**
boutique   **la boutique**
butcher's   **la carnicería**
cakeshop/store   **la pastelería**
car accesory/spares shop/store   **la tienda de repuestos/recambios**
charity shop/store   **la tienda de sociedad benéfica/de caridad**
chemist's/drugstore   **la farmacia**
clothes shop/store   **la tienda de modas/de ropa**
cobbler's   **la tienda del zapatero remendón, [la remontadora de calzado]**
cosmetics shop/store   **la tienda de estética, [el almacén de cosméticos]**
covered market   **la plaza del mercado**
dairy   **la lechería**
delicatessen   **el delicatessen**
department store   **los (grandes) almacenes, [el centro comercial]**
dress shop/store   **la casa de modas**
drugstore   **la farmacia, la droguería**
dry-cleaners   **la tintorería, [la lavandería]**
electrical shop/store   **la tienda de material eléctrico/de electrodomésticos**
estate/real estate agent   **el agente inmobiliario**

fast-food shop/store **la tienda de fast-food/[de comidas rápidas]**
fishmonger's **la pescadería**
fishstall **el puesto de pescado**
florist's **la floristería**
furniture shop/store **la tienda de muebles**
garden centre/center **el centro de jardinería**
greengrocer's **la verdulería, la verdurería, [la tienda de verduras]**
grocer **el tendero (de ultramarinos), el mantequero**
grocer's **la tienda de ultramarinos, la tienda de comestibles, [la tienda]**
hairdresser **el peluquero, la peluquera**
hairdresser's **la peluquería**
hardware shop/store **la ferretería**
health-food shop/store **la tienda de alimentos naturales**
hypermarket **el hipermercado**
indoor market **la plaza del mercado cubierta**
insurance agent/broker **el agente de seguros**
jeweller's/jewelry store **la joyería**
kiosk **el quiosco, el kiosco**
launderette **la lavandería automática**
market **el mercado**
menswear shop/store **la tienda de ropa de caballero**
model shop/store **la tienda de juguetes/miniatura**
music shop/store **la tienda de música**
newsagent's/newsstand **el vendedor de periódicos**
newspaper kiosk **el quiosco de periódicos**
open-air/outdoor market **el mercado**
optician's **la (tienda de) óptica**

petshop/pet store **la pajarería**
pharmacy **la farmacia**
photographic shop/store **la tienda de fotografía**
post-office **Correos, [la oficina de correos]**
pottery shop/store **la tienda de cerámica, [la alfarería]**
shoe repair shop/store **el zapatero remendón, [la remontadora de calzado]**
shoe shop/store **la zapatería, [el almacén de zapatos]**
shop/store **la tienda**
shopping centre/shopping mall **el centro comercial, la zona de tiendas**
souvenir shop/store la tienda de recuerdos
sports shop/store **la tienda de deportes***
stationer's/stationery store **la papelería**
store **la tienda, el almacén**
superstore **el hipermercado, [la supertienda]**
supermarket **el supermercado**
sweetshop/candy store **la confitería, [la dulcería]**
take-away food shop/store **tienda de comidas para llevar**
tobacconist's/tobacco store **el estanco, la tabaquería, [la cigarrería]**
toyshop/store **la juguetería**
travel agent's/store **la agencia de viajes**
vendor **el vendedor, la vendedora**
vending machine **la vendedora automática**
video-shop/store **la tienda de vídeo**

9a Currencies

dollar   el dólar
escudo   el escudo
florin   el florín
franc   el franco
lira   la lira
mark   el marco
peseta   la peseta
pound sterling   la libra esterlina
rouble   el rublo
yen   el yen

9c Jewellery/Jewelry

bangle   la esclava
chain bracelet   la pulsera
brooch   el broche
carat   el quilate
chain   la cadena
charm   el amuleto, [el dije]
cuff links   los gemelos, [las mancornas]
earring   los pendientes
engagement ring   la sortija de pedida, [el anillo de compromiso]
jewel   la joya
jewel box   el joyero
jewellery/jewelry   la joyería
medallion   el medallón
necklace   el collar
pendant   el medallón
precious stone/gem   la piedra preciosa
real   verdadero
ring   el anillo, la sortija
semi-precious stone   la piedra semipreciosa
tiara   la diadema
tie pin   el alfiler de corbata
wedding ring   el anillo de boda

9c Precious stones & metals

agate   la ágata
amber   el ámbar
amethyst   la amatista
chrome   el cromo
copper   el cobre
coral   el coral
crystal   el cristal
diamond   el diamante
emerald   la esmeralda
gold   el oro
gold plate   la lámina de oro
ivory   el marfil
mother of pearl   el nácar, la madreperla
onyx   el ónix
pearl   la perla
pewter   el peltre
platinum   el platino
quartz   el cuarzo
ruby   el rubí
sapphire   el zafiro
silver plate   la vajilla de plata
silver   la plata
topaz   el topacio
turquoise   la turquesa

10c Herbs & spices

aniseed   el anís
basil   la albahaca
bay leaf   la hoja de laurel
caper   la alcaparra
caraway   la alcaravea
chives   el cebollino
cinnamon   la canela
clove   el clavo
cumin   el comino
dill   el eneldo
garlic   el ajo
ginger   el jengibre
marjoram   la mejorana
mint   la menta
mixed herbs   las hierbas finas
mustard   la mostaza
nutmeg   la nuez moscada

oregano **el orégano**
parsley **el perejil**
rosemary **el romero**
saffron **la azafrán**
sage **la salvia**
tarragon **el estragón**
thyme **el tomillo**

10d Cooking utensils

alumin(i)um foil **el papel
aluminio/de estaño**
baking tray **la bandeja de horno**
carving knife **el trinchante**
colander **el colador**
food processor **el robot de cocina**
fork **el tenedor**
frying pan/fry-pan **la sartén**
grater **el rallador**
greaseproof/wax paper **el papel
apergaminado**
grill **la parrilla**
kettle **el hervedor**
knife **el cuchillo**
lid **la cobertera, la tapa**
pot **la olla**
rolling pin **el rodillo**
saucepan/casserole dish **el cazo,
la cacerola**
scales **la balanza**
sieve **la coladera**
skewer **la broqueta**
spatula **la espátula**
spoon **la cuchara**
tablespoon **la cuchara grande**
tablespoonful **la cucharada**
teaspoon **la cucharilla**
teaspoonful **la cucharadita**
tenderizer **el ablandador**
tin/can-opener **el abrelatas**

10d Smoking

ashtray **el cenicero**
box of matches **la cajita de
cerillas**
cigar **el puro**

cigarette **el cigarrillo**
cigarette butt/stub **la colilla**
lighter **el encendedor**
matches **las cerillas**
pipe **la pipa**
smoke **el humo**
I smoke **fumo**
(no) smoking **(no) fumadores**
tobacco **el tabaco**
tobacconist's **el estanco, la
tabaquería, [la cigarrería]**

11b Illnesses & diseases

AIDS **el SIDA**
angina **la angina**
appendicitis **la apendicitis**
arthritis **la artritis**
asthma **el asma** *(f)*
bacillus **el bacilo**
bacteria **la bacteria**
blister **la ampolla**
boil **el divieso, el furúnculo**
bronchitis **la bronquitis**
bruise **la contusión, el cardenal,
la magulladura, el magullón, el
moretón**
bubonic plague **la peste bubónica**
cancer **el cáncer**
catarrh **el catarro**
chickenpox **la varicela**
cholera **el cólera**
colic **el cólico**
cold **el resfriado, el catarro**
constipation **el estreñimiento**
corn **el callo**
cough **la tos**
deafness **la sordera**
death **la muerte**
depression **la depresión**
dermatitis **la dermatitis**
diabetes **la diabetes**
diarrhoea **la diarrea**
diptheria **la diftería**
disease **la enfermedad**
dizziness **el vértigo, el mareo**
earache **el dolor de oídos**

eczema   el eccema, el eczema
epilepsy   la epilepsia
fever   la fiebre
fit   el ataque
fleas   las pulgas
flu   el gripe
food-poisoning   la intoxicación
   alimenticia, la toxinfección
   alimenticia
gall-stones   el cálculo biliario
German measles   la rubéola
gingivitis   la gingivitis
gonorrhoea   la gonorrea
graze   el roce, la abrasión, [la
   raspadura]
haemorrhoids   las hemorroides
head-lice   el piojo
headache   el dolor de cabeza
heart attack   el ataque cardíaco
hepatitis   la hepatitis
hernia   la hernia
high blood pressure   la
   hipertensión
HIV-positive   (el virus de la
   inmunodeficiencia humana)
   VIH postive
illness/sickness   la enfermedad
incontinence   la incontinencia
influenza   la gripe
infection   la infección, el contagio
jaundice   la ictericia
leukaemia   la leucemia
lice   el piojo
malaria   la malaria, el paludismo
measles   el sarampión
meningitis   la meningitis
mental illness   la enfermedad
   mental
microbe   el microbio
migraine   la jaqueca
mumps   las paperas, las
   parótidas
nits   la liendre
overdose   la sobredosis
piles   las almorranas, las
   hemorroides

pneumonia   la pulmonía
polio   el polio
pregnancy   el embarazo, la
   preñez
rabies   la rabia
rheumatism   el reumatismo
salmonella   la salmonelosis
scabies   la sarna
seasickness   el mareo
sickness   la enfermedad, el
   malestar
smallpox   la viruela
stomach ache   el dolor de
   estómago
stomach upset   el trastorno
   estomacal
stroke   el ataque fulminante, la
   apoplejía
stye   el orzuelo
syphilis   la sífilis
temperature   la calentura, la fiebre
tetanus   el tétanos
thrombosis   la trombosis
tonsillitis   la amigdalitis
toothache   el dolor de muelas
tuberculosis   la tuberculosis
ulcers   las úlceras
urinary infection   la infección
   urinaria
venereal disease   la enfermedad
   venérea
whooping cough   la tos ferina
yellow fever   la fiebre amarilla

11c Hospital departments

Admissions   la Secretaría, las
   Admisiones
Blood Bank   el Banco de sangre
Casualty   (la Sección de)
   Accidentes
Consulting Room   el Consultorio,
   la Consulta
Coronary Care Unit   la Sección de
   Asistencia Cardíaca
Dialysis Unit   la Sección de

Diálisis
Emergency **las Urgencias**
Geriatric **la Geriatría**
Gynaecology **la Ginecología**
Infectious Diseases **las enfermedades infecto-contagiosas**
Intensive Care **la Asistencia Intensiva**
Maternity **la Maternidad**
Medical Ward **la Sala Médica**
Mortuary **el Mortuorio, el Depósito de Cadáveres, la Funeraria, [el Anfiteatro]**
Oncology **la Oncología**
Operating Theatre/Theater **el Quirófano, la Sala de Operaciones**
Orthopaedic **Ortopédico**
Out-Patients Department **el Departamento de Consulta Externa**
Paedeatric **la Pediatría**
Pathology **la Patología**
Pharmacy **la Farmacia**
Psychiatric **la Psiquiatría**
Reception **la Recepción**
Recovery Room **la Sala de Posoperatorio/Recuperación**
Surgery **la Cirugía**
Treatment Room **la Sala de Tratamiento/Cura/Medicación**
Ward **la Sala**
X-Ray **los Rayos-X, la Radiografía**

13b Holidays & religious festivals

All Saints (Nov 1) **el día de todos los Santos**
All Souls (Nov 2) **el día de los Difuntos**
Ascension Day **el día de la Ascensión**
Ash Wednesday **el Miércoles de Ceniza**
Assumption Day (Aug 15) **el día de la Asunción**
Candlemas **el día de la Candelaria**
Carneval **el Carnaval**
Christmas Day **el día de Navidad**
Christmas Eve **el día de Nochebuena**
Christmas **la Navidad**
at Christmas **en Navidad**
Corpus Christi **el Corpus Cristi**
Easter **la Semana Santa**
Easter Monday **el Lunes de Pascua de Resurreción**
Easter Sunday **el Domingo de Resurrección**
Eid **el Eid**
festival **el festival**
Good Friday **el Viernes Santo**
Hanukkah **el Hanukkah**
Labour/Labor Day **el día de los trabajadores, el día de San José obrero, el día del trabajo**
Lent **la Cuaresma**
New Year's Day **el día de Año Nuevo**
New Year's Eve **el día de Nochevieja**
Palm Sunday **el Domingo de Ramos**
Passover **la Pascua Judía**
Ramadan **El Ramadán**
Sabbath **el Sábado**
Shrove Tuesday **el martes de carnaval**
Whitsun **Pentecostés**
Whitsuntide **la semana de Pentecostés**
Yom Kippur **el Yom Kippur**

14b Professions & jobs

The arts

actor/actress   **el actor, la actriz**
announcer   **el presentador, el locutor, la presentadora, la locutora**
architect   **el arquitecto, la arquitecta**
artist   **el/la artista**
book-seller   **el vendedor de libros, el librero**
cameraman   **el cámara, el camarógrafo**
editor   **el editor**
film/movie director   **el director de cine/la directora de cine**
film/movie star   **la estrella de cine**
journalist   **el/la periodista**
musician   **el/la músico**
painter (*artist*)   **el pintor, la pintora**
photographer   **el fotógrafo/la fotógrafa**
poet   **el/la poeta**
printer   **el impresor**
producer (theatre/theater)   **el productor/la productora de teatro**
publisher   **el editor**
reporter   **el reportero, la reportera**
sculptor   **el escultor, la escultora**
singer   **el cantante, la cantante**
TV announcer   **el presentador/la presentadora de televisión**
writer   **el escritor, la escritora**

Education & research

headteacher/principal   **el director, la directora, el rector, la rectora**
lecturer   **el profesor universitario, la profesora universitaria**
physicist   **el físico, la física**
primary teacher   **el profesor/la profesora de escuela primaria, el maestro, la maestra**
researcher   **el investigador, la investigadora**

scientist   **el científico, la científica**
secondary teacher   **el profesor/la profesora de escuela secundaria**
student   **el/la estudiante**
technician   **el técnico, la técnica**

Food & retail

baker   **el panadero, la panadera**
brewer   **el cervecero, la cervecera**
butcher   **el carnicero, la carnicera**
buyer   **el encargado/la encargada de compras**
caterer (*supplying meals*)   **el abastecedor de comidas**
chemist   **el químico, la química**
cook   **el cocinero, la cocinera**
farmer   **el granjero, la granjera**
fisherman   **el pescador, la pescadora**
fishmonger   **el pescadero, la pescadera**
florist   **el/la florista**
greengrocer   **el verdulero, la verdulera, [el vendedor/la vendedora de verduras]**
grocer   **el tendero/la tendera (de comestibles)**
jeweller/jeweler   **el joyero, la joyera**
pharmacist   **el farmacéutico, la farmacéutica**
pork-butcher   **el carnicero, la carnicera**
representative   **el representante, el diputado, la diputada**
shop assistant   **el dependiente/la dependienta de comercio**
shopkeeper/storekeeper   **el tendero, la tendera**
tobacconist   **el tabaquero, el estanquero**
waiter   **el camarero, la camarera**
wine-grower   **el vinicultor, la vinicultora**

Government service

civil-servant **el funcionario, la funcionaria**
clerk **el/la oficinista**
customs officer **el/la agente de aduanas**
fireman **el bombero, la mujer bombero**
judge **el/la juez**
member of Parliament/senator **el diputado, la diputada, el senador, la senadora**
minister **el ministro, la ministra**
officer **el oficial, la oficial**
policeman **el policía**
policewoman **la mujer policía**
politician **el político, la política**
sailor **el marino, la marino, el marinero**
secret agent **el agente secreto, la agente secreta**
serviceman **el/la militar**
soldier **el/la soldado**

Health care

dentist **el/la dentista**
doctor (Dr) **el médico, la médica, el doctor, la doctora**
midwife **la comadrona**
nurse **el enfermero, la enfermera**
optician **el/la óptico, [el optómetra]**
physician **el físico**
psychiatrist **el/la psiquiatra**
psychologist **el psicólogo/la psicóloga**
surgeon **el cirujano, la cirujana**
vet **el veterinario, la veterinaria**

In manufacturing & construction

bricklayer **el/la albañil**
builder **el constructor**
carpenter **el carpintero, la carpintera**
engineer **el ingeniero, la ingeniera**

foreman **el/la capataz**
industrialist **el/la industrial**
labourer/laborer **el trabajador, la trabajadora, el obrero, la obrera**
manufacturer **el/la fabricante**
mechanic **el mecánico, la mecánica**
metalworker **el trabajador/la tragajadora del metal**
miner **el minero, la minera**
plasterer **el yesero, la yesera, el enlucidor, el albañil**
stonemason **el cantero**

Services

accountant **el/la contable, el contador, la contadora**
actuary **el actuario/la actuaria de seguros**
agent **el/la agente**
bank-manager **el director/la directora de banco**
business-man **el hombre de negocios**
business-woman **la mujer de negocios**
careers adviser **el consejero/la consejera profesional**
caretaker **el/la vigilante, el conserje**
cleaner **el limpiador, la limpiadora**
computer programmer **el programador/la programadora de ordenadores**
counsellor **el asesor, la asesora, el consejero, la consejera**
draughtsman **el/la delineante**
dustman/garbageman **el basurero, la basurera**
electrician **el/la electricista**
furniture remover **el empleado/la empleada de la mudanza**
gardener **el jardinero, la jardinera**
gasman **el trabajador/la trabajadora del gas**

guide **el/la guía**
hairdresser **el peluquero, la peluquera**
insurance agent **el/la agente de seguros**
interpreter **el/la intérprete**
lawyer **el abogado, la abogada, el letrado/la letrada**
librarian **el bibliotecario, la bibliotecaria**
office worker **el/la oficinista**
painter & decorator **el pintor, la pintora, el decorador, la decoradora**
plumber **el fontanero, la fontanera**
postman **el cartero, la cartera**
priest **el sacerdote**
receptionist **el/la recepcionista**
servant **el criado, la criada**
social worker **el/la asistente social**
solicitor **el abogado, la abogada**
stockbroker **el/la agente de bolsa**
surveyor **el topógrafo, la topógrafa**
tax inspector **el inspector/la inspectora de impuestos/ hacienda**
trade-unionist **el/la sindicalista**
translator **el traductor, la traductora**
travel agent **el agente de viajes**
typist **el mecanógrafo, la mecanógrafa**
undertaker **el director de pompas fúnebres**

Transport

airhostess **la azafata**
busdriver **el conductor/la conductora de autobuses**
driver **el conductor, la conductora**
driving instructor **el profesor/la profesora de autoescuela/ conducción**

lorry/truck-driver **el camionero, la camionera**
pilot **el/la piloto**
taxi-driver **el/la taxista**
ticket inspector **el revisor, la revisora**

14b Places of work

blast furnace **el alto horno**
branch office **la sucursal**
brewery **la cervecería**
business park **el centro de negocios**
construction site **la obra**
distillery **la destilería**
factory **la fábrica**
farm **la granja**
foundry **la fundición**
head office **la oficina principal**
hospital **el hospital**
mill **el molino**
  paper mill **la fábrica de papel**
  rolling mill **el taller de laminación**
  sawmill **el aserradero**
  spinning mill **la hilandería**
  steel mill **la fábrica de acero, la fábrica siderúrgica, la fundidura**
  weaving mill **la fábrica de tejidos**
mine **la mina**
office **la oficina**
plant **la planta**
public company **la empresa pública**
shop/store **la tienda, el almacén**
steelworks/steel plant **la fábrica de acero, la fábrica siderúrgica**
sweatshop **la tienda de dulces**
theme park **el parque temático**
vineyard/winery **la viña**
warehouse **el almacén, el depósito**
workshop **el taller**

14b Company personnel & structure

accounts department **el departamento de cuentas/contabilidad**
apprentice **el aprendiz, la aprendiza**
assistant **el ayudante, el asistente**
associate **el asociado, el socio**
board of directors **el consejo directivo, la junta de directores**
boss **el jefe**
colleague **el colega, el compañero de trabajo**
department **el departamento**
director **el director**
division **la división**
employee **el empleado**
employer **el empresario, el patrón/la patrona**
executive **el ejecutivo**
foreman **el capataz**
labour/labor **el trabajo**
line manager **el encargado de sección**
management **la dirección, la gestión, la administración, la gerencia**
manager **el director, el encargado, el gerente**
manageress **la directora, la encargada, la gerente**
managing director/CEO **el director/la directora general**
marketing department **el departamento de márketing/mercadeo**
personal assistant **el asistente personal**
president **el presidente**
production department **el departamento de producción**
sales department **el departamento de ventas**
secretary **el secretario, la secretaria**
specialist **el especialista**
staff/personnel **el personal**
team **el equipo**
trainee **el empleado en período de aprendizaje, el aprendiz**
vice president **el vicepresidente**

15c Letter-writing formulae

Dear … **Querido/a …**
Dear Madam **Muy señora mía, Estimada**
Dear Mr. and Mrs. … **Estimados Señores …**
Dear Peter **Querido Pedro, Mi querido amigo Pedro**
Dear Sir **Muy señor mío, Estimado señor**
greetings from **recuerdos de**
I am pleased that **Me alegro de**
I enclose **Remito adjunto/a**
All the best to **Recuerdos para**
Best wishes from **Saludos de**
Love from **Besos, Un abrazo de**
…, Un cariñoso saludo de …
With best wishes from **Saludos de, Un cordial saludo de**
With kind regards **Con muchos recuerdos**
Yours faithfully **Le saluda atentamente**
Yours sincerely **Le saluda atentamente/cordialmente**

15d Computer hardware

adaptor **el adaptador**
back-lit screen **la pantalla a iluminación trasera**
battery **la pila, la batería**
brightness **el brillo**
brightness control **el botón de ajuste del brillo**
charger **el cargador**
central processing unit **la unidad procesadora central**

chip **el chip, la micropastilla, el microplaquete, el circuito integrado**

colour/color monitor **el monitor en color**

computer **el ordenador, la computadora**

computer system **el sistema de ordenadores**

delete key **la tecla de borrado**

desk-top **... de escritorio**

disc/disk drive **la unidad de disco, el disk drive**

disc/disk **el disco**

diskette **el disquete, el diskette, el disco flexible**

display **la visualización, el despliegue**

double density disc/disk **el disco de densidad doble**

drive **la unidad de disco, el disk drive**

escape key **la tecla de escape**

exit key **la tecla de salida**

floppy disk **el disco flexible, el floppy, el disquete, el diskette**

floppy drive **la unidad de disco, el disk drive**

function key **la tecla de función**

hard disk **el disco duro, el disco Winchester**

hard disk drive **la unidad del disco Winchester**

hardware **el hardware, el material informático**

high density disk **el disco de densidad alta**

IBM clone **el clónico de IBM**

IBM-compatible **compatible con IBM**

integrated circuit **el circuito integrado**

interface **la interfaz, el interface**

keyboard **el teclado**

lap-top **el ordenador portátil plegable**

liquid crystal display **el visualizador de cristal líquido**

local Area Network/LAN **la red de área local**

main-frame computer **la computadora central, el ordenador central**

micro-processor **el microprocesador**

mini computer **el miniordenador, la minicomputadora**

modem **el módem**

monitor **el monitor**

mouse **el ratón**

network **la red**

personal computer/PC **el ordenador personal, la computadora personal**

plug-in drive **la unidad de disco enchufable**

port **la puerta, el puerto, el port**

portable **portátil**

processor **el procesador**

random access memory/RAM **el RAM/la memoria de acceso directo**

resolution **la resolución, la definición**

return key **la tecla de retorno**

screen **la pantalla**

scroll bar **la barra de desplazamiento**

socket/port **la puerta, el puerto, el port**

space-bar **el espaciador, la espaciadora**

terminal **la terminal**

touch screen **la pantalla de toque**

visual display unit/VDU **la unidad de presentación visual, la unidad de despliegue visual**

viewdata system **el sistema de videodatos**

Wide Area Network/WAN **la red de área amplia**

15d Computer software

algebraic   **algebraico**
algorithm   **el algoritmo**
BASIC   **el BASIC**
bug   **el duende, el fallo, el error**
byte   **el byte, el octeto**
coding   **la codificación**
command   **el comando**
compatible   **compatible**
compatibility   **la compatibilidad**
computer aided design/CAD   **el diseño asistido por ordenador/ DAO**
computer aided learning/CAL   **la instrucción asistida por ordenador/IAO**
computer aided language learning/ CALL   **la enseñanza de lenguas asistida por ordenador**
computer animation   **la animación por ordenador**
computer graphics   **las gráficas por ordenador**
computer language   **el lenguaje de ordenador**
computer literacy   **la competencia en la informática**
computer literate   **competente en la informática**
copy   **la copia**
corrupted   **degradado**
data capture   **la formulación de datos**
data logging   **la entrada de datos**
data   **los datos**
data processing   **el tratamiento de datos**
database   **la base de datos**
default option   **la opción por defectos**
double clicking   **el doble pulsar, el doble clic (del ratón)**
drive   **la unidad de disco**
escape   **el escape**
exit   **la salida del sistema**
file   **el fichero**

flow chart   **el diagrama de flujo, el organigrama, el ordinograma**
format   **el formato**
function   **la función**
graphical   **gráfico**
graphical application   **la aplicación gráfica**
graphics   **los gráficos**
graphics accelerator   **el acelerador de gráficos**
help   **ayuda, asistencia, auxilio**
help menu   **el menú de asistencia**
incompatible   **incompatible**
IT   **la informática**
language   **el lenguaje**
logic circuit   **el circuito lógico**
low/high density   **la densidad baja/alta**
macro   **macro**
memory   **la memoria**
menu   **el menú**
operating system   **el sistema de explotación, el sistema operativo**
on line   **on-line, en línea**
output   **la salida, el output**
output unit   **la unidad de salida, el dispositivo de salida**
password   **la contraseña de acceso**
program(me)   **el programa**
programmable   **programable**
programmer   **el programador**
programming   **la programación**
pull-down menu   **el menú desplegable**
reference archive   **el archivo de referencias, el archivo de consulta**
return   **el retorno**
software   **el software, los elementos de programación**
software package   **el paquete de programas**
sort   **la ordenación**
space   **el espacio**
spreadsheet   **la hoja electrónica,**

la hoja de cálculo
statistics package **el paquete estadístico**
update **la actualización**
user-friendly **fácil de utilizar**
virus **el virus**

15d Computer printing

continuous paper **el papel continuo**
dot matrix **la impresora matricial de puntos, la impresora de matriz de puntos**
font **la fuente, el tipo de letra**
hard copy **la copia impresa**
ink cartridge **el cartucho/el recambio de tinta**
inkjet **la impresora de chorro de tinta**
laser printer **la impresora (por) láser**
A4 paper **el papel tamaño A4**
paper feed **el alimentador de papel**
paper tray **la reserva de papel**
ribbon **la cinta (de impresora)**
roller **el rodillo**
sheet feeder **el alimentador de papel**
style **el estilo**
toner **el virador**

16a Hobbies

angling **la pesca con caña**
archeology **la arqueología**
archery **el tiro con arco**
ballroom dancing **el baile de salón**
bee-keeping **la apicultura**
birdwatching **la ornitología, la observación de aves**
carpentry **la carpintería**
collecting antiques **la colección de antigüedades**
collecting stamps **la colección de sellos/[estampillas]**

dancing **bailar**
fishing **la pesca**
gambling **el juego**
gardening **la jardinería**
going to the cinema/movies **ir al cine**
knitting **el tejido de punto**
listening to music **oír música**
photography **la fotografía**
playing chess **el ajedrez**
reading **la lectura**
sewing **la costura**
spinning **hilar**
walking **pasear**
watching television **ver la televisión**

17b Architectural terms

alcove **el hueco, el nicho**
arch **el arco**
architrave **el arquitrabe**
atrium **el atrio**
bas relief **el bajorrelieve**
battlement **la almena**
buttress **el contrafuerte**
capital **el capitel**
caryatid **la cariátide**
colonnade **la galería**
column **la columna**
  doric **dórica**
  ionic **jónica**
  corinthian **corintia**
concave **cóncavo**
convex **convexo**
corner-stone **la piedra angular**
cupola **la cúpula**
dado **el zócalo, el friso**
diptych **el díptico**
drawbridge **el puente levadizo**
eaves **el alero**
façade **la fachada**
fanlight **el montante de abánico**
gable **el frontón**
gargoyle **la gárgola**
half-timbered **con entramado de madera**

haut-relief   el altorrelieve
headstone   la lápida
herringbone *(adj)*   de espinapez
moulding/molding   el zócalo
nave   la nave
ogive   la ogiva
oval   ovalado
overhanging   sobresaliente, voladizo
pagoda   la pagoda
pilaster   la pilastra
pinnacle   el pináculo
plinth   el plinto
porch   el pórtico, la entrada
portico   el pórtico, la arcada
rear arch   el arco trasero
roof   el tejado
rosette   el rosetón
rotunda   la rotonda
sacristy   la sacristía
spire/steeple   la aguja
triumphal arch   el arco triunfal, de triunfo
tryptych   el tríptico
vault   la bóveda
vaulted   abovedado
volute   la voluta
wainscot   el revestimiento

17c Publishing

abridged version   la versión abreviada
acknowledgement   el agradecimiento
appendix   el apéndice
artwork   la obra de arte
author   el autor
best-seller   el best-seller, el libro de más venta
bibliography   la bibliografía
book fair   la feria del libro
catalogue   el catálogo
chapter   el capítulo
contents   el contenido
contract   el contrato
copy   la copia

copyright   el derecho de autor
cover *(of book)*   la cubierta, la tapa
deadline   el plazo
dedicated to   dedicado a
edition   la edición
   first edition   la primera edición
   latest edition   la última edición
editor   el editor
   literary editor   el editor literario
footnotes   las notas a pie de página
illustrations   las ilustraciones
manuscript   el manuscrito
paperback   la cubierta rústica, el libro en rústica
preface   el prefacio
proof-reading   la corrección de textos
publication date   la fecha de publicación
publisher   el editor
publishing house   la casa editorial
quote   la cita
review   la revisión, la revista
reviewer   el crítico, el reseñante
subtitle   el subtítulo
translation   la traducción
version   la versión
with a forward by   con prólogo escrito por

17d Musicians & instruments

accordionist   el acordeonista
alto *(singer)*   el contralto
bagpipe   la gaita
baritone   el barítono
bass *(singer)*   el bajo
bass clarinet   el clarinete bajo
basset horn   el cuerno de bajo
bassoon   el fagot
bassoonist   el fagotista
bells   las campañas tubulares
bugle   la corneta, el clarín
busker   el músico ambulante
castanets   las castañuelas

celeste   la celesta
cellist   el violonc(h)elista
cello   el violonc(h)elo
cembalo   el cémbalo
chorister   el corista
clarinet   el clarinete
clarinettist   el clarinetista
clarion   la trompeta
classical guitar   la guitarra clásica
clavicord   el clavicordio
conductor   el director de orquesta
contralto   el contralto
cornet   la corneta
cymbal   el cimbal
double bass   el contrabajo
double bassoon   el contrafagot
drum   el tambor
drummer   el batería
dulcimer   el salterio, el dulcémele
flautist   el flautista
flute   la flauta
French horn   el cuerno francés
grand piano   el piano de cola
guitar   la guitarra
guitarist   el guitarrista
harmonium   el armonio
harp   el arpa *(f)*
harpist   el arpista
harpsichord   el clavicordio
horn   el cuerno
hurdy-gurdy   el organillo
instrumentalist   el instrumentalista
jews' harp   el birimbao
librettist   el libretista
lyre   la lira
mandolin   la mandolina
mezzo-soprano   la mezzosoprano
mouth-organ   la armónica
oboe   el oboe
oboe player   el oboe
orchestra leader   el primer violín
orchestra players   los músicos de
   la orquesta
organ   el órgano
organist   el organista
percussion   los instrumentos de
   percusión

percussionist   el percusionista
pianist   el pianista
piano   el piano
pipe   la gaita, el tubo
recorder   la flauta dulce, la flauta
   de pico
saxophone   el saxofón
saxophonist   el saxofonista
soprano   el soprano
spinet   la espineta
squeeze-box   la concertina
string instruments   los
   instrumentos de cuerda
synthesizer   el sintetizador
tenor   el tenor
tin whistle   la flauta metálica
triangle   el triángulo
trombone   el trombón
trumpet   la trompeta
tuba   la tuba
tuning fork   el diapasón
tympani   los tímpanos
viol   la viola
viola   la violeta, la viola
viola player   el músico de viola
violin   el violín
violinist   el violinista
violoncello   el violonc(h)elo
vocalist   el cantante
Welsh harp   el arpa *(f)* galesa
xylophone   el xilófono

17d Musical forms

aria   el aria *(f)*
ballad   la balada
cantata   la cantata
canzonetta   la canzoneta
chamber music   la música de
   cámara
choral music   la música coral
concerto   el concierto
   piano concerto   el concierto
   para piano
duet   el dúo
fugue   la fuga
madrigal   el madrigal

march **la marcha**
music drama **el drama musical**
musical (comedy) **la comedia musical**
nocturne **el nocturno**
octet **el octeto**
opera **la ópera**
operetta **la opereta**
oratorio **el oratorio**
overture **la obertura**
piano trio **el trío de piano**
plainsong **el canto llano**
prelude **el preludio**
quartet **el cuarteto**
quintet **el quinteto**
recitative **el recitativo, el recitado**
requiem Mass **la misa de réquiem**
sacred music **la música sacra**
serenade **la serenata**
sextet **el sexteto**
septet **el septeto**
sonata **la sonata**
song-cycle **el ciclo de canciones**
suite **la suite**
symphonietta **la sinfonieta**
symphony **la sinfonía**
string quartet **el cuarteto de cuerda**
trio **el trío**

17d Musical terms

accompaniment **el acompañamiento**
accompanist **el acompañante**
arpeggio **el arpegio**
bar **el compás**
beat **el compás, el ritmo**
bow **el arco**
bowing **la técnica del arco**
cadence **la cadencia**
chord **el acorde**
clef **la clave**
  bass **de bajo**
  treble **de soprano**
discord **la disonancia**
improvisation **la improvisación**

key **la clave, la nota**
  major **mayor**
  minor **menor**
note **la nota**
  breve **la breve**
  minim/half note **la blanca**
  crotchet/quarter note **la negra**
  quaver/eighth note **la corchea**
  semiquaver/sixteenth note **la semicorchea**
mute **sorda**
scale **la escala**
score **la partitura**
sharp **sostenido**
sheet (of music) **la partitura**

17e Film/Movie genres

adventure film/movie **la película de aventuras**
animation **la animación**
black and white **blanco y negro**
black comedy **la comedia negra, el cine negro**
cartoons **los dibujos animados**
comedy **la comedia**
documentary **el documental**
feature film/movie **el largometraje**
horror film/movie **la película de terror**
low-budget **de bajo presupuesto**
sci-fi **la ciencia ficción**
short film **el corto de cine**
silent cinema/movies **el cine mudo**
thriller **la película de intriga**
video-clip **el vídeo-clip**
war film/movie **la película de guerra**
western **la película del oeste**
weepie **la película lacrimosa**

19a Means of transport

by air **por aire, por avión**
in an ambulance **en una ambulancia**

by bicycle **en bicicleta**
by bus **en autobús**
by cable-car **en teleférico**
by car **en coche**
by coach **en autobús**
in a dinghy **en barca**
by ferry **en ferry**
by helicopter **en helicóptero**
by hovercraft **en hidrodeslizador/
aerodeslizador**
by hydrofoil **en hidroala**
in a lorry/truck **en camión**
by plane **en avión**
by ship **en barco, en buque**
by taxi/cab **en taxi**
by tram **en tranvía**
by trolleybus **en trolebús**
in a truck **en camión**
by jumbo jet **en jumbo**
by underground/subway **por metro**

19b Ships and boats

aircraft carrier **el porta(a)viones**
canoe **la canoa**
cargo boat **el barco de
mercancías, el buque mercante**
dinghy **el bote**
ferry **el ferry**
hovercraft **el hidrodeslizador**
hydrofoil **el hidroala**
life boat **el bote salvavidas**
merchant ship **el barco mercante**
ocean liner **el transatlántico**
petrol tank **el tanque de petróleo**
rowing boat **el bote de remo**
sailing boat **el barco de vela**
ship **el barco, el buque, la nave**
speed-boat **la lancha rápida**
submarine **el submarino**
towboat **el remolcador**
warship **el buque de guerra**
yacht **el yate**

19c Parts of the car

airconditioning **el
aireacondicionado**
alternator **el alternador de
corriente**
automatic gear **la marcha
automática, el cambio
automático**
back wheel **la rueda de atrás, la
rueda trasera**
battery **la batería**
bodywork **la carrocería**
bonnet/hood **el capó**
boot **el maletero**
brake **el freno**
bumper/tender **el parachoques**
carburettor **el carburador**
catalytic converter **el convertidor,
el catalizador**
choke **el obturador, el estárter**
clutch **el embrague**
dashboard **el cuadro de mandos,
el tablero (de instrumentos)**
door **la puerta**
  front **delantera**
  passenger **del pasajero**
engine **el motor**
exhaust pipe **el tubo de escape**
front seats **los asientos
delanteros**
front wheel **la rueda delantera**
gearbox **la caja de marchas/de
cambios**
headlights **los focos, los faros**
horn **la bocina, el pito**
hood/top **la capota**
indicator **el indicador de
dirección, el intermitente**
lights **las luces**
motor **el motor**
number/license plate **la matrícula**
passenger seat **el asiento de
pasajero**
pedal **el pedal**
  accelerator **el pedal de
  aceleración, el acelerador**

brake **el pedal de freno, el freno**

clutch **el pedal de embrague, el embrague**

plug **la bujía**

rear-view/rear mirror **el espejo retrovisor**

registration number **el número de matrícula, [las placas]**

roof **el techo**

roof-rack **la baca, la canasta**

safety belt **el cinturón de seguridad**

spares **las piezas de repuesto**

spare wheel **la rueda de repuesto**

speedometer **el velocímetro, el cuentakilómetros**

starter **el arranque**

steering wheel **el volante**

tank **el depósito de gasolina**

throttle valve **la válvula reguladora**

tyre/tire **la cubierta, la llanta, la neumática**

back tyre/tire **la cubierta/llanta trasera**

front tyre/tire **la cubierta/llanta delantera**

spare tyre/tire **la cubierta/llanta de repuesto**

tyre/tire pressure **la presión de las ruedas**

wheel **la rueda**

windscreen/windshield **el parabrisas**

windscreen/windshield wiper **el limpiaparabrisas**

19c Road signs

Cross now **cruzar ahora**

Danger! **peligro!**

Diversion **la desviación**

End of diversion **fin de la desviación**

End of roadworks **fin de las obras**

de la carretera

End of motorway/expressway regulations **fin de la regulación/señalización**

Free parking **aparcamiento gratuito, parqueadero gratis**

Keep clear **dejar libre el paso**

Loading bay **la zona de carga y descarga**

Maximum speed **la velocidad máxima**

Motorway/Expressway entrance **acceso a la autopista**

Motorway/Expressway junction **cruce de autopistas**

No entry **prohibida la entrada**

No parking **no aparcar**

Pedestrians crossing **el cruce de peatones**

Residents only **sólo residentes**

Road closed **carretera cerrada**

Roadworks **carretera en obras**

Stop **stop, parar**

Toll **el peaje**

20a Tourist sights

abbey **la abadía**

adventure playground **el parque infantil**

amphitheatre, amphitheater **el anfiteatro**

aquarium **el acuario**

art gallery **la galería de arte**

battle field **el campo de batalla**

battlements **las almenas**

boulevard **el bulevar**

castle **el castillo, el alcazar**

catacombs **las catacumbas**

cathedral **la catedral**

cave **la cueva**

cemetery **el cementerio**

city **la ciudad**

chapel **la capilla**

church **la iglesia**

concert hall **la sala de conciertos**

convent **el convento**

exhibition   la exhibición
fortress   la fortaleza
fountain   la fuente
gardens   los jardines públicos
harbour/harbor   el puerto
library   la biblioteca
mansion   el palacio
market   el mercado
monastery   el monasterio
monument   el monumento
museum   el museo
opera   la ópera
palace   el palacio
parliament building   el edificio de
   las Cortes/[del Parlamento]
pier   el embarcadero
planetarium   el planetario
ruins   las ruinas
shopping area   la zona de tiendas
square   la plaza
stadium   el estadio
statue   la estatua
temple   el templo
theatre/theater   el teatro
tomb   la tumba
tower   la torre
town centre/downtown   el centro
   de la ciudad
town hall   el ayuntamiento, [la
   alcadía]
university   la universidad
zoo   el parque/jardín zoológico

20a On the beach

bathing hut/cabana   la cabina, la
   cabaña, la caseta de playa
beach   la playa
beach ball   la pelota de playa
bucket and spade/pail and shovel
   el cubo y pala
deck-chair   la silla de lona
I dive   me tiro al agua
diver   el buceador
sand   la arena
   grain of sand   el grano de
   arena

sandcastle   el castillo de arena
sandy (beach)   arenoso
scuba diving   la natación
   submarina
sea   el mar
sea shore   la costa
snorkel   el tubo snorkel, el
   esnórquel
I snorkel   nado respirando por un
   tubo
sun-tan lotion   la loción
   solar/bronceadora
sunshade (umbrella)   la sombrilla
I surf   hago surf
surfboard   la tabla deslizadora
surfboarder   el surfista
surfing   el surf, el acuaplano
I swim   nado
water-skiing   el esquí acuático
windsurfing, sailboarding   el
   windsurf, el surf a vela
I go windsurfing   practico el
   windsurf

20a Continents & regions

Africa   **Africa**
Antarctica   **Antártida**
Arctic   **Ártico**
Asia   **Asia**
Australasia   **Australasia**
Balkans   **los Balcanes**
Baltic States   **los estados bálticos**
Central America   **América Central**
Eastern Europe   **Europa del este**
Europe   **Europa**
European Union   **la Unión Europea**
Far East   **el Extremo Oriente**
Middle East   **el Medio Oriente**
North America   **América del Norte**
Oceania   **Oceanía**
Scandinavia   **Escandinavia**
South America   **América del Sur**
former Soviet Union   **la ex-Unión
   Soviética**
West Indies   **las Antillas
   Occidentales**

former Yugoslavia   **la ex-Yugoslavia**

20a Countries

Afghanistan   **Afganistán**
Albania   **Albania**
Algeria   **Argelia**
Argentina   **Argentina**
Austria   **Austria**
Belgium   **Bélgica**
Bolivia   **Bolivia**
Bosnia   **Bosnia**
Brazil   **Brasil**
Bulgaria   **Bulgaria**
Canada   **el Canadá**
Chile   **Chile**
China   **China**
Colombia   **Colombia**
Costa Rioa   **Costa Rica**
Croatia   **Croacia**
Cuba   **Cuba**
Cyprus   **Chipre**
Czech Republic   **la República Checa**
Denmark   **Dinamarca**
Ecuador   **Ecuador**
Egypt   **Egipto**
England   **Inglaterra**
Estonia   **Estonia**
Finland   **Finlandia**
France   **Francia**
Germany   **Alemania**
Great Britain   **Gran Bretaña**
Greece   **Grecia**
Guatemala   **Guatemala**
Hungary   **Hungría**
Iceland   **Islandia**
India   **India**
Indonesia   **Indonesia**
Iran   **Irán**
Iraq   **Irak**
Ireland   **Irlanda**
Israel   **Israel**
Italy   **Italia**
Japan   **el Japón**
Jordan   **Jordania**

Kampuchea   **Kampuchea**
Kenya   **Kenia**
Korea (North/South)   **Corea (del Norte/del Sur)**
Kuwait   **Kuwait**
Latvia   **Latvia**
Lebanon   **Líbano**
Libya   **Libia**
Lithuania   **Lituania**
Luxemburg   **Luxemburgo**
Malaysia   **Malasia**
Mexico   **México**
Mongolia   **Mongolia**
Morocco   **Marruecos**
Netherlands   **los Países Bajos**
New Zealand   **Nueva Zelandia**
Nicaragua   **Nicaragua**
Norway   **Noruega**
Pakistan   **Pakistán**
Palestine   **Palestina**
Paraguay   **Paraguay**
Peru   **el Perú**
Philippines   **las Filipinas**
Poland   **Polonia**
Portugal   **Portugal**
Romania   **Rumania**
Russia   **Rusia**
Saudi Arabia   **Arabia Saudita**
Scotland   **Escocia**
Serbia   **Serbia**
Slovakia   **Eslovaquia**
Slovenia   **Eslovenia**
South Africa   **Africa del Sur**
Spain   **España**
Sri Lanka   **Sri Lanka**
Sudan   **Sudán**
Sweden   **Suecia**
Switzerland   **Suiza**
Syria   **Siria**
Taiwan   **Taiwán**
Tanzania   **Tanzania**
Thailand   **Tailandia**
Tibet   **el Tibet**
Tunisia   **Túnez**
Turkey   **Turquía**
Uganda   **Uganda**
Ukraine   **Ucrania**

United States **los Estados Unidos**
Uruguay **Uruguay**
Venezuela **Venezuela**
Vietnam **Vietnam**
Wales **el País de Gales**
Zaire **Zaire**
Zimbabwe **Zimbabue**

20a Oceans & seas

Adriatic Sea **el Mar Adriático**
Arctic Ocean **el Océano Glacial Ártico**
Atlantic Ocean **el Océano Atlántico**
Baltic Sea **el Mar Báltico**
Bay of Biscay **la Bahía de Vizcaya**
English Channel **el Canal de la Mancha**
Gulf of Mexico **el Golfo de México**
Indian Ocean **el Océano Indico**
Mediterranean Sea **el Mar Mediterráneo**
Pacific Ocean **el Océano Pácifico**

21a Main language families

Afro-asiatic **afroasiático**
Altaic **altaico**
Austronesian **austronesiano**
Australian **australiano**
Caucasian **caucasiano, caucásico**
Central and South **central y del sur**
Eskimo **esquimo**
Indo-European **indoeuropeo**
  Baltic **báltico**
  Celtic **céltico**
  Germanic **germánico**
  Hellenic **helénico**
  Indo-iranian **indoiraní**
  Italic **itálico**
  Romance **romance**
  Slavic **eslavo**
Independent **independiente**
North American-Indian **indio**

norteamericano
Paleo-asiatic **paleoasiático**
Papuan **papúa**
Sino-Tibetan **sino tibetano**
Uralic **urálico**

21a Languages & nationalities*

Afrikaans **el africano**
Albanian **el albanés**
Arabic **el árabe**
Armenian **el armenio**
Basque **el vasco**
Bengali **el bengalí**
Breton **el bretón**
Bulgarian **el búlgaro**
Burmese **el birmano**
Catalan **el catalán**
Chinese **el chino**
Coptic **el copto**
Czech **el checo**
Danish **el danés**
Dutch **el holandés**
English **el inglés**
Eskimo **el esquimo**
Estonian **el estonio**
Finnish **el finés, el finlandés**
Flemish **el flamenco**
French **el francés**
Gallegan **el gallego**
German **el alemán**
Greek **el griego**
Hebrew **el hebreo**
Hindi **el hindú**
Hungarian **el húngaro**
Icelandic **el islandés**
Indonesian **el indonesio**
Irish Gaelic **el gaélico irlandés**
Italian **el italiano**
Japanese **el japonés**
Korean **el coreano**
Kurdish **el kurdo**
Latin **el latín**
Majorcan **el mallorquín**
Mongolian **el mongol**
Norwegian **el noruego**
Persian **el persa**

➤ *Where applicable, the adjective of nationality (masculine form) is the same as the language.

Polish   el polaco
Portuguese   el portugués
Punjabi   el punjabí
Rumanian   el rumano
Russian   el ruso
Scottish Gaelic   el gaélico
   escocés
Slovak   el eslovaco
Somali   el somalí
Spanish   el español
Swahili   el swahilí
Swedish   el sueco
Thai   el tailandés
Tamil   el tamil
Tibetan   el tibetano
Turkish   el turco
Urdu   el urdú
Valencian   el valenciano
Vietnamese   el vietnamita
Welsh   el galés

Latin-American languages

Aztec   el azteca
Guaraní   el guaraní
Inca   el inca
Nahuatl   el nahuatl
Pampa   el pampa
Quechua   el quechua

Other nationalities

Algerian   argelino
American   americano
American Indian   indio, indígena
Argentinian   argentino
Australian   australiano
Austrian   austríaco
Belgian   belga
Bolivian   boliviano
Brazilian   brasileño
Canadian   canadiense
Chilean   chileno
Colombian   colombiano
Costa Rican   costarricense
Ecuadorean   ecuatoriano
Egyptian   egipicio
French-Canadian
   francocanadiense

Guatemalan   guatemalteco
Indian   indio
Iraqi   iraquí
Iranian   iraní
Irish   irlandés
Israeli   israelí
Lebanese   libanés
Mexican   mexicano, mejicano
Moroccan   marroquí
New Zealander   neozelandés
Nicaraguan   nicaragüense
Pakistani   pakistaní
Palestinian   palestino
Panamanian   panameño
Paraguayan   paraguayo
Peruvian   peruano
Puerto Rican   puertorriqueño
Saudi   saudí, saudita
Scottish   escocés
South African   sudafricano
Swiss   suizo
Syrian   sirio
Uruguayan   uruguayo

21b Grammar

accusative   el acusativo
   accusative *(adj)*   acusativo
adjective   el adjetivo
adverb   el adverbio
agreement   la concordancia
   it agrees with   concuerda con
article   el artículo
   definite article   el artículo
   definido
   indefinite article   el artículo
   indefinido
case   el caso
case ending   la terminación del
   caso
clause   la claúsula
comparative   el comparativo
conjunction   la conjunción
dative   el dativo
definite   el definido
demonstrative   el demostrativo
direct object   el objeto directo

ending **la terminación**
exception **la excepción**
gender **el género**
genitive **el genitivo**
indefinite **el indefinido**
indirect object **el objeto indirecto**
interrogative **el interrogativo**
negative **el negativo**
nominative **el nominativo**
noun **el nombre, el sustantivo**
object **el objeto**
phrase **la frase, la oración**
plural **el plural**
 plural *(adj)* **plural**
possessive **el posesivo**
prefix **el prefijo**
preposition **la preposición**
pronoun **el pronombre**
 demonstrative **el pronombre demostrativo**
 indefinite **el pronombre indefinido**
 interrogative **el pronombre interrogativo**
 personal **el pronombre personal**
 relative **el pronombre relativo**
 subject **el pronombre sujeto**
reflexive **el reflexivo**
 reflexive *(adj)* **reflexivo**
rule **la regla**
sequence **la concordancia, la sucesión**
singular **el singular**
suffix **el sufijo**
superlative **el superlativo**
 superlative *(adj)* **superlativo**
word order **el orden de las palabras**

Verbs

active voice **la voz activa**
auxiliary **auxiliar**
compound **compuesto**
conditional **el condicional**
defective **el defectivo**
formation **la formación**

future **el futuro**
gerund **el gerundio**
imperative **el imperativo**
imperfect **el imperfecto**
impersonal **el impersonal**
infinitive **el infinitivo**
intransitive **el intransitivo**
irregular **irregular**
passive voice **la voz pasiva**
participle **el participio**
past **el pasado**
 past *(adj)* **pasado**
perfect **el perfecto**
present **el presente**
reflexive **el reflexivo**
 reflexive *(adj)* **reflexivo**
regular **regular**
sequence **la concordancia, la sucesión**
simple **simple**
strong **fuerte**
subjunctive **el subjuntivo**
system **el sistema**
tense **el tiempo**
transitive **el transitivo**
use **el uso**
verb **el verbo**
weak **débil**

21b Punctuation

apostrophe **el apóstrofe**
asterisk **el asterisco**
bracket **el paréntesis**
colon **los dos puntos** *(pl)*
comma **la coma**
dash **el guión**
exclamation mark **el signo de exclamación/admiración**
full stop/period **el punto final**
inverted commas **las comillas**
(in) parentheses **(entre) paréntesis**
question mark **el signo de interrogación**
semicolon **punto y coma**

22b Stationery

adhesive tape   la cinta adhesiva, el papel celo, [la cinta pegante]
board-rubber/eraser   el borrador de la pizarra
carbon paper   el papel carbón
card index   el fichero, el tarjetero
chalk   la tiza
clip board   la tablilla con sujetapapeles
compasses   el compás
correction fluid   el líquido corrector
diary/datebook   la agenda
drawing pin   la chincheta, el chinche
envelope   el sobre
exercise book   el cuaderno de ejercicios
felt-tip   el rotulador
file   la carpeta archivadora
filing cabinet   el archivador
fountain pen   la pluma
glue   el pegamento, [el pegante]
guillotine   la guillotina
highlighter   el rotulador fluorescente, el marcador
hole punch   la taladradora, el taladro, [la perforadora]
ink   la tinta
ink refill   la mina de bolígrafo
in-tray/out-tray   la bandeja de entradas/de salidas
label   la etiqueta
marker   el rotulador
note book   el cuaderno, el block
OHP   el proyector de transparencias
paper   el papel
paper clip   el clip, el sujetapapeles
pen   el bolígrafo
pencil   el lápiz
photocopier   la fotocopiadora
pocket calculator   la calculadora de bolsillo
protractor   el transportador de ángulos
ring binder   la carpeta de anillos
rubber band/elastic band   la gomilla, la gomita
rubber/eraser   la goma de borrar, el borrador
ruler   la regla
scalpel   el escalpelo
scissors   las tijeras
screen   la pantalla
set square   el juego de escuadra y cartabón, el cartabón, la escuadra
sheet of paper   la hoja de papel
shredder   la trituradora de papel, el desfibrador
stamp   el sello, el tampón, la estampilla
stapler   la grapadora, la cosedora
staple remover   el quitagrapas
text-book   el libro de texto
typewriter   la máquina de escribir
typewriter ribbon   la cinta de la máquina de escribir
transparency   la transparencia
waste-paper basket   la papelera
whiteboard   la pizarra blanca

23a Scientific disciplines

applied sciences   las ciencias aplicadas
anthropology   la antropología
astronomy   la astronomía
astrophysics   la astrofísica
biochemistry   la bioquímica
biology   la biología
botany   la botánica
chemistry   la química
geology   la geología
medicine   la medicina
microbiology   la microbiología
physics   la física
physiology   la fisiología
psychology   la psicología
social sciences   las ciencias sociales

technology la tecnología
zoology la zoología

23b Chemical elements

aluminium/aluminum el aluminio
arsenic el arsénico
calcium el calcio
carbon el carbono
chlorine el cloro
copper el cobre
gold el oro
hydrogen el hidrógeno
iodine el yodo
iron el hierro
lead el plomo
magnesium el magnesio
mercury el mercurio
nitrogen el nitrógeno
oxygen el oxígeno
phosphorus el fósforo
platinum el platino
plutonium el plutonio
potassium el potasio
silver la plata
sodium el sodio
sulphur el sulfuro
uranium el uranio
zinc el zinc, el cinc

23b Compounds and alloys

acetic acid al ácido acético
alloy la aleación
ammonia el amoniaco
asbestos el amianto, el asbesto
brass el latón
carbon dioxide el dióxido de carbono
carbon monoxide el monóxido de carbono
copper oxide el óxido de cobre
hydrochloric acid el ácido clorhídrico
iron oxide el óxido de hierro
lead oxide el óxido de plomo
nickel el níquel

nitric acid el ácido nítrico
it oxidizes oxida, se oxida
ozone el ozono
propane el propano
silver nitrate el nitrato de plata
sodium bicarbonate el bicarbonato de sodio
sodium carbonate el carbonato de sodio
sodium chloride el cloruro de sodio
sulphuric acid el ácido sulfúrico
tin el estaño

23c The Zodiac

Aries Aries
Taurus Tauro
Gemini Géminis
Cancer Cáncer
Leo Leo
Virgo Virgo
Libra Libra
Scorpio Escorpio
Sagittarius Sagitario
Capricorn Capricornio
Aquarius Acuario
Pisces Piscis

23c Planets and stars

Earth Tierra
Venus Venus
Mercury Mercurio
Pluto Plutón
Mars Marte
Jupiter Júpiter
Saturn Saturno
Uranus Urano
Neptune Neptuno
Pole star la Estrella Polar
Halley's comet el Cometa Halley
Southern cross la Cruz del Sur
Great Bear la Osa Mayor

24b Wild animals

baboon   **el mandril**
badger   **el tejón**
bear   **el oso**
beaver   **el castor**
bison/buffalo   **el búfalo**
camel   **el camello**
cheetah   **el leopardo cazador**
chimpanzee   **el chimpancé**
cougar   **el puma**
coyote   **el coyote**
deer   **el ciervo, el venado**
elephant   **el elefante**
elk   **el alce, el anta**
fox   **el zorro**
frog   **la rana**
giraffe   **la jirafa**
gorilla   **el gorila**
grizzly bear   **el oso pardo**
hare   **la liebre**
hedgehog   **el erizo**
hippopotamus   **el hipopótamo**
hyena   **la hiena**
jaguar   **el jaguar**
leopard   **el leopardo**
lion   **el león**
lizard   **el lagarto**
lynx   **el lince**
mink   **el visón**
mole   **el topo**
monkey   **el mono**
moose   **el alce de América**
mouse   **el ratón**
otter   **la nutria**
panther   **la pantera**
polar bear   **el oso polar**
puma   **el puma**
rat   **la rata**
reindeer   **el reno**
rhinoceros   **el rinoceronte**
snake   **la serpiente, la culebra**
squirrel   **la ardilla**
tiger   **el tigre**
toad   **el sapo**
whale   **la ballena**
wildcat   **el gato montés**

wolf   **el lobo**
zebra   **la cebra**

24b Birds

albatross   **el albatros**
blackbird   **el cuervo**
bluetit   **el herrerillo**
chaffinch   **el pinzón**
crow   **el grajo, la corneja**
dove   **la paloma**
eagle   **el águila** (f)
   golden eagle   **el águila real**
emu   **el emú, el dromeo**
hawk/falcon   **el halcón**
heron   **la garaza**
hummingbird   **el colibrí, el picaflor**
kingfisher   **el martín pescador**
magpie   **la urraca**
osprey   **el águila** (f) **pescadora**
ostrich   **el avestruz**
owl   **el búho, la lechuza, el mochuelo**
parrot   **el loro**
peacock   **el pavo real, el pavón**
pelican   **el pelícano**
penguin   **el pingüino**
pigeon   **la paloma**
robin   **el petirrojo**
seagull   **la gaviota**
sparrow   **el gorrión**
starling   **el estornino**
swallow   **la golondrina**
swan   **el cisne**
swift   **el vencejo**
thrush   **el tordo**
woodpecker   **el pájaro carpintero**
wren   **el troglodito**

24b Parts of the animal body

beak   **el pico**
claw   **la garra, la zarpa**
comb   **la cresta**
feather   **la pluma**
fin   **la aleta**
fleece   **la lana, el vellón**

fur   el pelo
gills   la branquia, la agalla
hide   el pellejo, la piel
hoof   la pezuña
mane   la melena, la crin
paw   la pata, la garra
pelt   el pelo, el pelaje
scale   la escama
shell *(oyster, snail)*   la concha
   shell *(tortoise, crab)*   el
   caparazón
tail   el rabo, la cola
trunk   la trompa
tusk   el colmillo
udder   la ubre
wing   el ala

24c Trees

apple tree   el manzano
ash   el fresno
beech   la haya
cherry tree   el cerezo
chestnut   el castaño
cypress   el ciprés
eucalyptus   el eucalipto
fig tree   la higuera
fir tree   el abeto
fruit tree   el árbol frutal
holly   el acebo
maple   el arce, el maple
oak   el roble
olive tree   el olivo
palm   la palmera
peach tree   el melocotonero
pear tree   el peral
pine   el pino
plum tree   el ciruelo
poplar   el chopo, el álamo
redwood   la secoya
rhododendron   el rododendro
walnut tree   el nogal
willow   el sauce
yew   el tejo

24c Flowers & weeds

azalea   la azalea
cactus   el cactus, el cacto
carnation   el clavel
chrysanthemum   el crisantemo
clover   el trébol
crocus   la flor del azafrán
daffodil   el narciso
dahlia   la dalia
daisy   la margarita
dandelion   el diente de león
fern   el helecho
flax   el lino
foxglove   la dedalera
geranium   el geranio
hydrangea   la hortensia
lily   la azucena
nettle (stinging)   la ortiga
orchid   la orquidia
poppy   la amapola
rose   la rosa
snowdrop   la campanilla de
   invierno, la flor de nieve
sunflower   el girasol
thistle   el cardo
tulip   el tulipán
violet   la violeta

25b Political institutions

assembly   la asamblea
association   la asociación
cabinet   el gabinete
   shadow cabinet *(UK)*   el
   gobierno en la sombra
confederation   la confederación
congress   el congreso
council   el consejo, la junta
federation   la federación
House of Representatives   la
   cámara de los representantes
local authority   la autoridad local
Lower House/Lower Chamber   la
   cámara baja
parliament   el parlamento
party   el partido político

Senate **el senado**
town council   **la junta local, el consejo de gobierno local**
town hall   **el ayuntamiento, [la alcadía]**
Upper House   **la cámara alta**

27b Military ranks

admiral   **el almirante**
air marshal   **el mariscal de aire**
brigadier   **el brigadier, el general de brigada**
captain   **el capitán**
   captain *(Naval)*   **el capitán de navío**
commander   **el capitán general del ejército**
   commander *(Naval)*   **el capitán de fragata**
commanding officer   **el comandante**
corporal   el cabo
fieldmarshal   **el mariscal de campo**
general   **el general**
lieutenant   **el teniente**
lieutenant commander   **el capitán de corbeta**
major   **el comandante**
private   **el soldado raso**
rear-admiral   **el contraalmirante**
sergeant   **el sargento**
sergeant-major   **el sargento mayor, el brigada**
sergeant-major *(US)*   **el primer sargento**

27c International organizations

ASEAN/Association of South-East Asian Nations   **ANSA/Asociación de Naciones del Sureste Asiático**
Council of Europe   **el Consejo de Europa**
EC/European Community   **CE/la Comunidad Europea**
EU/European Union   **UE/la Unión Europea**
IMF/International Monetary Fund   **FMI/el Fondo Monetario Internacional**
NATO/North Atlantic Treaty Organization   **OTAN/la Organización del Tratado del Atlántico Norte**
OECD/Organization for Economic Cooperation and Development   **OCDE/la Organización de Cooperación y Desarrollo Económico**
OPEC/Organization of Oil Exporting Countries   **OPEP/la Organización de Países Exportadores de Petróleo**
Security Council   **el Consejo de Seguridad**
UNO/United Nations Organization   **ONU/la Organización de las Naciones Unidas**
WHO/World Health Organization   **OMS/la Organización Mundial de la Salud**
World Bank   **el Banco Mundial**

D
SUBJECT INDEX

Subject index

References refer to Vocabularies